W9-BAL-895

What's in the Bible for Teens

What's in the Bible for Teens

Mark Littleton
and
Jeanette Gardner Littleton
Larry Richards, General Editor

BETHANYHOUSE
MINNEAPOLIS, MINNESOTA

What's in the Bible™ for Teens

Published by Bethany House Publishers
11400 Hampshire Avenue South
Bloomington, Minnesota 55438

Bethany House Publishers is a division of Baker Publishing Group, Grand Rapids, Michigan.

Originally published by Starburst Publishers. Now revised and updated.

General Editor: Larry Richards
Managing Editor: Lila Empson
Associate Editor: Natasha Sperling
Scripture Editor: Deborah Wiseman
Assistant Editor: Amy Clark
Design: Diane Whisner

Printed in the United States of America

ISBN 978-0-7642-0386-2

Library of Congress Cataloging-in-Publication Data

Littleton, Mark R., 1950—
What's in the Bible for teens : life's questions, God's answers / Mark Littleton and Jeanette Gardner Littleton ; Larry Richards, general editor. — [Rev. and updated ed.]
p. cm. — (What's in the Bible for—)
Summary: "Bible-based information relevant to today's teens. Arranged topically, material includes Scripture and analysis, character studies, personal application, illustrations, quotations, and more. Suitable for individual or group study"—Provided by publisher.
Includes bibliographical references and index.
ISBN-13: 978-0-7642-0386-2 (pbk. : alk. paper)
ISBN-10: 0-7642-0386-X (pbk. : alk. paper)
1. Teenagers—Religious life. 2. Teenagers in the Bible. I. Littleton, Jeanette Gardner. II. Richards, Larry, 1931- III. Title.

BV4531.3.L58 2007
248.8'3—dc22

2007028742

---

08 09 10 10 9 8 7 6 5 4 3

Introduction

"My biology teacher is on the evolution stuff again."

"My boyfriend keeps putting more pressure on me to have sex. How do I deal with this?"

"I find the Bible boring. How can I get more interested in it?"

These are the kinds of questions perhaps you or your friends ask about God, the Bible, Christian faith, and the many other issues you face in trying to live a life that pleases God. Where do you get answers?

This book is a start. *What's in the Bible for Teens* will take you through many of the greatest concerns and issues that you as a teen face today. You will soon find the Bible a very readable book when you use a modern translation. You will also discover that the Bible speaks to many of the most modern and controversial problems people struggle with today. The Bible is a book from God, and we believe he knew all the difficulties teens like you would face from the earliest times to today. As a result, you will find that the Bible has insight and help for you and your friends at every level. It's the most relevant book of all time and speaks to people of every time and age.

We Will Look at the Bible!

In this book, you will not find a lot of human opinion and views. Instead, we'll look directly at what the Bible says about each issue and subject. Remember, this is a book about what is in the *Bible* for teens! Therefore, we won't dwell on the opinions and ideas of modern adults. At times we will look at what teens have to say about a topic, and you'll read about their ideas. Ultimately, however, we'll focus on the Bible's opinions, ideas, concerns, and thoughts.

Are you a little skeptical about that? "The Bible? Why use that?" you might ask.

That's a good question. Just what is so significant about the Bible? Perhaps your parents have taken you to church for years, but you may wonder just what the big deal is. We'll look at why you should make the Bible your number one resource for getting your questions answered. In fact, we are convinced that you'll find the Bible offers you stronger, better, more-relevant, and more-promising answers to the issues in your life than any other kind of book.

What Will You Find in This Book?

This book will look at many classic issues as well as contemporary ones. For instance:

- How did we get the Bible?

- Is it worth reading? Will it help me? How?
- What teens are found in the Bible? Is there anyone in there like me?
- Who was Jesus? What did he come to do?
- What are the primary teachings of the Bible? What about things like prayer, faith, and reaching out to my friends?
- How about my family? How can I relate better to my parents?
- What does the Bible say about dating and relationships?
- How can the Bible help me in school? At work? With friends?
- In what ways will the Bible help me achieve success in life?
- What does the Bible offer me about dealing with issues like drugs, drinking, sex, gambling, other religions, blended families, money, the latest fads, prayer, and worship, to name just a few?

You will find many other issues faced in this book, and you will find genuine help and guidance as you live in your world.

A Word of Encouragement

Ally Littleton, our seventeen-year-old daughter, has recently undergone a complete turnaround in her life. Though we didn't know it, her wild high school friends had been leading her to try alcohol and drugs, become more open to sex, and use filthy language when she wasn't at home. But this summer she got into trouble with us about these friends, and we grounded her for three weeks. We told her that if she attended a local Christian camp called "God's Mountain," we would reduce her grounding by a week. She went and worked with kids in third through sixth grade.

To our surprise, she asked if she could go again the next week to work with junior high kids. That week something clicked in her heart, and she underwent a deep, personal heart change. She came home full of enthusiasm about her faith. She came to me asking, "What book of the Bible should I start with? What would be a good version to use? What verses should I start memorizing?"

I was astonished and asked her what happened. She told me about one day at camp where she broke down and admitted to all the bad things she'd been into. The leader helped her get back into a right relationship with God.

"I've got my joy back," she told me. "I feel like I'm going right now."

She made new friends, and though she reaches out to her old wild friends, she no longer hangs out with them as she did before. She told me one day, "God is so awesome. I saw his glory tonight at church." She had gotten to know another committed Christian named Sarah, and they decided to be accountability partners. She simply bubbled over with excitement when she came home.

Then she told us another story. "It was so cool, Dad," she said. "Last week I was reading in the Bible about speaking in tongues and things like that. Then last night, one of my friends called. She was having problems at college because everyone was trying to get her to do that. She tried, but it wasn't working. Then she called me, and I was able to explain to her what I read in 1 Corinthians. It was so awesome. I was able to help her from the Bible. She really listened, agreed, and said it made sense. Now she's not so scared and worried about it. In fact, she's taking the people who are putting pressure on her to the verses I showed her."

I sat there almost in tears as I listened. This was my daughter, who in recent months had become disobedient and hard to get along with. But this change in her had brought us a closeness and a love and joy that we'd never felt before.

As you read this book, if you seek God and ask him to speak to your heart, I am convinced you'll find in the Bible the most powerful help, encouragement, and insight you could ever wish or pray for.

The beautiful thing here is that joy, love, and peace are available to every teen in every place and at every time. Give the Bible your best effort, and you will find it rewarding you with more than you could ever ask or think.

About the Authors

Mark Littleton is the author of eighty-eight books and more than two thousand magazine articles, poems, and interviews. He has a teenage daughter who occasionally gives him fits, but for the most part is building her life on Christ. He also has three other children who mostly just give him fits.

Jeanette Littleton is an author of five books and more than three thousand articles, devotionals, and interviews. She is married to Mark; they collaborated on this book, and their marriage survived. She works as a volunteer in the library at her son's local elementary school, helps out in her church bookstore, and recently completed several books of stories about teens, mothers, and converts to Christian faith.

About the General Editor

Dr. Larry Richards is a native of Michigan who now lives in Raleigh, North Carolina. He was converted while in the Navy in the 1950s. Larry has taught and written Sunday school curriculum for every age group, from nursery through adult. He has published more than two hundred books, and his books have been translated into twenty-six languages. His wife, Sue, is also an author. They both enjoy teaching Bible studies as well as fishing and playing golf.

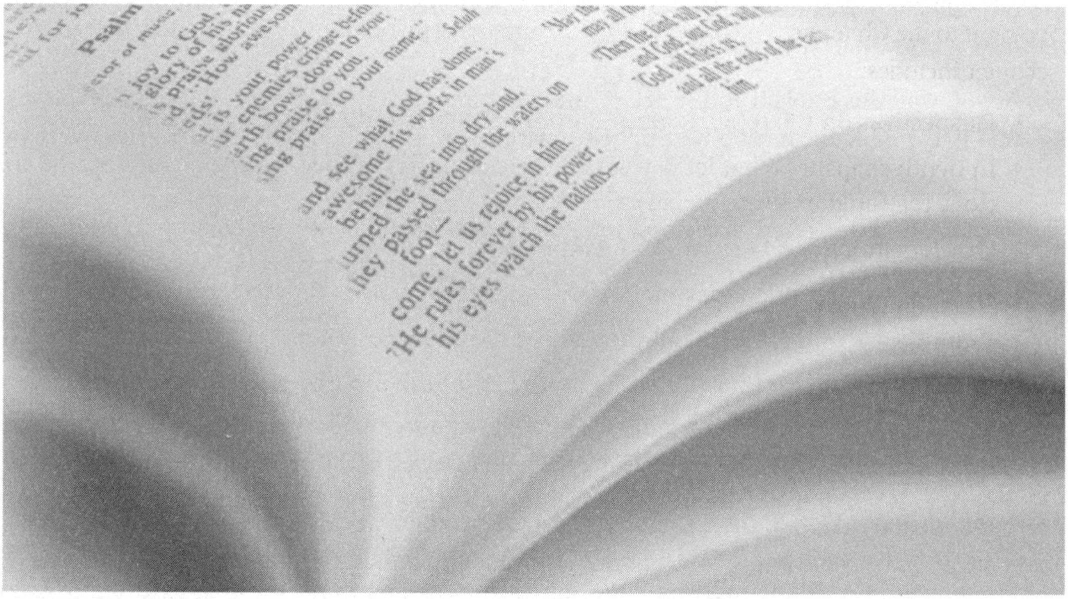
Psalm
and see what God has done,
awesome his works in man's
behalf!
turned the sea into dry land,
passed through the waters on
foot—
come, let us rejoice in him.
He rules forever by his power,
his eyes watch the nations—

What's in the Bible for You? This Series Will Help You Find Out

For every situation you face and for every stage of life, there's no better place than the Bible to turn for answers and advice. This book in the What's in the Bible™ series guides you from life's questions to God's answers by tackling the topics that matter to you most. Its organization allows you to quickly and easily find the godly wisdom you need to be your best in every area of your life.

You can start with chapter 1 and read straight through the whole book, or if you prefer, you can go right to the Chapters at a Glance to find the topic you're looking for. The friendly format in each chapter includes:

- Perspectives on the topic, examples from the Bible, and real-life stories
- In-depth snapshots that let you see the true character of men, women, couples, and teens from the Bible in situations just like yours
- Quick definitions of key words and concepts
- Helpful insights and additional information from experts on the topic
- Examples of God's power and promises throughout history
- Ways your topic fits into context with the rest of the Bible to give you the bigger picture
- How-to suggestions for putting biblical truths into action
- End-of-chapter reflections and questions

On page after page, you'll meet real people just like you who dealt with real issues just like yours. So take heart and take hope. You're about to find out that the Bible has everything you need.

Special Features for Each Topic

sovereign
Psalm 141:8

More information is at your fingertips! Look up the Bible verse listed in the margin to better understand the underlined word in the text you just read. The underlined words are key concepts that will help you build your faith.

When you see this icon, you'll know you're about to read something especially important for your mind, your heart, your soul, your whole life.

This icon is a signal for you to take time to consider the ideas in the passage. You'll want to savor the insights and consider how you can live out the truths and practical suggestions.

The Bible is full of wisdom you'll want to take to heart. But how do you move it from your heart to your life? This icon gives you guidelines and encouragement for jump-starting your faith into action.

How does God work in people's lives? Look for this icon to see encouraging examples of God's power and promises throughout history.

Want to make your day better? Insights and stories come alongside you like an old and trusted friend, and they offer timely advice for putting biblical truths into daily practice.

What else is there to read on the topic? Look for this icon at the end of each chapter for the authors' recommendations for further reading on the topic.

It's time to get real. Personal. Unguarded. Authentic. Here you'll read true stories of how people dealt with the same issues you're struggling with. Be encouraged. You're not alone.

Examples From the Bible

Suffering was a common experience for many people in the Bible:

- Job, a wealthy man of God, lost his children, his possessions, and his health when Satan took them all away. Yet he stayed true to God and praised him during his suffering. (Job 1:1, 21)
- The apostle Peter suffered the consequences and pain of his denying he knew Jesus. (Luke 22:55–62)

There's nothing like a good example to drive home an important point. Biblical examples of the godly and the ungodly will empower you to respond wisely to the situations and relationships you face each day.

Snapshots of Women in the Bible

The Widow of Zarephath (1 Kings 17:1-24)

The widow of Zarephath was no stranger to pain and suffering. But God rescued her from eternal suffering by showing her his power through the prophet Elijah.

Who were the men, women, couples, and teens of the Bible? Informative snapshots give you a close, personal look into their minds, hearts, and lives so you can be inspired to live in a way that pleases God.

How Others See It

Jill Briscoe

Nobody knows what is around the corner of tomorrow. But one thing we can know: God will be waiting there for us. He is a God of comfort, a God well acquainted with grief and suffering. A god who knows what it is to have the forces of hell do their worst. Because God inhabits our future, he is never surprised by the magnitude of the troubles waiting for us. We may be surprised, but our heavenly Father never is.[5]

What do others have to say about the topic? This icon highlights the opinions and perspectives of others to increase your understanding of the topic.

Chapters at a Glance

Part Three: Living It Up

Part Four: Stressed to the Max

Part One

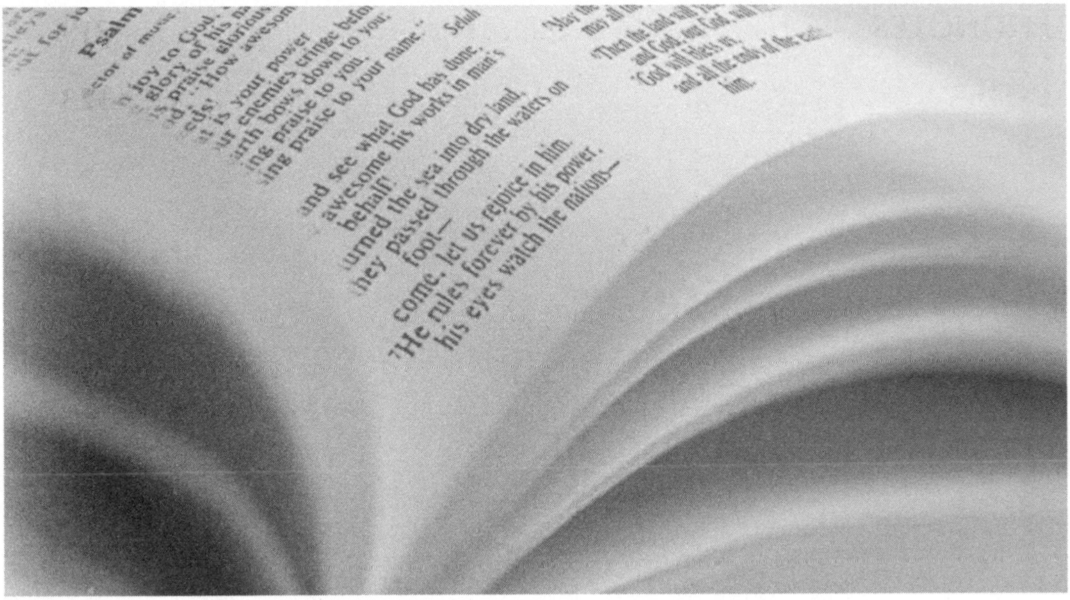

A Powerful Book for Teens

Chapter 1: Is the Bible Worth Reading?

Opening Your Bible and Being Amazed

What's in This Chapter

- The Bible—Life's Tour Book
- I Love This Book!
- The Languages of the Bible
- History in the Making

Here We Go

All right. You've bought this book or it's been given to you. Either way, you should read something, so let's start with a question: Is the Bible worth reading? It's an old book, right? It was written by guys with beards and gray hair who had no clue what it's like to be in high school, right?

Good questions, and they deserve some answers. Yes, the Bible is old, written from about 1400 to 400 BC (the **Old Testament**) and from AD 45 to AD 100 (the **New Testament**). And yes, though some authors of the Bible were very young (it's possible that **David** wrote some of the **Psalms** during his teen years), the Bible was written mostly by older men a long time ago. That doesn't mean the Bible isn't important to us today, whatever our age. If the Bible is God's Word—God's very thoughts—then surely he wrote it so everyone would enjoy or learn something from it.

Old Testament
the thirty-nine books of the Bible written before Christ came to earth

New Testament
the twenty-seven books of the Bible written after Christ died

David
king of Israel around 900 BC

Psalms
song book in Bible

Jews
God's "chosen people"

divine
of God or from God

As you can see, the Bible was written for everyone everywhere—in every age and in every situation!

Just imagine: a book that tells you everything you need to know to have an excellent life. That's what the Bible is. Amazingly, the Bible speaks to people from every age and country, every color and culture. Why? Because it's not a human book. If it were, it would only reflect the thoughts of a few humans, and because all the writers were **Jews**, it would probably speak mainly to Jews. But because the Bible is a **divine** book, it is God's way of speaking to everyone, including you!

Who the Bible Is For

	Sections of Scripture Especially for . . .
Genesis 1–11	Scientists, archaeologists, philosophers, dreamers, and people who like to imagine
Genesis 12–50	People who recorded history, Jewish people

Who the Bible Is For (cont'd)

Sections of Scripture Especially for . . .

Leviticus	Priests
Numbers	People interested in genealogy (family history) and world history
Joshua	Generals, fighting men, adventurous and courageous guys
Ruth	Women interested in relationships and women who don't have husbands
1 and 2 Kings	Kings, political leaders, and people who like to be in charge
Nehemiah	People who like to be leaders or work with others, encouragers
Esther	Risk-takers, queens-to-be, and girls who want to know if they can make a difference in the world
Job	People who are sad and have been through tough times
Psalms	Singers, musicians, worshipers
Ecclesiastes	Skeptics, cynics, philosophers, and people who like to think about life
Song of Solomon	People in love; those who are married or engaged especially
Isaiah	People who are discouraged and need to know that God cares and wants them in his family
Daniel	Dreamers, prophets, and guys who like to be in tip-top shape
Hosea	Guys who know what it's like to have a girl turn on them
Matthew, Mark, Luke	People who want to know about Jesus
John	People who want to know what God is like
Acts	People who want to make a difference in the world
Romans	People who love to study what God's like
Philippians	People who want to have a fun, happy life
Revelation	Anyone who wants to know where we're all going

think about it

About a thousand years passed from the time the first pages of the Bible were written to the last pages. God pulled more than forty different authors together during that time to tell a message that all these authors agreed on—a message that everyone needs to know about. However, talk about "everyone" and "everywhere" may keep you from remembering that this book is actually for you. What kinds of things do you think God wants to teach you through his Word?

The Bible—Life's Tour Book

Scripture
another word for Bible

2 TIMOTHY 3:16–17 ***All Scripture is God-breathed and is useful for teaching, rebuking, correcting and training in righteousness, so that the man of God may be thoroughly equipped for every good work.***

Why did God give us the Bible? These verses in 2 Timothy give us some ideas. God uses the words in the Bible to train us in the way we should go. He gave us the Bible to help us. To guide us into the truth. To tell us about who God is and what he is like. In fact, the Bible is God's divine way of communicating with us. However, the best way to answer this question is to go directly to the Scriptures and see what they say about why they were written. Let's look at some of the exact words the Bible uses to reveal those reasons.

Why God Gave Us the Bible

Verse	Reason
I have hidden your word in my heart that I might not sin against you. (Psalm 119:11)	To help keep us from sinning
Your word is a lamp to my feet and a light for my path. (Psalm 119:105)	To keep us safe and to guide us
For everything that was written in the past was written to teach us, so that through endurance and the encouragement of the Scriptures we might have hope. (Romans 15:4)	To teach us and encourage us when life gets rough
Do not think that I have come to abolish the Law or the Prophets; I have not come to abolish them but to fulfill them. (Matthew 5:17, Jesus speaking)	To show that Christ's life was a fulfillment of all God's promises
But these are written that you may believe that Jesus is the Christ, the Son of God, and that by believing you may have life in his name. (John 20:31)	To help us to believe in Christ and to receive the gift of eternal life
For the word of God is living and active. Sharper than any double-edged sword, it penetrates even to dividing soul and spirit, joints and marrow; it judges the thoughts and attitudes of the heart. (Hebrews 4:12)	To help us see sin for what it really is
And we have the word of the prophets made more certain, and you will do well to pay attention to it, as to a light shining in a dark place, until the day dawns and the morning star rises in your hearts. (2 Peter 1:19)	To encourage us to study and apply God's Word until Christ returns, when a supernatural transformation will take place in the hearts of believers

check this out

sneak away
Matthew 14:23; 26:36; Mark 6:46; Luke 6:12; 9:28

teachers of the law
Luke 2:46–47

wilderness
Matthew 4:1–11

Jesus had to sneak away from the crowds to spend time with God too. So when you feel a need to get closer to God and his Word, get away from the pressures of life and read!

A Passage for Every Occasion

Different biblical passages speak to different needs for different people. Sometimes a **Proverb** will address your need. Other times it will be something from **Paul's epistles** or the **books of Moses**. When you study the Bible, you need to ask this question: What does God want to say to me today? You can find the answer to that question by first becoming familiar with the whole Bible. Then you can delve deeper into one section when a specific need arises.

Proverb
a short popular saying; a saying from the book of Proverbs

Paul
a man who eventually became Christianity's chief theologian and missionary to the Gentiles

epistles
letters to churches in the New Testament

books of Moses
first five books of the Old Testament

Satan
angelic adversary of God

I Love This Book!

> MARK **1:35** ***Very early in the morning, while it was still dark, Jesus got up, left the house and went off to a solitary place, where he prayed.***

Jesus knew how important it was to spend time alone with God. He made it a priority to get away from other people, to find a "solitary place." This text says Jesus prayed. We can do the same, and we can also study the Bible. Jesus certainly knew the Old Testament Scriptures (New Testament Scripture wasn't around yet, of course). When he was a boy, Jesus confounded the teachers of the law so thoroughly that they wondered who he was and where he learned what he knew. When **Satan** tempted him in the wilderness, Jesus recited a number of verses from memory.

How Others See It

Mark Twain

It ain't those parts of the Bible that I can't understand that bother me, it's the parts that I do understand.[1]

Terry Jones

I dug into God's Word. I studied the Bible every chance I got. I remember reading the book of James and getting a lot of comfort from it.[2]

Billy Graham

[The Bible] is the blueprint of the Master Architect.[3]

The Playbook

Ever thought of comparing your Christian life to sports? Doug Pelfrey, a kicker for the Cincinnati Bengals, says that football's a lot like our Christian lives. To be a successful sportsman, you have to know the playbook. Pelfrey likens God to a team's coach, with the team being the body of Christian believers. He feels the Bible is like a team's playbook that gives specific goals and outlines a game plan.

Doug also points out that we can't neglect our workout. He says Christians reading their Bibles and praying are much like a football workout. And when we don't do our workout, our enemy, Satan, is more likely to tackle us.

Reading the Bible can be tough if you're like Doug and don't like to read. But that's where strength and perseverance come in. Doug has found he can read the Bible from cover to cover and learn in the process. So can we![4]

In the *Guinness Book of World Records*, you'll find an entry on how long it takes to read the Bible straight through. Reverend Don Taggart of Pontotoc, Mississippi, invited his students from the high school youth group to read the Bible aloud without stopping. It took fifty-two hours for the Old Testament and fourteen hours for the New.

What? No TV?!

> EXODUS 34:27 ***Then the Lord said to Moses, "Write down these words, for in accordance with these words I have made a covenant with you and with Israel."***

Moses was the first person God gave the Bible to. God dictated; Moses wrote. And wrote. And wrote. In fact, Moses wrote the first five books of the Old Testament!

Think about this for a moment: How could God best communicate his thoughts, concerns, and ideas to people from the beginning to the end of time?

He used three things: a person, a language, and the written word. That's all.

His Source: The Bible

The music group dc Talk hit almost instant fame after the release of Jesus Freak. *Turning out a popular album is a wonderful, fulfilling accomplishment, but it also brings some pressure to make sure your next project is as excellent. After all, what if you turn out one great album, and the next CD is a total flop?*

After Jesus Freak, *Toby McKeehan of dc Talk didn't let the pressure get to him or hinder his work. He went back to what he feels is the source of great music: the Bible.*

Toby says, "The only pressure I felt is just the normal pressure of wanting twelve great songs, songs that are a true depiction of what's going on in our hearts, things that make you ask questions and go to the Bible and look up the answers. If we can get twelve songs that do that, that's a great record."[5]

How Others See It

Danny Stephens

Keith Green's biography, *No Compromise*, is the best. The only book that's had a greater impact on my life would be the Bible.[6]

Lost and Then Found

Have you ever been lost? Like in the woods with some bozo who's missed the trail? Being lost can be terrifying.

When I graduated from college with a degree in physical sciences (math, chemistry, and physics), for the first time in my life I had to make it on my own. Dad said to me, "Now you're on your own, kid. Go to it!"

I was frightened. What made it worse was how many of my friends seemed to know just what they wanted to do. One planned to be a neurological surgeon. Another, a corporate tax lawyer. How could anyone be that specific? I wasn't sure I even wanted to be alive, and here were people who had it all sketched out.

When people asked me what I planned to do, I told them I planned to become a doctor, but in my heart, I didn't want to be a doctor. I couldn't face four more years of raw grind. Besides, looking into hairy ears and armpits didn't appeal to me.

It was a frustrating time in my life. Later that summer, though, I became a Christian. Everything in my life changed, especially the fact that God was a real friend and presence. He led me day by day. One afternoon, I found the verses, "'For I know the plans I have for you,' declares the Lord, 'plans to prosper you and not to harm you, plans to give you hope and a future. Then you will call upon me and come and pray to me, and I will listen to you. You will seek me and find me when you seek me with all your heart'" (Jeremiah 29:11–13). I marveled. "God has a plan for me?" Yes, he did, and soon he revealed it to me as I prayed and sought him.

He has a plan for you too. Of course, you won't find "I want YOU to be an engineer" in the Bible. But you can trust your Bible to provide answers for you about whatever searing questions you're asking. Just seek, pray, read, and believe. And God will speak, if you're listening.

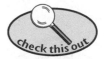

check this out

God sent
Genesis 42:1–7

Jacob
the grandson of Abraham

Joseph
son of Jacob who became prime minister of Egypt

Genesis
the first book of the Old Testament

Moses
the first leader of the Jews

The Languages of the Bible

The Jews perfected the Hebrew language during their captivity in Egypt (see Illustration #1) from about 1860 to 1440 BC. That may be part of the reason God sent his people to Egypt, not only to save them from a severe famine in their homeland (during the time of **Jacob** and **Joseph** in the book of **Genesis**), but to put them in a situation where they could develop and grow as a community. By the time of **Moses** (1440 BC), Hebrew was a written language. That's when God first began communicating his Word to Moses.

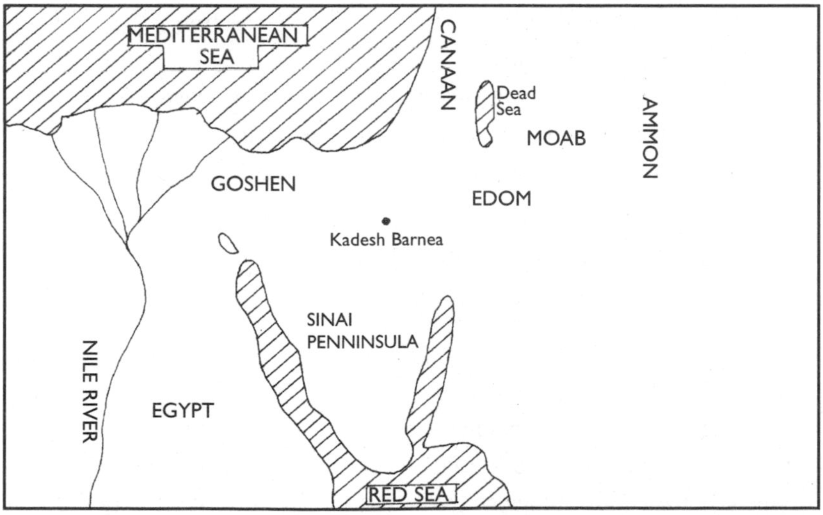

Illustration #1
Egypt and Surrounding Areas—The book of Genesis tells the story of Joseph, who went from slavery to political leadership in Egypt. He eventually brought his family to Egypt too and settled them in the land of Goshen. For about four hundred years, the Israelites remained in Egypt, where eventually they were enslaved. During their captivity, the Jews perfected the Hebrew language.

How Others See It

Michael Johnston

It's not enough to keep the bad stuff out of your mind; you've got to put the right stuff in. . . . I spend a lot of time reading my Bible. God's Word is a real source of moral strength. Out on the road, there are plenty of long travel hours. I'm learning to make good use of them.[7]

The Bible in Fifty Words

1. God made
2. Adam bit
3. Noah arked
4. Abraham split
5. Jacob fooled
6. Joseph ruled
7. Bush talked
8. Moses balked
9. Pharaoh plagued
10. People walked
11. Sea divided
12. Tablets guided
13. Promise landed
14. Saul freaked
15. David peeked
16. Prophets warned
17. Jesus born
18. God walked
19. Love talked
20. Anger crucified
21. Hope died
22. Love rose
23. Spirit flamed
24. Word spread
25. God remained

check this out

inspired
2 Peter 1:20–21; 2 Timothy 3:16–17; Matthew 5:18

genealogies
ancestral lines

prophecies
predictions of the future

sermons
theological lectures

inspired
moved or influenced

Holy Spirit
the Spirit of God

The Men With a Pen

LEVITICUS 1:1–2 *The Lord called to Moses and spoke to him from the Tent of Meeting. He said, "Speak to the Israelites and say to them: 'When any of you brings an offering to the Lord . . ."*

Moses was the first of over forty Bible writers. The Bible contains history, laws, rules for living, **genealogies**, stories, poetry, memoirs, songs, letters, love songs, lectures, **prophecies**, **sermons**, and numerous other types of writing. Though God used imperfect people to write the Bible, they were **inspired** by the **Holy Spirit** so that what came out were the very thoughts and utterances of God.

That's exactly why the Bible is the most important book on earth. If you want to know what God thinks about the world, life, death, or whatever, read the Bible. It will tell you the straight truth. You won't have to look anywhere else.

You Talkin' to Me?

The written word was not the only way God communicated. The Bible records numerous conversations between God and people. The record begins with Adam and Eve in Genesis and ends with the last book of the Bible, Revelation. Sometimes he appeared as an angel. Other times he spoke from various objects or things. God spoke to Moses, for example, from a burning bush, and to **Job** from a storm.

> **How Others See It**
>
> **A. C. Green**
>
> As I attended church and followed my spiritual coaches, God purified my mind and ego. . . . First John 1:9–10 says that if we confess our sins, God will forgive us and cleanse us from unrighteousness—the habits of sin. Many Christians are forgiven, but they aren't cleansed, so they stay in old physical and mental habit patterns. My mind had to be renewed by daily Bible reading and attending church. My ego had to be humbled. . . . I began to see victory not as a stroke to my own ego but as a witness for God, something that proved how great He was within me. A new purer drive for winning branched out in other areas. . . . I wanted to achieve all that He had created me to achieve.[8]

If the Bible really is God's way of talking to us, do you think learning and knowing what's in the Bible should be a priority? If you want to "walk the talk" and show the world you're the real thing—one of God's children—the best way is to let the Bible influence and color your life. Let its teachings affect every part of who you are.

The Power of the Bible in My Life

As a little kid, I was in Sunday school every week of my life. My church believed in Scripture memory and in contests. We got cool little pins and prizes (okay, they aren't cool now, but they were cool in elementary school) for the Scriptures we memorized. I can't tell you how many verses from the Bible I tucked away in my brain. I became a Christian when I was a teenager and memorized more verses. Then I was a youth worker and a Sunday school teacher and memorized the verses I helped kids learn.

Adam and Eve
Genesis 2:15–3:19

angel
Genesis 16:7–11; Judges 13

burning bush
Exodus 3:1–4:17

storm
Job 38:1

Adam
first man created by God

Eve
first woman

angel
a supernatural messenger from God

Job
a man who suffered in the Old Testament

archaeology
the scientific study of historic peoples and their cultures by analysis of their artifacts, inscriptions, monuments, etc.

Dead Sea Scrolls
a group of ancient manuscripts discovered near the Dead Sea in 1947

Masoretic text
our master copy of the Old Testament, standardized in AD 1100

Greek
language of the original New Testament

It's been a while since I was a kid or a teen, but those verses still pop up in my mind thirty years later. Sometimes a Scripture I've read but never consciously memorized will come to me out of nowhere.

That doesn't happen because I have a great brain. In fact, my sixteen-year-old, Nicole, could give plenty of examples of my less-than-great brain. It happens because if we put Scriptures in our mind, the Holy Spirit will bring those Scriptures to us when we need them most. Like when we're being tempted. Or when we're feeling sad. Or when we're ticked off. God reassures us, encourages us, warns us, and helps us make it through the day by bringing his Word into our heads. But he can't really do that if we're not studying, memorizing, or at least reading his Word. Just as Nicole could give you examples of my brain fogs, Nicole could also give you examples of how this has happened in her life since she started reading her Bible this year. Through the Bible, God gives her strength to deal with her strict parents, a tough school, and annoying siblings.

Make the Bible a regular part of your day, and it will change your life—both now and thirty years in the future!

History in the Making

Many people assume the Bible we read today must be a lot different from the original, but **archaeology** tells us something very different.

Take the **Dead Sea Scrolls** for instance. Our master copy of the Old Testament is called the **Masoretic text**, which dates back to about AD 1100. In 1947, the Dead Sea Scrolls were discovered (see Illustration #2), which were written or copied anywhere from 250 BC to AD 68. The biblical texts of the Dead Sea Scrolls are almost identical to the Masoretic text of a thousand years later. Moreover, what few differences there are have to do with grammatical things that don't affect the meaning of the text.

What does this tell us? It tells us that though the Bible we use today was handed down from generation to generation, it was copied so carefully that we can be reasonably certain the Old Testament we have today is essentially the same as it was in the very beginning.

The New Testament is even more amazing. We have more than five thousand manuscript copies of the New Testament written in the original **Greek** before the invention of the printing press. One script, from the book of John, is dated at AD 125. That copy is from just thirty years after the book of John was originally written! We have several complete copies of the New Testament from around AD 400, which means we have copies that were made only 350 years or so after the original. This is significant because we do not have copies that close in time to the original of any other book in the history of the ancient world.

> **How Others See It**
>
> **Josh McDowell**
>
> After personally trying to shatter the [historical proof for the] validity of the Scriptures, I have come to the conclusion that they are historically trustworthy.[9]

The Plan of Attack

2 Timothy 2:7 ***Reflect on what I am saying, for the Lord will give you insight into all this.***

As you read this book, it would be a good idea to go back to the Bible and make sure we're telling you the truth. Why? Because ultimately, even this book is just one of many. The Bible, however, is timeless and will give you the wisdom you need to see the difference between God's truth and people's opinions.

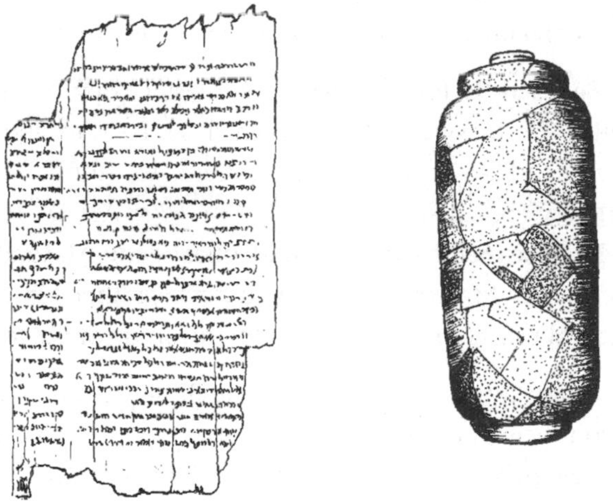

Illustration #2
Dead Sea Scrolls—The Dead Sea Scrolls were discovered in 1947 in caves near Qumran on the northwestern shore of the Dead Sea. The scrolls were preserved in clay jars. Inside the jars were a number of scrolls that included fragments of every book of the Old Testament except Esther.

In the pages ahead, we'll look at many of the main subjects found in the Bible, from its teachings on its authenticity to what it says about alcohol, relationships, and friendship, to name only a few. We'll select issues that relate to you as a teen and skip the parts for grandmothers, kings, and princes. We want to show you that the Bible really does have something to say to you where you are today and about what you're facing in school, at work, on the ball field, and in the midst of a party. You will be surprised that the Bible even has anything to say about these subjects, I'm sure. Nevertheless, the answers may be even more surprising. So read on, and share what you're learning with your friends.

How Others See It

Rebecca St. James

Hopefully my music is becoming more and more affected by the Bible. As I go I hope the lyrics and the songs get deeper into His Word.[10]

Jerry Manuel

I gave them mostly biblical principles in the interview (being a servant, for example). Most of the things I had on my outline were based on the Bible, but were put into baseball terms.[11]

Final Thoughts

- The Old Testament and the New Testament were written over a period of sixteen hundred years by more than forty different authors. Yet the Bible is amazingly consistent from start to finish.
- The Holy Spirit was behind everything written in the Bible. He inspired people so the words they wrote were actually God's words.
- The Bible is for anyone and everyone who wants to know God.
- God put many different kinds of literature in the Bible: sermons, histories, poems, songs, prophecies, promises, and so on. He did this to ensure that Scripture would contain something for everyone.
- Archaeology offers evidence that supports the historical reliability of the Bible. We need to pay attention to everything in the Bible, for all of it is God's Word and has the power to transform our lives.

Questions to Deepen Your Understanding

1. In what ways do you think the Bible is unique and speaks to you personally?
2. Name some people you know and suggest ways the Bible might help them.

3. What teachings from the Bible have helped you in the past, and which ones do you rely on for the future?

4. What verses of the Bible have you memorized? Name one and list several ways you've seen it become real in your life.

read on

Some of Mark and Jeanette's favorite books about opening your Bible and being amazed:

- *Don't Jump to Conclusions Without a Bungee Cord,* Martha Bolton, Vine Books
- *Evidence That Demands a Verdict,* Josh McDowell, Thomas Nelson
- *More Than a Carpenter,* Josh McDowell, Tyndale House
- *NIV Teen Devotional Bible,* Carla Barnhill, ed., Zondervan
- *Stuff You Don't Have to Pray About,* Susie Shellenberger, Broadman & Holman

Part Two

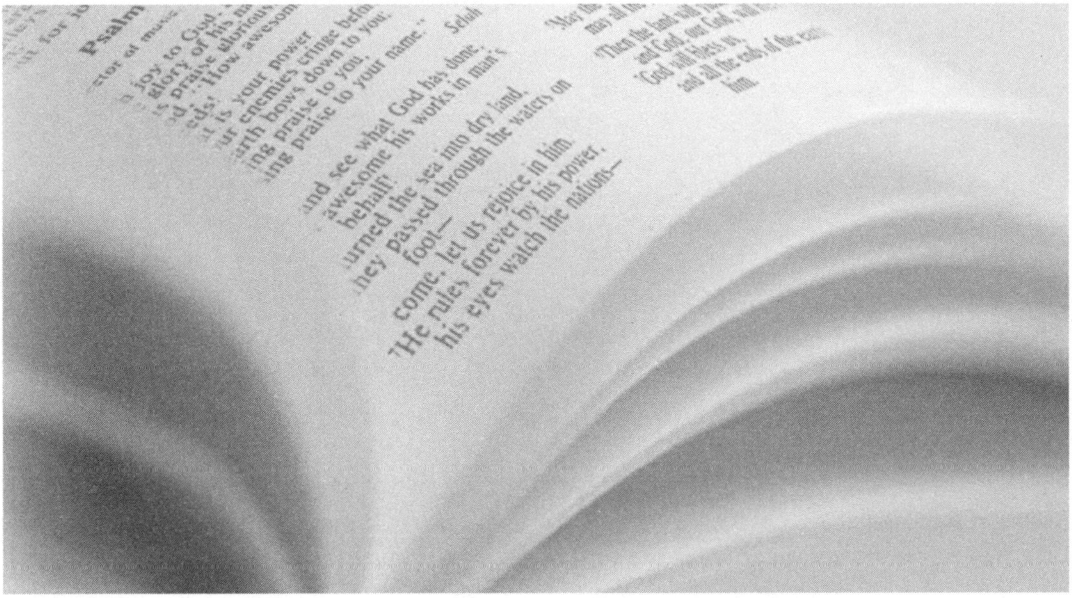

Great Teens of the Bible

Chapter 2: Teens Who Helped Found Judaism

Becoming Acquainted With Old Testament Teens

What's in This Chapter

- A Cheering Crowd
- The Miracle Child
- Sure, I'll Marry Him . . . What's His Name?
- God Loves Cheaters Too
- The Slave Who Led a Country
- The Slave Who Told Her Master What to Do

Here We Go

If you think the Bible is full of old guys with long beards . . . uh, you're right. But it includes stories about other folks too. Bible stories feature people of all ages, including a group of guys and gals we like to call "great teens of the Bible."

Judaism
religion of the Jewish people

But these weren't just "great teens." The ones we'll look at in this chapter founded **Judaism**, the Jewish faith. They gave God's people their start in knowing him.

The Bible writers recorded these stories to encourage and warn future generations. In this chapter, we'll see biblical teenagers perform great exploits, make tragic mistakes, commit grave sins, and accomplish amazing deeds. Some of the teens glorified God, and some of them sinned big-time! Yet even when they were weak, God stood by them.

Try to look at these teens as friends who will help you on your faith journey. Remember that they were imperfect people. Like you, they were human. And, like you, they experienced the Father's love.

A Cheering Crowd

Hebrews 12:1–3 ***Therefore, since we are surrounded by such a great cloud of witnesses, let us throw off everything that hinders and the sin that so easily entangles, and let us run with perseverance the race marked out for us. Let us fix our eyes on Jesus, the author and perfecter***

of our faith, who for the joy set before him endured the cross, scorning its shame, and sat down at the right hand of the throne of God. Consider him who endured such opposition from sinful men, so that you will not grow weary and lose heart.

This quote from Hebrews 12 reveals what kind of people support us from the past. In fact, according to Hebrews, these people make up a "cloud of witnesses" who cheer us on as we race for the Lord in this life. Some think these "witnesses" watch us now. Others say they are merely witnesses from the past to God's truth. Either way, they tell the story of who God is and what he can do in our lives.

Imagine people of the Bible, like those we're talking about in this chapter, are watching your life unfold and they're cheering you on. "Great move." "Hey, look at this. He's really trusting God this time." "Don't give up now." "Get up, get up. You can do it." While we don't know how much those in heaven see what's going on down here, we can be sure that some day our lives will unfold before others. That's not to strike fear into us, but it is a sober reminder that everything counts. You can't slide through life as though what you did doesn't matter. Everything matters, and when you get to heaven, you'll see just how much.

Who are your favorite characters in the Bible? Choose one you enjoy reading about, and imagine what he or she was like as a teen. What encouragement do you glean from their lives? What warnings?

---

everyday insights

Heather Floyd of Point of Grace found life-changing truth in the Bible, especially in the lives of Peter, Paul, and John. She used to put these apostles on pedestals, but she realized as she read more that the main point of Scripture was not how wonderful they were but how wonderful God is. Peter, Paul, and John were obedient to God, and so God did miracles through them. Learning this scriptural truth compelled Heather to commit herself to do whatever God wanted her to do. She recognized it was her responsibility to obey the Lord and avoid focusing on others or on herself. The Bible has a continual impact on her life, enabling her to find in its pages resources to encourage, build up, convict, and direct her to do the very important work of God.[1]

The Miracle Child

> ### The Big Picture
>
> **Genesis 21**
>
> Isaac is the son of Abraham, the father of the Jews. In this Scripture, Abraham and his family have entered a foreign land through God's leading. For years, God told Abraham he would have a son through his wife, Sarah. Abraham failed once to believe this and fathered a son through Sarah's servant. The son God had promised Abraham wasn't born until fourteen years later. Isaac's name means "laughter," because his mother thought God was joking when he sent angels to tell her that she was finally going to become a mother at ninety. He was named laughter also to symbolize the joy his parents felt when he was born.

ISAAC: One of the **Patriarchs** of the Jewish race (see appendix A). Isaac was the second generation of Jews in the world. Isaac's father, Abraham, was the beginning of the Jewish race and, accordingly, the foundation of Christian history. Isaac continued the family traditions his father taught him and launched the race of the Jews into history.

Miracle Boy

Isaac was a miracle baby. He was born to one-hundred-year-old Abraham and ninety-year-old **Sarah** twenty-five years after God's promise that Abraham's descendants would be as numerous as the stars in the sky. Before Isaac's birth, Abraham and Sarah had been unable to have children. Desperate, Sarah persuaded Abraham to go to bed with her servant, **Hagar**, and get her pregnant. Sarah hoped her servant's child would be counted as her child. But it didn't work out that way. Hagar did get pregnant and **Ishmael** was born. However, Sarah and Hagar no longer got along, and Ishmael was always considered the enemy of the household.

Isaac was born fourteen years later to Sarah and Abraham. He was the child God had promised Abraham.

Isaac was not a perfect man. He played favorites with his children, and he lied to a king, but despite his faults, God appeared to Isaac as he had appeared to Abraham. God made the same covenant, the promise that his children would inherit the land of Canaan and that he would have as many children as the "stars in the sky" (Genesis 22:15; 26:4).

check this out

descendants
Genesis 22:17; 26:4

Hagar
Genesis 16

fourteen
Genesis 16:16;21:5

Patriarchs
fathers; in this case, fathers of the Jews

Sarah
the wife of Abraham

Hagar
slave maiden to Sarah

Ishmael
son of Hagar

check this out

trick
Genesis 20:1–18;
26:1–11

How Others See It

Steve Crawford

When you understand the grace and mercy of God in your own life—and you're aware of your own weaknesses and struggles that He allows you to overcome on a daily basis—then you're able to be a little bit more compassionate.[2]

The life of Isaac is an example of someone who lived in contrasts. Even though he was the person who was to be the beginning of a completely new race of God's chosen people, he was not a perfect man. On one hand, he was very courageous. When he was a young boy, his father took him at God's command to sacrifice him. (More on that in a minute.) It took a lot of faith and courage to trust his dad like that—and to trust God. On the other hand, later in life, he lied to a king because he was afraid the king would kill him.

(The king thought Isaac's wife, Rebekah, was attractive. The king could have killed Isaac and taken Rebekah as his wife. Instead, he courted Rebekah, not knowing she was Isaac's wife. Isaac had apparently learned this trick from his father.) And he was undisciplined enough to play favorites with his own kids. Isaac seemed to be strong in his faith in some ways, but miserably weak in other ways.

heart to heart

Isn't that the way it is for most of us? We have some times when we really seem to be trusting God, and then we blow it. Amazingly, Isaac seemed to have more faith when he was a teenager than he did as an adult. That happens. Look at yourself. Perhaps you feel you're a committed follower of Christ. That's great. But don't just surf through the future on that assurance. You can lose your excitement about serving Christ if you don't purposely try to keep your commitment strong and fresh. You can be caught up in the things of this world—in possessions, in money, in power, in popularity—and you can end up a tired man or woman with little or no faith. We must always keep nurturing our faith and believe, like Isaac, that God is in charge of our lives.

How Others See It

Ruthie Bolton-Holifield

I know I have to keep things in perspective spiritually, because it's easy to get lost in the world's ideas and attitudes and lose your focus.[3]

Paul Molitor, at one time an MLB player, sensed Satan's attacks as a new Christian. "At that point in my life, I really started to realize my need for Christ. I began to read the Bible and think about Him a lot more. But I struggled with some spiritual warfare. I don't think Satan wanted me to get serious about my commitment to Christ."

How, then, did he overcome the problem? "Through God's persistent love," he says, "I was able to give myself up to Him."[4]

How Others See It

Rebecca St. James

Sometimes I get a bit bothered by the limelight—when people treat me differently—like I don't make mistakes. I had a girl come up to me and say, "I used to be really good like you," and I was like, "I'm not that good. We all make mistakes. We all sin. We all fall short. It's only God's love, grace, and mercy that bring us through." I just want to be faithful to God one day at a time.[5]

God Suggesting Murder?

HEBREWS 11:17–19 ***By faith Abraham, when God tested him, offered Isaac as a sacrifice. He who had received the promises was about to sacrifice his one and only son, even though God had said to him, "It is through Isaac that your offspring will be reckoned." Abraham reasoned that God could raise the dead, and figuratively speaking, he did receive Isaac back from death.***

This might be one of the strangest events in the Bible. After all, it looks like God was ordering Abraham to murder Isaac, his teenage son. Moreover, Isaac was specifically supposed to be sacrificed to God! Nowhere in biblical history before or after this time did God say human sacrifice was okay, even though it was practiced by many of the **heathen** people in Canaan at that time.

When God commanded Abraham to take Isaac up on the mountain and sacrifice him, according to Scripture, Abraham did not flinch at this task. In fact, he probably thought about it a long time as he made the fifty-mile trek from his home to the mountains of Moriah. From this passage we know that Abraham believed God could raise Isaac from the dead. Abraham might have guessed that he could sacrifice Isaac, slit his throat,

heathen
unbelieving, godless people

angel of the Lord
Jesus Christ in angelic form

pour out his blood, and fulfill the obligation. Then God would resurrect the young man. But that's not what happened.

When Isaac's father was ready to sacrifice him, what did Isaac do? He submitted to his father, perhaps with the same faith his father exhibited. He lay on the wood, had his hands and feet tied, and presented his neck for the slaughter. Imagine what faith this young man must have had! Where had that faith come from? Undoubtedly, Isaac learned it from his father. He had observed how his father approached problems and situations. He had seen his father pray and seek God in the problems of life. He had witnessed how his father worshiped when the old man made other sacrifices. If your parents know God, you can follow Isaac's example by asking God to teach you through your parents, as he did through Abraham. If your parents aren't Christians, you can be sure God has placed others in your life to be "spiritual parents" and to teach you.

And, in turn, you're also a spiritual example to those who are your age and younger than you—maybe siblings or kids in church. What kind of faith are you showing those who look up to you?

Boy Saved, All Is Well

> GENESIS 22:11–14 ***But the angel of the Lord called out to him from heaven, "Abraham! Abraham!" "Here I am," he replied. "Do not lay a hand on the boy," he said. "Do not do anything to him. Now I know that you fear God, because you have not withheld from me your son, your only son." Abraham looked up and there in a thicket he saw a ram caught by its horns. He went over and took the ram and sacrificed it as a burnt offering instead of his son. So Abraham called that place The Lord Will Provide. And to this day it is said, "On the mountain of the Lord it will be provided."***

Abraham is about to cut his son's throat. He believes God can raise the boy from the dead, yet he also can't be sure what God will do. He has faith in God and he trusts him. He raises his arm. The knife glints in the sunlight.

Isaac is lying on this pile of sticks. He knows he is about to die. He knows his father loves him. Yet he doesn't struggle. He is unafraid. He knows God is in charge. What happens? As Abraham is about to cut Isaac's throat with the knife, even as his hand raises to make the cut, the **angel of the Lord** calls out to Abraham. He says, "Now I know that you fear God, because you have not withheld from me your son, your only son"

(Genesis 22:12). Abraham sacrifices a **ram** instead, which he finds caught in some bushes shortly after the angel speaks.

The interesting thing here is that at one point Isaac asks, "Where is the sacrifice?" He saw that his father had the knife for killing the animal and wood for the fire, but he saw no animal present. Abraham responded that God would provide the sacrifice. Human sacrifice was condemned by God. Abraham's faith was rewarded. When we obey God and wait on him with faith, he provides for us. When you don't obey God, you disobey the only one who can bless you.

What does Isaac teach us about faith? Perhaps this: Sometimes God will ask us to do strange or difficult things in his name, like sharing Christ with the person we think would be least interested in hearing about him, giving up some activity to spend more time in God's Word, or obeying our parents when we don't agree with them. We may not understand why he wants us to do such things, but we must obey, or disobey to our own peril. Isaac and his father were greatly blessed by God because of their obedience. God promises to bless us when we obey, even when we don't understand why he's asking what he's asking.

words to live by

Sure, I'll Marry Him . . . What's His Name?

> GENESIS 24:61–67 *Then Rebekah and her maids got ready and mounted their camels and went back with the man. So the servant took Rebekah and left. Now Isaac had come from Beer Lahai Roi, for he was living in the Negev. He went out to the field one evening to meditate, and as he looked up, he saw camels approaching. Rebekah also looked up and saw Isaac. She got down from her camel and asked the servant, "Who is that man in the field coming to meet us?" "He is my master," the servant answered. So she took her veil and covered herself. Then the servant told Isaac all he had done. Isaac brought her into the tent of his mother Sarah, and he married Rebekah. So she became his wife, and he loved her; and Isaac was comforted after his mother's death.*

REBEKAH: An attractive cousin of Isaac's. Her mother's name was **Milcah**, and her father was **Nahor**, who was Abraham's (Isaac's father's) brother. Although Rebekah was Isaac's cousin, she had never met him.

check this out

human sacrifice
Judges 11:30–40; 2 Kings 3:27; 16:3

condemned
Leviticus 18:21; 20:2–5; Jeremiah 7:31–32; 19:5–6

search
Genesis 24

ram
male sheep

Milcah
wife of Nahor

Nahor
brother of Abraham

Love at First Sight

When the time came for Abraham's son Isaac to find a bride, Abraham sent his servant to search in Haran. The servant, Eliezer, was to seek a

Haran
ancient city

woman from the family of Nahor and bring her home to marry Isaac (see Illustration #3).

When Eliezer arrived in **Haran**, he stopped by a well to pray for success in finding Isaac's bride. He asked that God would send the woman to the well, and that when he asked for a drink, she would offer to water his camels as well. Soon a beautiful young woman appeared. She carried a water pot on her shoulder, and when Eliezer asked for a drink, she offered to serve his camels. Eliezer asked the girl's name and told her he needed a place to stay for the night. The girl welcomed him to stay with her family and said her name was Rebekah. She was Isaac's first cousin (in ancient times, it was not uncommon for members of the same family to marry). Eliezer praised God for answering his prayer and showered Rebekah with gifts. When Eliezer explained his mission to Rebekah and her family, she agreed to travel to Canaan and marry Isaac, sight unseen (see appendix A).

How old was Rebekah at this time? We don't know for sure, but the Bible says that Rebekah was a virgin. At that time girls typically married by thirteen or fourteen, so chances are Rebekah was much younger than Isaac, who was forty at the time. But Isaac didn't care! This Scripture tells us that he loved her. It looks like Isaac and Rebekah experienced the unusual—love at first sight!

Illustration #3
The Search for Rebekah—This map shows Eliezer's journey to the well where he found Rebekah, Eliezer's return with Rebekah, and Isaac's journey to the wedding.

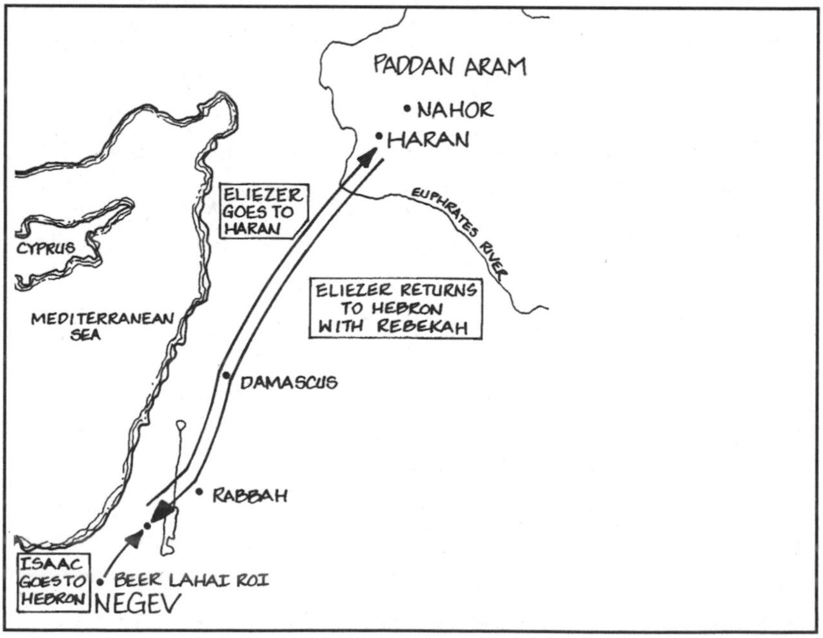

What can we learn from Rebekah's response to Eliezer and his requests? First, we see that Rebekah cared about strangers and was willing to serve others. When Eliezer approached her and asked for a drink, she received him immediately. She also willingly offered to water his camels, showing that she was a woman of care and compassion. Second, it is clear that Rebekah had great faith. When Eliezer told of his mission and of God's answer to his prayer, she agreed to travel to Canaan without hesitation. She sensed God's hand on her life and was willing to follow his leading. She and Isaac later had two children, Jacob and Esau. There would be problems galore, but this godly couple sought to please God, which is what it's all about.

---

everyday insights

When I (Mark) met my wife, Jeanette, I was teaching at a writer's conference. So was she. We talked after the conference. I went out to my car afterward, sat in the driver's seat, and whooped, "God, I'm going to marry that woman!" I think that's about the same kind of reaction Isaac had to Rebekah and Rebekah to Isaac.

Romance doesn't always happen like that, but an important step like marriage is always an act of faith—faith in the other person to be a good husband or wife and faith that God has led you together.

It may be a few years before you get married, but in the meantime, God will place plenty of little steps of faith into your life. As you learn to trust God in the little things, you'll learn to hear his voice and trust him when you face the big ones.

God Loves Cheaters Too

GENESIS 25:21–28 ***Isaac prayed to the Lord on behalf of his wife, because she was barren. The Lord answered his prayer, and his wife Rebekah became pregnant. The babies jostled each other within her, and she said, "Why is this happening to me?" So she went to inquire of the Lord. The Lord said to her, "Two nations are in your womb, and two peoples from within you will be separated; one people will be stronger than the other, and the older will serve the younger." When the time came for her to give birth, there were twin boys in her womb. The first to come out was red, and his whole body was like a hairy garment; so they named him Esau. After this, his brother came out, with his hand grasping Esau's heel; so he was named Jacob. Isaac was sixty years old when Rebekah gave birth to them. The boys grew up, and Esau became a skillful hunter,***

check this out

Esau
Romans 9:6–13;
Hebrews 12:15–17

Messiah
the Anointed One

a man of the open country, while Jacob was a quiet man, staying among the tents. Isaac, who had a taste for wild game, loved Esau, but Rebekah loved Jacob.

JACOB: The third-generation Jew from his grandfather, Abraham. Jacob married two women, Leah and Rachel, and had several of his twelve sons through each of their servants. He was the last individual Jew—after him, twelve sons carried on the heritage (see appendix A).

Sibling Rivalry to the Extreme

From this passage we can see that God chose Jacob to be the person through whom the **Messiah**, Jesus, would eventually be born. Yet the Bible is clear that Jacob wasn't a perfect man either. Even at birth, Jacob seemed to be wheeling and dealing. When his twin brother, Esau, was being born, Jacob's hand was gripped on Esau's heel, as if to say, "I won't let you get ahead of me!" And Jacob didn't. All his life he ripped off his brother and managed to create so much tension in the family that he eventually had to be sent to his mother's family in Haran to keep the peace.

We see much of Jacob's life from the time he was born. One of the main events comes early on, perhaps when he was a teenager. The reason Jacob's mother, Rebekah, favored him was because he was a homebody—he liked nice things, cooking, and living in tents. She probably pampered him and introduced him to all her favorite subjects. Esau, on the other hand, was a hunter, a rough-and-tumble party boy, a man of the mountains—the kind of guy who plays hard and works hard. His father favored him, but God let his blessing come through Jacob.

How Others See It

Michelle Akers

Only two things last forever: God and people. In time, everything else will fade away. Striving for power, possessions, and popularity is ultimately a waste of time and effort. I've found the initial excitement that comes with a new championship vanishes soon thereafter. The thrill of being the best can't be sustained. Possessions rust, break, and wear out. These things have no power nor worth in light of eternity.[6]

Weatherworn Word

for real

I (Mark) knew Steve was smart, one of the smartest guys in the senior class at his school. In the high school Sunday school class, he asked tough questions and didn't let me get away with simplistic answers. At first I thought he was a rather skeptical character, convinced the whole Christianity idea was a dead-end excursion.

One weeknight I called him up and asked if I might come out and visit him in his home. He said sure. We made a date, and the following week I went by his house. When we sat down in his living room, we talked about school, his interests, and the debate team of which he was a prime member. He showed me his bedroom, his rock music CDs, several books he liked from Tolkien to a number of authors I didn't recognize, and his monstrous "debate" file. In it he had cards with quotes and data from all sorts of sources on the subject they were debating that year nationally. I was astounded at the research he'd done.

"These guys in debate are fanatics," he told me. "They'll do anything to win. You can't let a fact get by. You have to back everything up."

He told me about his style and how he approached a debate, how he had to be able to argue from both sides of an issue. It occurred to me how difficult it could be to convince him of the issues of faith and Christ, if that was where he stood.

Later, with some cake and cola under our belts, we sat again in the living room and talked quietly. I asked him specifically about his faith in Christ. He didn't know exactly what he believed, although his parents were ardent believers and very active in the church. I tried to make clear what the Gospel was, then rounded it off, saying, "Anytime you want to talk, let me know."

We talked many times over the next few months. One Sunday Steve came up to me in Sunday school and said he'd accepted Christ. In fact, he and several other students at his high school had become Christians, and they wanted to start a Bible study in school. "Would you like to come?"

I said yes.

Over the next year and a half, we met, discussed the Bible, ate pizza, laughed, told jokes, and went on trips. We built some strong relationships. There were strong differences among members of the group. One spoke in tongues. Another struggled with parents who were splitting up.

Others faced dating, school, and other personal problems. But they were all students who stayed at the top of the class. They didn't let anything go by without making sure "the Bible really said it."

Later that year Steve was accepted at college. He wanted to go. He went off to a secular college still committed to Christ, but I knew it could be a struggle. I had also attended a secular school and knew well how it might affect his faith.

When I stopped by to see him off to school, I gave him a little pocket Bible. "It's good because you can carry it around with you if you want. When a prof says something you know isn't true, just pop it out and read off a line. See what happens. Just like in a debate."

He laughed. "I don't know about that. I don't want to get them all on my case right away. But it is a nice Bible. I guess that's about par from a youth pastor."

I smiled. We hugged and I wished him God's best.

Over the next month we talked on the phone a few times. "They really hit Christianity around here," he told me. "Evolution is another big subject. I've met a few other Christians though. We meet for a Bible study."

I felt some relief. I visited him later, and he showed me around campus. We talked about many things. As we walked through campus, he reached into his back pocket to pull out the little Bible. Then he read me a verse he'd found about what we'd been talking about.

I didn't even hear him. I was staring at the Bible I'd given him less than a month before. It was dog-eared, mangled, beat up. It looked like three Doberman pinschers had fought over it for three hours.

I exclaimed, "Steve, what on earth happened to your Bible?"

He glanced at it, then shrugged. "Hey, I carry it with me all the time. I'm always looking up stuff in it. Even in the middle of meals and in the rain. I guess it got that way because it goes with me wherever I am."

On the way home, I had to laugh. I knew if that was his attitude, he was in good hands. He was seeking Jesus as his primary discipler. Jesus, I knew, would guard him, lead him, and challenge him every step along the way.

"How can a young man keep his way pure?" Psalm 119:9 asks. It answers, "By living according to your word."

You might wonder how people like Isaac, Rebekah, Joseph, and the other teens in this chapter kept close to God. There is one answer: They kept what they knew of his Word tight in their hearts. If you want to be anything like them in your relationship with God, keep the Bible in your heart. Know it. Think about it. Live it. And it will live in you!

The Way to a Man's Birthright Is Through His Stomach

GENESIS 25:29–34 ***Once when Jacob was cooking some stew, Esau came in from the open country, famished. He said to Jacob, "Quick, let me have some of that red stew! I'm famished!" (That is why he was also called Edom.) Jacob replied, "First sell me your birthright." "Look, I am about to die," Esau said. "What good is the birthright to me?" But Jacob said, "Swear to me first." So he swore an oath to him, selling his birthright to Jacob. Then Jacob gave Esau some bread and some lentil stew. He ate and drank, and then got up and left. So Esau despised his birthright.***

One time Esau returned from the fields desperately hungry. Jacob stood at the soup pot making some bean stew. Esau probably would have preferred venison, but he didn't want to cook it. He was hungry. You know the feeling—when you're so hungry you think you're going to die. So Esau said to his brother, "Quick, let me have some of that red stew! I'm famished!"

Jacob was smart at figuring people out. He sensed this was the perfect time to spring something on Esau that Jacob had probably thought about all his life. You see, Esau was the firstborn son. That meant that up to two-thirds of the family inheritance belonged to him. The rest would go to Jacob—he would only inherit one-third of his father's money, which was still substantial, but not enough for Jacob.

Maybe Jacob felt irked that he wasn't first, especially since he must have known that God had chosen him. After all, before the boys were even born, God had told Rebekah that the second son would eventually rule over the firstborn. Rebekah had probably told Jacob that God favored him and promised to bring the Messiah through his line. Perhaps Jacob became a bit arrogant after that. Maybe he thought he was better than his brother. Pride stepped in and derailed his faith. When things didn't go his way, he didn't trust God; he trusted his own wits, himself. And he engineered circumstances to go in his favor.

So Jacob got Esau to trade his birthright to his brother for a bowl of soup. We have to realize not only that was Jacob smart, but also that Esau apparently didn't value his inheritance too highly. He seemed to make the trade gladly. And Jacob got what he valued. Later, Jacob and his mother went to extremes to trick the near-blind Isaac into also giving Jacob the blessing that normally went to the firstborn. When the time came for Isaac to give Esau the blessing, he'd told him to first go into the fields, kill an animal, and prepare him a meat stew. While Esau was out hunting, Rebekah and Jacob killed a goat and attached its hair to Jacob's arms so he would feel like the hairy Esau to their blind father. Jacob put on Esau's clothes so he would smell like his brother. His mom made a meat stew, just as Esau would. The trick worked. Isaac gave the blessing of the family to the wrong son. Jacob not only got his brother's financial inheritance, but he also got the spiritual inheritance as well.

Later, though, Jacob had an encounter with the angel of the Lord in which he persistently asked for God's blessing.

think about it

What can we learn from the life of Jacob? Perhaps the best lesson of all is that God can still love us even when we don't trust him, even when we disobey him, even when we sin atrociously. God loved Jacob so much that he ultimately changed his name from Jacob to Israel. Israel means "he fights or persists with God." Hanging in there with God, even when you don't like him very much, impresses God greatly. He loves a person who perseveres. It also shows that your teen years aren't all that God looks at. Maybe you think, *I've blown it with God!* If that's you, then take heart from Jacob. God can bring good out of your situation, if you trust him.

How Others See It

Michelle Akers

I am significant simply because I am created by and owned by God. He calls me His jewel, His treasured possession (Malachi 3:17). God rejoices over me. His love for me will never end, nor can He love me more (or less) than He does this very minute.[7]

Before we get too self-righteous about how we'd never act like Jacob, we can take a look at these statistics on honesty, according to the George Barna Research Group:[8]

- One-third of the public said lying is sometimes necessary, but more than half (52 percent) said they sometimes lie.

- The older a person was, the more likely they were to state they are completely satisfying the commandment to always tell the truth. . . . Deceitful language was more common among men than women; among college-educated adults than those with less formal education; among people without young kids than among parents; among people in metropolitan areas than among rural residents; among people who do not attend church and those who do not read the Bible.
- Just over half of the born-again adults (53 percent) said they were completely fulfilling this commandment; 44 percent of the non-Christians claimed compliance. Remember, God honors honesty!

Reuben
first son of Jacob by Leah

The Slave Who Led a Country

The Big Picture

Genesis 37–50

Joseph was one of the twelve sons of Jacob. Just as Jacob's mom, Rebekah, favored him, Jacob also had favorites among his kids. Jacob's favorite child was Joseph because he was the first son of Jacob's beloved wife, Rachel. Joseph's half brothers hated him for this favoritism and sold him as a slave. He eventually landed in jail for being falsely accused of molesting his boss's wife. But Joseph trusted God, and God was with him even in prison. Joseph eventually became prime minister in Egypt. During a famine, Joseph's brothers visited Egypt looking for food. There they met Joseph and feared retribution. Joseph told them that what they meant for evil (selling him into slavery), God had meant for good. God used that event to save Jacob's family.

JOSEPH: The eleventh son of Jacob, favored greatly by his father. He was referred to as the dreamer because of dreams he had in which his brothers and father bowed down to him as one would to a king. Joseph's brothers sold him into slavery, and he was taken to a foreign country. While there, he achieved a position of great authority in the government and was responsible for saving many lives during a worldwide famine (see appendix A).

Dad's Favorite!

Joseph is one of the greatest figures in the entire Bible. His ten older brothers hated him for his prophetic dreams and his status. They eventually conspired to kill him, but **Reuben**, Joseph's oldest brother, persuaded them to

bad things
Romans 8:28; Jeremiah 29:11–13

Potiphar
Joseph's master in Egypt

Pharaoh
ruler of Egypt

sell him as a slave. Joseph was taken to Egypt and became the leading caretaker of his master's house. Joseph was a handsome young man, and his master's wife wanted to have an affair with him. Many times, she tried to get him to sleep with her. He refused every time. On one occasion, she was insistent and grabbed him. He ran out of the house, leaving his coat in her hands. The angry woman told her husband that Joseph had tried to rape her. **Potiphar**, Joseph's master, had Joseph thrown in prison.

Joseph was probably in his teens when this happened. Think about it. He was a young man who had great gifts and talents: looks, intelligence, and the ability to lead. Yet he kept his eyes on God. But everything didn't go smoothly for him. His own family hated him and sold him into slavery. He ended up a slave in Egypt, enticed by a beautiful woman. He could have been very angry with God that he got in trouble when he wasn't doing anything wrong. He could have said, "God, you obviously don't care about me, so why should I listen to or follow you? You've let my life end up in a mess." Joseph didn't. Instead, he continued to love God and do what was right. And God blessed him for it.

How Others See It

Napoleon Kaufman

But before I got saved, it was hard when I didn't have good days. I would constantly beat myself up if it looked like I wasn't going to make my goals. But now that I'm working for the Lord, I know that everything that happens to me is in accordance with the will of God. The steps of a righteous man are ordered by the Lord. And just knowing that has brought me peace.[9]

How do you respond when <u>bad things</u> happen in your life? Do you see it as God's plan or as a meaningless problem that neither you nor God can do anything about? When you walk with Jesus, you know that he will pull you through even hard times because he loves you.

Hey! Who Cleaned Out the Refrigerator?

The Big Picture

Genesis 41–45

Joseph, through interpreting **Pharaoh**'s dream and offering advice about what to do, becomes prime minister of Egypt. He organizes a plan to store grain because of the seven years of famine that are coming. For seven years he stores the grain, builds great cities, and taxes the people. Then the seven years of famine come. Much of the Middle Eastern world begins turning to Egypt for help. That is when Joseph's brothers come to Egypt looking for food.

As Pharaoh's prime minister, Joseph ran things well. He also had God's blessing and help, making him the most powerful man in the world at that time. Joseph stored up grain in Egypt, and when the years of famine came, everyone was fed. The famine also came to the land of Canaan, where Joseph's brothers lived with their father. They learned of grain in Egypt, and when they came there, Joseph met them, though they didn't know who he was. After a series of tricks and chicaneries, Joseph revealed that he was their brother. They were shocked and afraid, but Joseph assured them he would take care of them. Later, when Israel, their father, died, Joseph had to reassure his brothers that he wouldn't kill them, making one of the greatest statements of faith in all the Bible about having bad things happen to good people. He said, in Genesis 50:20, "You intended to harm me, but God intended it for good to accomplish what is now being done, the saving of many lives."

When bad things happen to good people, do not fear. God is with good people even when bad things happen to them. A good verse to memorize in this context is Psalm 27:14: "Wait for the Lord; be strong and take heart and wait for the Lord."

True Staying Power

for real

Bryan Allen had a dream: to power a self-propelled plane across the English Channel from England to France. He powered the plane by a bicycle-type arrangement in a small cabin in the midsection of the slight plane, called the Albatross. *As he neared France, he was exhausted, driven to ground by thirst, pain in his legs, and dehydration. He dipped to within six inches of the water. Finally, defeated eight miles out, he signaled to the rescue craft nearby to send out a line that he would use to tow himself in. He had to climb ten feet for the boat to come in close. There, he found calmer air, and a new burst of energy swelled through him.*

By the last quarter mile, Allen's legs were useless. But he kept pumping, even when painful cramps crackled through his shins. When he finally landed on the coast to the cheers of spectators, he said he couldn't *have gone another ten feet. Radio, television, and other media caught the story of the $1,600 plane that had been powered across the Channel. They took it off to the Paris Air Show, where it would sit among million-dollar marvels. Allen's first words when he touched down were, "Wow! Wow!"*[10]

That's the kind of perseverance it takes to serve God in this world. However, it can be done only with God's help. It's the kind that Joseph had as he worked as a slave and then as a prisoner in Egypt. He knew God had a plan and that he would bring it about. All Joseph had to do was stick to the rules and not give up.

heart to heart

Joseph's faith and perseverance are two things he learned in his youth. He hung in there even when his brothers hated him. Joseph stands out in Scripture as a premier man of faith because of his attitude of forgiveness. In addition, he saw that God was in charge even of the bad things that happened to him. What about you? Are you living out that kind of faith? It's difficult, but with God's help it can be done. Are you angry about how things have not gone your way? God says, "Trust me, and I'll lead you into an adventure you would not want to miss."

Are you upset because a situation in which you were innocent has left you rejected and hated? If you're feeling that way, remember, Jesus knows exactly how you feel—he was innocent but was killed. In his despair, he turned to his Father.

We can do that too. When you're hurting, trust God. He is with those who love him, and he will lead them to glory. It's an old story, but one worth repeating: When you trust God, even the bad things turn out for good. When you don't trust God, often the good things turn out for bad!

How Others See It

Michael W. Smith

God is a deeply compassionate Father. He cares about us when we suffer. He understands our anger and our confusion. His grief is just as real as ours. . . . If you plan on living here in this world, then you'd better figure out how you're going to deal with crises. Suffering is unavoidable for the human race; it touches us all. Jesus warned his disciples with these words: "I have told you these things, so that in me you may have peace. In this world you will have trouble. But take heart! I have overcome the world" (John 16:33).[11]

The Slave Who Told Her Master What to Do

> 2 Kings 5:1–5 *Now Naaman was commander of the army of the king of Aram. He was a great man in the sight of his master and highly regarded, because through him the Lord had given victory to Aram. He was a valiant soldier, but he had leprosy. Now bands from Aram had gone out and had taken captive a young girl from Israel, and she served Naaman's wife. She said to her mistress, "If only my master would see the prophet who is in Samaria! He would cure him of his leprosy." Naaman went to his master and told him what the girl from Israel had said. "By all means, go," the king of Aram replied. "I will send a letter to the king of Israel." So Naaman left, taking with him ten talents of silver, six thousand shekels of gold and ten sets of clothing.*

SERVANT GIRL: The servant girl in this passage worked for Naaman's wife. We don't even know her name. Servants in those days had about the same experience as slaves did in America. Many were taken into slavery when their nation was conquered by a larger nation. How they were treated depended on their masters. Some were beaten. Some were treasured. For most, it was not a pleasant life. Apparently, this servant girl valued her master because she told his wife where he could get help.

Renewed Love

for real

I (Jeanette) have experienced some tough times with the teens in my life. Nicole, my stepdaughter, was one of them. I came into her life when she was twelve years old, after her father had been through a harrowing divorce. For six years she had been the "queen of the house," living with her dad and her sister, Alisha. Then I came along, and sparks began to fly.

"I know you hate me," Nicole sobbed. "I've been so horrible lately. I don't blame you for not liking me at all."

It had been a rough couple of weeks for us. Nicole had been dating her first steady boyfriend for about a month. A good kid, and sixteen, she didn't understand why we had rules about how often she could see her boyfriend and how long they could talk on the phone. As a result, nearly every night, we had a "boyfriend battle." Now Nicole was feeling badly about our arguments. As I hugged her, I reassured her of my love. I meant it. Nicole is my daughter. Sure, she messes up sometimes. So do I. So does her dad and her sister and her brother. Even though we're trying to be a family that loves God and one another, we still have times of anger, disobedience, ugliness, and sin.

God doesn't stop loving any of us, any more than Mark and I stop loving Nicole or our other kids when they behave badly or disobey us. They may have to suffer the consequences of their actions, or we may discipline them, but we never stop loving them.

You know, if you and I were writing the stories of the people in the Bible, we'd probably write mainly about all the interesting and amazing things they did right. But God didn't want the Bible written that way. God didn't try to hide the mistakes, sins, and ugliness of his people. Instead, he let us see them for what they truly were—human, fallible, and sinful. But he also showed us how he can use imperfect people to make neat things happen.

God can do the same thing with us. As we strive to live for him, even if we blow it sometimes, he can use us to make his will happen.

Caring Enough to Get Involved

Years passed in Israel. People did God's thing. Then people did their own thing. Israel suffered many experiences of being carried into slavery. Here we see one of those slaves helping a friend.

This is a remarkable situation. A girl, perhaps a teen (we don't know for sure), is captured by Aramaeans marauding into the land of Israel. She's taken to Aram, and there she's put into the household of a great captain of the Aramaeans, a man named Naaman. This captain happens to be a leper. In those days, leprosy was a terrible disease physically and socially. Lepers were required to stay away from everyone else. Whenever they approached nonleprous people, they had to ring bells and shout "unclean!" so others would know to stay away from them. Naaman's family was probably devastated when he contracted the disease.

The servant girl in Naaman's household had been raised to know of the great prophet of God, Elisha, who lived in Israel. He performed miracles—including healing—and pointed people to God. When Naaman became a leper, the slave girl told her mistress about Elisha. In a sense, that was a risky thing to do. After all, who expected a young girl, and a slave at that, to know anything valuable or helpful? What if Naaman went to Elisha and didn't get any help? Would he be angry and beat the girl? It was a chance. But the servant had faith that her God could help the master she served.

Naaman got a letter from the king of Aram to introduce him to Israel's king. The story unfolds in the Bible in 2 Kings 5. Naaman ultimately is healed of his leprosy and all is well. Even Jesus once referred to Naaman and Elisha in the book of Luke.

Naaman and Elisha
2 Kings 5:8–27;
Luke 4:27

What does this little girl teach us? Perhaps the main lesson is one of witness. When we see an opportunity to speak up for God and his people, we should take it. Witnessing is an intimidating, hard thing for many Christians. They're afraid of being hated or made fun of, or worse.

The Bible clearly teaches that God puts opportunities to witness right in our path. He wants us to take those opportunities and use them to tell the world about him and his love for people. What about you? Are you willing to tell the good news of Christ to anyone and everyone every chance you get? How do you get those opportunities? Ask God for them. Get on your knees each night before bed and say, "God, tomorrow show me opportunities to speak up for you." God will give you some, so take heart. Tomorrow is the first day of the rest of your life as a witness for Jesus!

How Others See It

Larry Sutton

I need to be aware of those people around me who God wants me to spend time with and witness to.[12]

Telling the World

The story of seventeen-year-old Cassie Bernall shows us the way of witnessing during a moment of absolute persecution. She was in the Columbine High School library on April 20, 1999, as two murderous teenagers swept through the halls shooting everyone in sight. Christians, classmates, and even several members of her own church were hiding in the library with her. As the trench-coated killers approached, Cassie dove under a table, clutching the Bible she'd brought to the library to read. The killers played cruel games with different people, shooting them or leaving them alive for no apparent reason. One gunman asked Cassie, "Do you believe in God?" At first, she didn't respond. Onlookers said the still-smoking gun was pointed right at her.

"Yes, I believe in God," she said finally. The gunman laughed and said, "Why?" Then he shot her in the face. She died immediately.

Other witnesses said that Cassie, who only a few years before had been dabbling in the occult and considering suicide, also said, "There is a God and you need to follow along God's path." The killer reportedly answered, "There is no God," and pulled the trigger.

One other student, eighteen-year-old Valeen Schnurr, also faced this question in the hallway. She also replied "Yes" and was shot. She was found with nine bullet and shrapnel wounds in her body, but she was alive.

It could happen to me or you. How would you answer? The truth is, though you might like to say you know exactly what you'd say, you don't. All you have from God is a promise that he will give you the words to say when they are needed. That's the witness. That's the trust. God will give you the words. That's what telling the world about Jesus is all about.

Final Thoughts

- Isaac, also a great teen of the Bible, showed the true meaning of obedience when his father, Abraham, took him on the mountain to sacrifice him to God. Isaac complied, showing that obedience, even to the point of death, is what God values.
- Rebekah, one of the great mothers of the children of Israel, led an exemplary life. She trusted God to provide her husband for her. She was God's match for Isaac and a mother to be reckoned with.
- Jacob demonstrates that you don't have to be perfect to get God on your side. He was a cheat and a doubter, and yet he still pursued God. God worked with him until he became a man of faith.
- Joseph was not only a great teen of the Bible, but one who also grew up to become a great leader of Egypt and Israel. He is one to be studied as an example of a man who followed God and was strong in resisting temptation.
- Naaman's wife's maid shows us something of what it means to witness. Just point others to God, no matter what your status in life.

Questions to Deepen Your Understanding

1. How did God lead Rebekah? Have you ever seen him lead you like that?
2. How was Isaac an example of dedication to God? What would you have done if Abraham had been your father and had taken you to sacrifice on the mountain?
3. What imperfections do you have that you think God will have to deal with as he did with Jacob's?
4. Why do you think Joseph continued to trust God even though so many things went wrong for him?
5. What principles do you see active in the witness of Naaman's wife's maidservant?

read on

Some of Mark and Jeanette's favorite books about becoming acquainted with Old Testament teens:

- *Bible Heroes: Abraham, Joseph and Moses,* (no author given), Shining Star
- *Encounters With Truth: Bible Characters Tell Their Own Story,* Joseph R. Cooke, Good Samaritan Ministries
- *Joseph: How God Builds Character,* Paul Borthwick, InterVarsity
- *Joseph: A Man of Absolute Integrity* (Great Lives from God's Word, vol. 3), Charles R. Swindoll, Word
- *New International Encyclopedia of Bible Characters,* Paul D. Gardner, Zondervan
- *A Treasury of Miracles for Teens: True Stories of God's Presence Today,* Karen Kingsbury, FaithWords
- *What's in the Bible for Women,* Georgia Curtis Ling, Bethany

Chapter 3: Teens Who Were Leaders in the Old Testament

Becoming a Leader for God

What's in This Chapter

- David, God's Guy
- Josiah, the Teen King
- Daniel, the Man of the Future
- Esther, Too Young to Be Queen

Here We Go

Teens were not only involved in founding Israel, the Jewish nation, but also in leading it. Some of the greatest people of faith began living for God while they were teens, and they rocked their world. In this chapter, we'll look at four more teens who show us how to lead, serve, and give.

These teens really existed. They struggled with the same challenges you face: girls, guys, school, math, pleasing God, witnessing, and serving others. As you study these teens, you'll see gutsy, realistic, red-blooded people who wanted to walk with God. Ultimately, that is what life is all about, and young people have wondered and pondered these things from the beginning. Look at these teens not through rose-colored glasses, but through eyes of admiration and respect. They served God at a time when it was hard, if not harder, to survive in the world. They knew what it was to be rejected, hated, persecuted, and, in some cases, killed for their faith. Listen to their heartbeats, and as you do, begin to trust their judgments.

David, God's Guy

> ACTS 13:22 ***After removing Saul, [God] made David [Israel's] king. He testified concerning him: "I have found David son of Jesse a man after my own heart; he will do everything I want him to do."***

DAVID: He was the youngest of Jesse's eight sons. He was a shepherd who composed psalms and fought off wild animals as he watched his flocks. Later he killed the giant Goliath. God chose David to be the second king of Israel. He led the country during a time of growth and prosperity (see appendix A).

Loved by One and All

David was praised for being the greatest king, warrior, and psalm writer of the Bible. But most of all, he was chosen by God because he was "a man after God's own heart." What does that mean? It means David had the same purposes, plans, commitments, loves, and hates as God did. And he had these attitudes at an early age, for when the above comment was made, David was still a teenager—he had not yet killed **Goliath**, led Israelites in battles, or accomplished anything great in the eyes of man or God. God is always looking for people who have his heart, who want what he wants.

What would it mean for you to be a person "after God's own heart"? What changes might come into your life? Do you think you'd tell others about Jesus more than you do now? Would you pray more or study Scripture more persistently? To be a person after God's own heart is a great honor, but it is also a major responsibility. God never complimented any other person in the Bible like this, except Jesus, of whom he said, "This is my Son, with whom I am well pleased."

What about you? If you'd like to become a man after God's heart, begin praying about it today. Seek God and ask him to transform you into being the kind of person of whom he might say, "This is a person after my own heart!"

David Fights the Giant

The Big Picture

I Samuel 17

Goliath, the champion of the **Philistines**, steps out and challenges any Israelite to personally battle him to decide which nation would rule the other. David, a shepherd, heard the giant and decided to offer his services. In an amazing battle, the shepherd boy of sixteen or seventeen defeated one of the greatest warriors in history.

heart
2 Chronicles 16:9

David
the greatest king of Israel

Goliath
A giant who was nine feet nine inches in height; he was killed by David.

Philistines
enemies of the Jews

One of the greatest episodes from David's outstanding life occurred when he was a teenager. King Saul was leading the Israelite army as they fought the Philistines. Every day, a champion from the Philistine army named Goliath stepped into the battleground between the two armies and made a challenge. He wanted Israel's champion to come out and fight him. Whoever won their individual contest would win the whole battle, and the loser's army would become slaves of the winners.

But no Israelites would accept Goliath's challenge. After all, he had a sword as long and thick as a man and a spear that looked like an intercontinental ballistic missile. He was nine feet nine inches tall. He probably weighed six hundred pounds, most of it solid muscle. Who could take on this monster?

in people
I Timothy 3:1–8; Philippians 3:1–14

Saul
first king of Israel

Here comes David. A sixteen-year-old. A shepherd. A little fella. He'd left his shepherding job to take some food to his brothers who were in Saul's army. When he heard Goliath's challenge, David became angry. He wasn't afraid of Goliath because he knew God. He knew a God who could do anything. And he didn't like Goliath's boastful, scorning words about his God.

David accepted the challenge that older and more experienced men were too afraid to tackle. He went to face the Philistine with courage and confidence. David prepared himself for battle with five round stones from a nearby brook. When Goliath saw his opponent, he was so angry at the size of this pipsqueak kid Saul had sent against him that he must have forgotten how deadly a slingshot could be. You could kill with a slingshot at a much greater distance than with a sword or spear. Goliath, proud and arrogant, must have cursed and thrown off his helmet. David whipped a stone between his eyes and knocked him down. As he thudded to the ground, David took Goliath's own sword and cut off his head. Even then, though, David didn't boast. He knew God had given him, and Israel, the victory.

Pride always leads to a fall. If you don't want to fall, don't be proud.

How Others See It

Max Lucado

David swung. And God made his point. Anyone who underestimates what God can do with the ordinary has rocks in his head.[1]

God's eyes "range throughout the earth" to strengthen the one whose heart is "fully committed to him." The reason for David's greatness in God's eyes wasn't because David was to become a king or accomplish anything great. It was because David was a man after God's own heart.

What does God look for <u>in people</u>? The answer is found in another part of 1 Samuel, where Samuel was sent to anoint a king in **Saul**'s place.

Jesse
David's father

Samuel knew one of **Jesse**'s sons was to be the king, but as Jesse's handsome, impressive sons paraded by him, Samuel kept receiving indication from the Lord that none of the promising-looking boys was the one. Then Samuel learned there was one more son, the youngest, David, who was out tending the sheep. David's family mentioned him as kind of an afterthought. The young man was the one God had selected.

What can we learn from David's early years? That going all out for God is no waste of time, no foolish pastime, no useless endeavor. David worshiped God through singing and composing music. Is that your desire? Ever want to be in a rock band? Sing in the choir? Be a soloist at Talent Night? Why not go all out for God and glorify him through your music? Some people will call you foolish. Some will say it's a waste of time. But you know the truth. The God of the universe is worthy of our best.

David also faced a formidable enemy with courage and amazing fearlessness. What enemies assault you? Does a bully around school make your life miserable? Do some teens mock you and God? Stand up for God and stand up to them, and you'll be amazed what God does. If God can stop a Goliath through a teen like David, imagine what he can do through you!

How Others See It

Jody Davis

There are plenty of busboys in Nashville who are better guitar players than I am. And there are plenty of Christians who are more spiritually mature than I am. I look at what I'm doing for a living and I see grace. It's just a wonderful gift from God to be able to do what I do for a living and feel that God is using it for some sort of good. It's just a beautiful thing. It's God's grace, because he knows my heart, and he knows I'm not perfect, but he still chooses to love me and use me.[2]

It's "Bass-ic"

for real

Lack of confidence demolishes many young people who want to cruise the road of success. They just don't believe they can pull it off. They spend their youth wishing and hoping for some breakthrough or for "being discovered," but they never develop the confidence it takes to try something new on their own.

Every sports person who succeeded, every rock singer who sought stardom, every poet who put pen to paper had to believe in himself or her-

self. That does not negate Christ or suggest that we can go it alone. We can't. But it also means confidence is an essential tool in your mental kit of drives and emotions. Without it, we are little more than marshmallows. With it, we can be dynamos, potent weapons in God's hands for the work of the kingdom.

For some, confidence comes with seemingly little to no effort. They were born that way. "There's not an unconfident bone in his body," my grandma used to say of a neighbor boy who exuded raw, soaring confidence from the gangly way he walked down the street to his stalwart boasts of winning the next game!

An example is a friend named Ryan. We played in a praise band at our church, leading children in the third through fifth grades. Every week, about forty or fifty of these kids showed up, and we had to play them a series of songs that would get them roused up and looking forward to the rest of the meeting and teachings. Ryan played bass in the band, and I always marveled at his tremendous confidence in his abilities. I soon found out he not only played bass for our band but also played piano for his high school jazz ensemble and for another band that performed on weekends at local hangouts.

One day I was asked to teach the band a new song. I said, "I don't know. I don't have the music for you."

Everyone just said, "Play it, and we'll pick it up."

I played the song, and soon the whole band—Ryan on bass, the pianist, the lead guitarist, the rhythm guitarist, and the singers—were getting it. But what really got me was Ryan. In only seconds, ahead of everyone else, he had picked out a bass line for the song, and it sounded perfect.

"How do you do that?" I asked him.

"I just hear it, I guess," he said. I learned he did the same with the piano.

"But aren't you ever afraid you'll slip up or something?" I pressed.

"It's bass. That means 'bass-ic.' Basic. It's easy."

I stared at the long instrument in his hand. I couldn't have done what he did to save my life. But he did it every Saturday night without a skip or a hitch. He had real confidence, the kind only God can give.

Now that is confidence. Rip-roaring, in your face, pull no punches, take no prisoners confidence.

check this out

critics
Mark 12:13–17;
John 8:1–11

Caesar
Roman emperor

denarius
coin worth one day's wages

It's the kind of confidence I've found comes with a relationship with Christ. You know he's there with you, beside you, around you, ahead of you. Where you are, he is, and you can't go anywhere he isn't.

A great verse to know in this regard is Matthew 28:20: "I am with you always," Jesus said, "to the very end of the age."

It's when you know Jesus is with you that you can develop the confidence it takes to succeed in God's world. David, Josiah, Daniel, and Esther, the teens we're looking at in this chapter, all had that kind of confidence, because they knew God.

Let me ask you straight out: Do you know God as he is through Jesus Christ? If not, then consider three things. One, without him, you're lost and you'll never find your way in this difficult world. Everything you've ever done wrong will one day be scrutinized before God, and he will have to judge you. Two, God has made a way for us never to have to fear judgment or condemnation—through Jesus Christ. Jesus died to pay for the sins of the world. On that cross, he made possible a number of things: for us to be forgiven by God for everything; for us to come into a real relationship with God that will last forever; and for us to gain eternal life. If we believe these truths, then the third thing to do is to actually trust Christ. Tell him you believe and you want to follow him. No other decision in this life is as important as that one.

I hope if you haven't made that decision, you will now, or at least soon. I guarantee it will not only give you new confidence to face any trouble or problem in life, it will also open the doors to a relationship with God that will never be equaled by anyone else in this life.

If you think David had courage, consider Jesus. He faced up to thousands of critics and God-haters without batting an eye. For instance, on one occasion, the government men and the leading religious men banded together to try to trap Jesus in a statement about taxes. They asked, "Which is lawful, to pay taxes to **Caesar** or not?"

If Jesus answered, "No, it's not lawful," the government people would haul him away as a rebel. If he said, "Yes, it's lawful," the religious leaders would call him a heretic. He had nowhere to go. Or did he?

Jesus asked for a **denarius**, the common coin of the day, and said, "Whose image is on this coin?" They answered, "Caesar's." Then Jesus whammed both of his enemies with the words "Then give to Caesar what is Caesar's and to God what is God's."

You also see this kind of courage in Jesus as he faced being nailed to the cross to die for the world. In the Garden of Gethsemane, he sweat "drops of blood." That's how tense and anxious he was about going through a hideous execution in the next few hours. But when he got to the cross, his words revealed not only his courage but also his compassion. As the Romans pounded the spikes through his wrists, he cried out, "Father, forgive them, for they do not know what they are doing." Even in the midst of that pain, Jesus could look out on his executioners and offer them the greatest gift they could ever need or ask for. Like King David, he was a man with heart, and a man following God with "all his heart."

Judah
the southern kingdom of the Jews

mediums
people who mediate between a person and a demon

spiritists
people who talk to evil spirits

Pentateuch
first five books of the Bible, dictated by God to Moses on Mount Sinai

Josiah, the Teen King

> 2 KINGS 22:1–2, 10–13 *Josiah was eight years old when he became king, and he reigned in Jerusalem thirty-one years. His mother's name was Jedidah daughter of Adaiah; she was from Bozkath. He did what was right in the eyes of the Lord and walked in all the ways of his father David, not turning aside to the right or to the left. . . . Then Shaphan the secretary informed the king, "Hilkiah the priest has given me a book." And Shaphan read from it in the presence of the king. When the king heard the words of the Book of the Law, he tore his robes. He gave these orders to Hilkiah the priest, Ahikam son of Shaphan, Acbor son of Micaiah, Shaphan the secretary and Asaiah the king's attendant: "Go and inquire of the Lord for me and for the people and for all Judah about what is written in this book that has been found. Great is the Lord's anger that burns against us because our fathers have not obeyed the words of this book; they have not acted in accordance with all that is written there concerning us."*

JOSIAH: Became king of **Judah** when he was eight years old. The Bible says he did what was right in God's eyes. Josiah was killed in battle at the age of thirty-nine. His spiritual accomplishments for the nation included cleaning out the idol worship in the hills, planting Solomon's temple as the seat of worship for all the nation, and removing all the **mediums** and **spiritists** (see appendix A).

Doing What's Right

Josiah became king at an early age, and in his teens, when he heard the words of Moses (which we know as the **Pentateuch**, or first five books of

revival
making a fresh commitment to faith, sometimes as a group, like a church

apostasy
complete rejection of God by God's people

the Bible) being read, God moved in his heart. He was stricken with guilt and conviction. Years had passed since David's rule over Israel. The nation of the Jews had fallen into worshiping other gods, and God was angry that his people had forsaken him.

Josiah started to turn the nation around. He led his nation into a great revival, the last **revival** they would have before they were sent to Babylon in slavery in 586 BC.

What did Josiah do as a teen? We don't know of any specific events. His teen years were probably when he came into full maturity. But the Bible sums up God's opinion of Josiah's whole life and reign, teen and all, by saying he did what was right in God's eyes. God very strongly approved of this young man.

But isn't that enough? How many of us do right in God's eyes even when we've matured and grown past the time when we do stupid things and make bad decisions? Josiah came to power at a young age and didn't let his importance go to his head. He stuck with God even when his people left God behind. He brought about revival in a land where there had been fifty-seven straight years of **apostasy**. Josiah destroyed the idols that were filling the hillsides and got rid of all those who were leading the people to seek the guidance of demons (see Illustration #4) rather than the guidance of God. Imagine how much courage and commitment it took to face the wrath of those who were leading Israelites astray. But Josiah had the courage and commitment to fight evil and to lead his people to do what was right.

How Others See It

Joe Carter

One thing I like to do is lead by example. Some people take Christianity and say, "Ah, just another religion." But the real question they want to know is, "Are you living it?" A lot of people don't want to hear what you have to say—they want to see it in your life.[3]

What can we learn from Josiah's life? That God does care about the way we live when we're young. He doesn't support the theory of being wild while you're young and then turning to him later. No person is too young to live for God. Josiah was just a teen. Even though some may not have listened to him because of his age, Josiah decided to do what God commanded no matter what the cost. He went against tradition and history and stood firm for God.

That's a tough chore. When a person has been doing it one way, it's hard to get him or her to change. But Josiah called for the changes. Of course, you say, Josiah was a king. *I'm just an average kid, second-string tight end on the football team, Bs and Cs in school, and no great honors to my name.* But who knows what God can do through you? What if you make a stand? What if you tell your friends, "I'm going to serve God in all areas of my life, starting today"? What changes will occur in your life? Don't hesitate. No one who has ever lived for God has found that God cheated him. If you give God your best, God will give you his best.

heart to heart

Illustration #4
Mask of Humbaba—Pictured here is a drawing of a terra-cotta mask of the seventh-century Babylonian monster Humbaba, which was a symbol of supernatural or demonic evil. Every ancient culture we know of attests to the reality of supernatural evil.

Daniel, the Man of the Future

DANIEL 1:1–7 ***In the third year of the reign of Jehoiakim king of Judah, Nebuchadnezzar king of Babylon came to Jerusalem and besieged it. And the Lord delivered Jehoiakim king of Judah into his hand, along with some of the articles from the temple of God. These he carried off to the temple of his god in Babylonia and put in the treasure house of his god. Then the king ordered Ashpenaz, chief of his court officials, to bring in some of the Israelites from the royal family and the nobility—young men without any physical defect, handsome, showing aptitude for every kind of learning, well informed, quick to understand, and qualified to serve in the king's palace. He was to teach them the language and literature of the Babylonians. The king assigned them a daily amount of food and wine from the king's table. They were to be trained for three years, and after that they were to enter the king's service. Among these were some from Judah: Daniel, Hananiah, Mishael and Azariah. The chief*** *official gave them new names: to Daniel, the name Belteshazzar; to Hananiah, Shadrach; to Mishael, Meshach; and to Azariah, Abednego.*

DANIEL: Born in Israel, he was carried into slavery by the Babylonians in 586 BC. Because he was strong, handsome, and intelligent, the king drafted him for political service. Because of his ability to interpret dreams under God's leadership, Daniel rose to high positions of power. At one point, Daniel landed in the lions' den because of his faithfulness to God (see appendix A).

check this out

Revelation
Revelation 1:3

Babylon
Near Eastern kingdom, about 586 BC

King Nebuchadnezzar
king of Babylon

In the Lap of Luxury

Daniel and others were carried into slavery in Babylon. However, the king selected Daniel and three friends to be trained in the court of Babylon. These young men considered their situation and decided that they would do everything they could to follow the laws of Israel. In this chapter, we see them resisting the temptation to forget their homeland and its traditions and deciding to do what God wanted.

Some of the most popular stories in Scripture come from Daniel's life: the lions' den incident, Belteshazzar and the handwriting on the wall, and his friends landing in the fiery furnace.

The book of the Bible named after Daniel is full of information about the future of the world. In the Bible, it's second only to Revelation in specific truth about things to come. In fact, some say the book of Daniel is the key to understanding the book of Revelation. If you can get down with Daniel, you'll fathom Revelation.

Who is Daniel and what did he do? Daniel was born in Judah but was carried away to **Babylon** when **King Nebuchadnezzar** sacked and destroyed the nation. Nebuchadnezzar took most of the Israelites into slavery. But some select young men, like Daniel, were taken into the king's household and prepared to serve in his court. These were the handsomest, smartest, wisest, most athletic, and most intellectual young men the Babylonians could find. Daniel and three other young men came to the court of Babylon. There they would learn all the culture, languages, and wisdom of that land. The idea was that if Nebuchadnezzar could make the best and the brightest of each nation he conquered transfer allegiance to him, his kingdom would become rebellion-proof.

think about it

What principles from Scripture do you find today that interrupt your living a normal life of commitment to God? Premarital sex? Drugs?

Drinking? Parties? Obsession with the Internet? Have you decided to put God first in these areas? If you do, you can be sure God will honor you. You may not be sure of how, but the reward will come. And you would not have wanted to miss it for anything in this world.

In the 1924 Olympics, a young man named Eric Liddell was to race in the 100-meter sprint. He was the fastest man in the world at that time and all bets had him as winner of the race. But he had a problem. The heats for the 100-meter sprints were on a Sunday. Eric Liddell was a faithful Christian. He believed the Ten Commandments, and he wanted to keep the ***Sabbath*** *holy by not running in competition on a Sunday. His refusal to run was a national sensation. Many authorities of his country, Britain, criticized him for his "legalistic religion," but Christians all over the world admired him.*

What would happen, though? Was Liddell out? Instead of running the 100 meter, Liddell decided to run the 400, not his best event. He wasn't a favorite there, but at least he would run in the Olympics. (He also ran the 200.) When the final race of the 400-meter sprint arrived, Liddell ran as he'd never run before in his life. And he won. He had honored God with his stand on the Sabbath, so God honored him. This is a common occurrence in Scripture, and in real life!

Diet, Anyone?

DANIEL 1:8–21 ***But Daniel resolved not to defile himself with the royal food and wine, and he asked the chief official for permission not to defile himself this way. Now God had caused the official to show favor and sympathy to Daniel, but the official told Daniel, "I am afraid of my lord the king, who has assigned your food and drink. Why should he see you looking worse than the other young men your age? The king would then have my head because of you." Daniel then said to the guard whom the chief official had appointed over Daniel, Hananiah, Mishael and Azariah, "Please test your servants for ten days: Give us nothing but vegetables to eat and water to drink. Then compare our appearance with that of the young men who eat the royal food, and treat your servants in accordance with what you see." So he agreed to this and tested them for ten days. At the end of the ten days they looked healthier and better nourished than any of the young men who ate the royal food. So the***

honor
I Samuel 2:30; Galatians 6:7–8

Sabbath
day of rest

guard took away their choice food and the wine they were to drink and gave them vegetables instead. To these four young men God gave knowledge and understanding of all kinds of literature and learning. And Daniel could understand visions and dreams of all kinds. At the end of the time set by the king to bring them in, the chief official presented them to Nebuchadnezzar. The king talked with them, and he found none equal to Daniel, Hananiah, Mishael and Azariah; so they entered the king's service. In every matter of wisdom and understanding about which the king questioned them, he found them ten times better than all the magicians and enchanters in his whole kingdom. And Daniel remained there until the first year of King Cyrus.

check this out

unclean
I Corinthians 8; Romans 14

unclean
animals that God said were off-limits

eunuchs
men who had been surgically altered so that they wouldn't have a sex drive; they were often put in charge of the king's wives and concubines

This episode occurred when Daniel and his three friends were probably in their teens, maybe seventeen to nineteen. Daniel and his friends were faced with a difficult situation: obey the laws of Israel, or satisfy the king who had taken them into slavery and made them leaders-in-training for his kingdom. Daniel and his friends decided to follow Israel's laws. Because of their decision, they were blessed by God.

These young men were religious, and many of the foods that they might be served involved animals that Scriptures told Jews were **unclean**. To eat these foods was against Jewish law. So Daniel requested that they be served only vegetables. The chief of the **eunuchs**, who was in charge of Daniel and the other young men, denied their request, saying the Jews would look unhealthy and the king would get angry and have his head. Daniel suggested that the chief test his theory for ten days. If at the end of ten days the four boys didn't look healthier and more robust than the others, they would submit to the cuisine of the court. God honored Daniel's faith, and at the end of the ten-day test, the boys looked even better than the others did. They were allowed to continue their diet.

How Others See It

Michael Johnston

No matter what battle I've got to fight, no matter what I have to give up, peace with God has always got to be what guides my decisions in life.[4]

Shut Those Cats' Mouths

satraps
regional governors in Babylon

Darius
first king of Medo-Persia

Medes and Persians
conquerors of Babylon

The Big Picture

Daniel 6

The political bosses of Babylon hated Daniel and his faith. They wanted to get rid of him. So they devised a plot they thought was inescapable. They talked King Darius into signing into law an edict that would forbid worshiping anyone but King Darius. Daniel, being a Jew, worshiped God. When he continued with his normal routine of praying, he was sentenced to the lions' den.

Daniel, hated by the Gentile leaders in Babylon, was caught in a trap. The **satraps** thought the best way to destroy Daniel was to create a law by which no one could worship any other person except **Darius**, who was king. Darius passed the law, even though he liked Daniel. He just didn't make the connection that the law was designed to get rid of one of his favorite servants.

Daniel prayed three times a day in his upper chambers by his window. The satraps figured they'd nail him with a worship rap. When Daniel was caught, he was thrown into the lions' den. That was the method of capital punishment that the **Medes and Persians** used at that time. God shut the lions' mouths and Daniel was preserved. But the next day when he was released, Darius had all of Daniel's enemies thrown into the lions' den, and the Bible says, "And before they reached the floor of the den, the lions overpowered them and crushed all their bones" (Daniel 6:24).

The lions' den into which Daniel was thrown was probably a pit with an open top. Spectators would line up around the sides so they could watch the lions maul the prey as a warped kind of entertainment. The den probably also had a small entrance on the side—this was probably the entrance Darius sealed.

heart to heart

What does Daniel show us in this episode and others? The one who honors God will also be honored by God. When we follow God, he notices and he lifts us up before others as an example of faith. Daniel was in a tough predicament. He was a captive in a powerful kingdom, and in those days, their countries didn't often rescue POWs (prisoners of war). In a sense, it would have been easier for Daniel to just throw in the towel and not even try to buck his captors' system: Eat the food; follow the rules; worship the idols. Somewhere along the line, though, Daniel had committed his life to God and had learned that God was good and would watch out for him if he tried to serve God with all of his heart. When Daniel faced incredible pressure to conform to the rules of another culture, and to live the ways of pagan people, he resisted. He refused to knuckle under. He refused to just say, "What does it matter? God won't notice if I compromise on these issues." Daniel knew that what he did mattered. God would notice. So Daniel decided to put God first in everything he did.

We see this same illustration of courage in Jesus' life. Jesus stood for what was right and what his Father had directed, no matter who was upset by his doing so. It takes courage to stand for—and do—what's right when you know you're going to get in trouble for it. Are you courageous when it comes to doing what's right—like Daniel and Jesus?

How Others See It

Serene Campbell

There are many people who think they will start standing for Jesus when they get a little older and are more settled. I don't buy this concept of serving God when it's convenient. The longer they wait, the harder it gets, and many will never stand up at all. By the time they get around to it, a thousand seemingly tiny choices will have taken them so far off course that they will never be able to find their way back.[5]

You might have heard about the dreams Daniel had and the others he interpreted. For your own personal Bible studies sometime, you should look them up in the book of Daniel and see what they foretold. All of human history was encapsulated in those dreams.

So what does this have to do with us? God was organized enough and cared enough to outline the future of the whole world through the dreams. Likewise, he has our lives organized and planned out. We can rest secure in knowing he is in charge of the world and of our lives.

Esther, Too Young to Be Queen

The Big Picture

Esther 2

The first chapter of Esther sets up the story of how Esther got to be queen—King Xerxes got mad at his wife and decided to look for a new queen. Chapter 2 tells us how Esther was chosen. King Xerxes did not rule over Israel. He did not know that Esther was Jewish when he chose her, nor would he have probably cared. So as queen, Esther attained her level of power in the land of Persia, which then ruled the world. The rest of the book tells us about an intricate plot to kill all the Jews. Esther learns of it and decides to try to stop it, at risk to her own life.

ESTHER: This young woman became queen at an early age. Because Esther had no parents, her older cousin Mordecai raised her. Then she won a beauty pageant that landed her inside the palace walls in Persia. Besides being beautiful, the book of Esther shows us that she was smart and she valued advice. She was also courageous and committed to God. He used her to stop Satan's attempt to destroy the Jewish race. Esther was a favorite of the court (see appendix A).

The Girl Who Had It Made

You might not have heard of Queen Esther unless you know the Bible fairly well. She was a queen in **Persia** about 483 BC. How she became queen is an interesting story. Her predecessor, **Vashti**, was a beautiful woman. On one occasion, after a successful military campaign, King **Xerxes** (also known as Ahasuerus) threw a banquet and invited his nobles, while Vashti had a banquet for the women. After several days of partying, King Xerxes called for Vashti to come and display her beauty for the men. The men were all drunk, and some scholars speculate that Xerxes wanted Vashti to strip in front of these officials.

Whatever the king's reason for calling for Vashti's appearance, she refused to even poke her head into the event. Angered that his queen disobeyed him, and afraid other women in the nation would refuse to follow their husbands' guidance, King Xerxes decided Vashti was no longer suitable to be queen. After a royal beauty contest in which any lovely woman could participate, Xerxes chose Esther, a Jew, to be queen. He didn't know she was Jewish, but that probably didn't matter. Persia was a great kingdom with many different peoples in its grasp.

Esther was probably in her teens when the contest happened. Her older cousin Mordecai had raised her and treated her as his own daughter. When he learned of the contest, he may have entered Esther in it.

Esther did well in the palace. When Mordecai found out about a plot to kill the king, he told Esther, who in turn warned Xerxes, saving his life. In

check this out

queen
Esther 1:1–22

Persia
Middle Eastern empire in the 400s BC

Vashti
queen of Persia in 486 BC

Xerxes
king of Persia from 486 to 465 BC

the busy life of the kingdom, however, the good deed was overlooked and no reward was given to Mordecai.

Trouble came when Mordecai, a Jew, refused to bow to Haman, the prime minister of Persia, who was also an Amalekite. The Amalekites were enemies of the Jews, from the days of Moses. When Mordecai refused to bow down to Haman, Haman talked King Xerxes into signing an extermination notice for all Jews. King Xerxes didn't appear to have anything against the Jews—he didn't seem to care about them one way or the other. But Haman told him the Jews were against him, and Haman promised to put a lot of money into the king's treasury to help pay for eliminating the Jews. So the king agreed. The slaughter was to happen on an annual two-day holiday for Persia. This new law decreed that anyone could kill a Jew and take all his belongings.

check this out

Amalekite
Exodus 17:14; Deuteronomy 25:17–19; 1 Samuel 15:11, 26

scepter
a decorative rod the king held that symbolized his authority

Tough Spot for a Queen

> The Big Picture
>
> **Esther 4**
>
> In this chapter, Mordecai sent a message to Esther in the palace, telling her of Haman's plot to exterminate the Jews. Esther told Mordecai that she had not seen the king in thirty days. To approach the king without permission could mean her death. Mordecai responded that if Esther didn't help the Jews, God would raise help from another source, but she and her family might not survive. He also told her that perhaps the reason she was a queen at that time was to stop that very plot.

Not seeing the king for a month was a problem for Queen Esther. She might have wondered if she was out of favor with him (especially considering what had happened to his last wife), or if he'd simply been too busy to see her.

Anyone, even the queen, had to have permission to enter the king's presence. If someone walked into the king's presence and he lifted his **scepter**, everything was fine—the person was allowed to stay and speak with the king.

But if King Xerxes did not lift his scepter—if he was too busy talking to someone else, or just didn't feel like being bothered—the person was dragged away and killed for having the impudence to come to the king without being invited. So approaching the king was a dangerous choice.

Mordecai may have been sympathetic with Esther's plight, but he still talked bluntly and honestly to her. He pointed out that even though Esther was the queen, she wasn't necessarily safe. As much as any of the Jews, she was at risk. Mordecai realized that their God was all-powerful and could bring help from other directions. However, he also realized, and told Esther, that maybe God had allowed her to be chosen queen so that she could have an important part in saving her people.

Esther's response is one of sober faith: "If I perish, I perish" (Esther 4:16). She knew God could help, and she knew she was in God's hands. She asked all the Jews to fast and pray about her situation.

Sometimes, just like Esther, we'll be in a comfortable situation when it seems like God all of a sudden sends a tornado in to shake up our whole lives. Our security threatens to blow up around us.

Tornadoes are funny things. They usually make a path of destruction, turning everything topsy-turvy. But at the same time, in the very center of the tornado is an area called the eye. And in that area, everything is calm—no destruction, no winds whipping everything around. Just peace.

When tornadoes whip around in our lives, God can be that eye in the center of the turbulence. We can turn to him and find peace. Then, like Esther, we can calmly assess the situation and rest safe in the knowledge that what God allows to happen will happen, but, ultimately, we'll be okay.

heart to heart

The Unraveling of the Plot

The Big Picture

Esther 5–7

Esther invited the king to a banquet where she planned to reveal the truth about Haman, her enemy. But something stopped her at the first invitation. She didn't tell the king what she wanted at the first banquet. She merely asked him to come to another, the next day. That night, the king couldn't sleep, and he asked that the records be read to him. What he learned led to the unraveling of Haman's plot.

Everyone prayed and fasted, and when Esther appeared before the king, she was granted a hearing. But she didn't go into details with the king about what was bothering her. Her only request was that the king attend a small banquet she had prepared for him and Haman. After the banquet, Esther invited him to attend another banquet she had prepared for the next day.

check this out

providential acts
Isaiah 45:5–7;
Proverbs 16:9

providence
God's special work in the world to make things go his way

Purim
means "lot" as to "cast lots"

That night God's **providence** was put to work. The king couldn't sleep, so he studied some recent records of the kingdom. Amazingly enough, he learned of Mordecai's warning about the plot on his life. The king decided to honor Mordecai. The next day, Haman was commanded to march Mordecai through the streets, announcing that the king was honoring Mordecai. Imagine how angry Haman was to have to do that! Such providential acts have happened at other times in history.

That night, Xerxes and Haman again attended Esther's banquet. The king was in such a good mood that he pressed Esther to tell him what he could do for her. Esther simply requested that her life be spared. The king was horrified that someone would want to kill his wife. Then she revealed Haman's plot. The king was so furious that he had Haman hanged on the gallows Haman had built to hang Mordecai. Then he appointed Mordecai as prime minister. God had saved the people he loved once again. The Jews celebrated the two-day holiday on which they were to be killed, and they still celebrate those days now as their **Purim** celebration, when they remember how God saved them from Haman and the Amalekites in Persia.

This passage is an astonishing record of God's controlling history. When we read Esther, we see God behind the scenes, working events to go as he wants them to go. This is the way he works in all our lives, whether we know it or not.

What Is a Woman's Place in the World?

for real

Some people say a woman's place is in the kitchen. And some people say a Christian's place is out of politics and out of anything considered worldly. They're afraid that the world and sinful things in the world will too easily taint Christians. So some people cloister themselves off into a Christian corner, afraid of brushes with non-Christian life. I wonder what Esther would have thought of that. After all, she was in a beauty pageant and knew how to make her earthly good looks shine. She wanted to be the king's wife, and accordingly became totally embroiled in politics. She was smart enough to know how to best get the king's attention. She personally invited him to a banquet at the risk of her life, and then she didn't press her requests on him until just the right moment (like when your mom waits to ask your dad a question until he's in a good mood). She also apparently knew how to entertain well.

Because of being in the world, Esther made a huge impact and saved the people who served God.

So what's that mean for those of us who aren't queens? People who believe we should be separate from the world have a point—Scripture tells us to live like Christians so that we're different from those who don't know God. But as we circulate in the world, knowing what's going on in our society but still living for God, we can make a difference.

How can we be in the world, but not of it? It can be simple or drastic. For example, seventeen-year-old Alisha likes to carry her little prayer journal everywhere she goes. Then when friends and others ask her about it, she gains a chance to share her feelings and thoughts about Jesus. Or teens can be different by not being critical, mean, and ugly like other kids in their schools. We can be witnesses by holding our tongues and watching our language, by taking a stand for what's right, and by keeping our lives sexually pure (including in the movies we watch).

As we live in the world but not of it, we too can make a difference!

How Others See It

Ruthie Bolton-Holifield

[At first I thought] What did I do to deserve this? What did I do wrong? Then I thought about it and I said to myself, "Maybe I did everything right." Sometimes God allows things to happen to test you, as He did with Job. My favorite Bible verse is Romans 8:39. It says that nothing can separate us from the love of God—not trials or tribulations or the difficulties and obstacles that come our way—nothing! When things get tough, I remind myself that God is in control of my career and my life. He knows what's best.[6]

words to live by

What can we learn from Esther's life? That God is in charge of all things that happen, even bad things. This does not mean God causes bad things, but that he works around them to produce the results he wants. He will do that in your life if you ask him. Not everything that happens in your life will have a logical explanation, but everything should move you in the direction of loving God more, serving him joyfully, and sacrificing for his kingdom. God will never desert you. God will never leave you alone and lost in a dark place. He will provide the candlelight to get you out of it. He will show the way. Esther decided to trust God with her very life. When we do that, God is thrilled.

What do you need to trust God about today? What situations or people are threatening your happiness or existence? Remember Esther. Perhaps she had risen to royalty for "such a time as this." Perhaps you've been appointed to the yearbook team, or the newspaper, or the wrestling or hockey team for "such a time as this." Perhaps you've made friends with certain people "for such a time as this." Perhaps you've moved into a neighborhood for "such a time as this." Maybe your influence in these areas will lead others to turn to God. God will use you if you let him. Just look to him and expect to see him work. When he does, you will be amazed, and he will be pleased.

Courage to Share

i for real

Esther isn't the only one who's ever been challenged to find the courage to share her faith. Singer and songwriter Jennifer Knapp came to know God while in college. One Christmas shortly after she'd become a Christian, she went home to her grandmother's house for a couple of weeks. One day she wanted to read her Bible and pray, which was something that would have shocked the rest of her family. She scooted off to her room to spend some time with God.

When Jennifer left the room, her grandmother instantly asked what she'd been doing, and she gathered up her courage to tell Grandma she'd been reading her Bible.

When her grandmother asked why Jennifer wanted to do something like that, Jennifer replied by saying she guessed it was because she was a Christian.

Jennifer remembers this as probably the boldest thing she ever said to any of her family about what she was doing as a new believer.

Talking about Christ in secular surroundings was tough for Jennifer, but it's become easier with practice. Now she can readily talk to her family about how God is working in her life.[7]

It takes courage to share our faith sometimes, but go ahead and do it—even when you're in environments that are foreign to the gospel.

Final Thoughts

- David, perhaps the greatest teen in all of Scripture, shows us the way to defeat the giants in our lives. In his battle with Goliath, he demonstrates the meaning of true godly courage, courage based on a strong faith that God will protect, lead, and help in the midst of trouble.
- Josiah demonstrates how a young teen can have an impact on his culture. Josiah changed his world as a king, but anyone who will make a stand for God can change his or her world.
- Daniel, the man who went into the lions' den, is another of the brave, godly teens of the Bible who stood strong even when things went wrong.
- Esther, the teen queen, proved that following God's way is the only way, and through her example we see how to triumph when times are tough.

Questions to Deepen Your Understanding

1. How would you have faced a warrior like Goliath if you had been David?
2. Does Scripture ever convict you as it did Josiah? How and in what ways?
3. What did you learn from Daniel that will keep you through a bad night?
4. Would you be willing to risk your life for the people of God as Esther did? Why or why not?

read on

Some of Mark and Jeanette's favorite books about becoming a leader for God:

- *Bad to the Bone,* Miles McPherson, Bethany
- *Daniel in the Critics' Den: A Defense of the Historicity of the Book of Daniel,* Robert Anderson, Kregel
- *Daniel: God's Man in a Secular Society,* Donald K. Campbell, Discovery
- *David: A Man of Passion & Destiny,* Charles R. Swindoll, Word
- *Esther: A Woman of Strength & Dignity,* Charles R. Swindoll, Word
- *Teenage Guys: Exploring Issues Adolescent Boys Face and Strategies to Help Them,* Steve Gerali, Zondervan/Youth Specialities
- *Women of the Bible,* Ann Spangler and Jean E. Syswerda, Zondervan
- *Women of the Bible: The Life and Times of Every Woman in the Bible,* Sue Richards and Larry Richards, Thomas Nelson

Chapter 4: Teens Who Followed God in the New Testament

Becoming Acquainted With New Testament Teens

What's in This Chapter

- Mary, the Teen Chosen to Be Jesus' Mom
- John Mark, a Deserter Who Made Good
- Timothy, the Teen Who Became a Pastor
- Rhoda, the Teen They Should Have Taken Seriously

Here We Go

In this chapter we'll meet four more teens who affected their world for Christ—two girls and two guys. In the Bible, females are just as gutsy and committed as males. Whatever gender you are, you can be sure these teens will show you how to live in hard times and succeed.

Luke's genealogy
Luke 3:23–38

The teens in this chapter face troubles different from those in the last two. God specializes in dealing with different kinds of trouble. Some people believe trouble comes from God. Scripture reveals that God does not send trouble except when people sin. God's main relationship to trouble is how he helps us in the midst of the turmoil. When we face difficulties, God promises to guide us and go through it with us. God is worth trusting, as the teens in this section found out.

Mary, the Teen Chosen to Be Jesus' Mom

> LUKE 1:26–28 ***In the sixth month, God sent the angel Gabriel to Nazareth, a town in Galilee, to a virgin pledged to be married to a man named Joseph, a descendant of David. The virgin's name was Mary. The angel went to her and said, "Greetings, you who are highly favored! The Lord is with you."***

MARY: This girl was probably only thirteen or fourteen when she got pregnant with Jesus. King David was one of her ancestors, according to Luke's genealogy, but we know nothing about her family. Why God selected her, we do not know. From her words in Luke 1:46–55, we see that she knew Scripture well and that she was a believer in God (see appendix A).

check this out

Nazareth
John 1:46
Joseph
Matthew 2:23

Nazareth
small city of Galilee
betrothed
engaged or promised to be married

Unexpected Happenings

Mary was a Jewish woman living in Nazareth, a small city in the middle area of Galilee. Nazareth was not known for anything, and later the fact that Jesus was a "Nazarene" made people look down on him. A good man named Joseph, a carpenter, noticed Mary and decided he wanted to marry her. They were **betrothed** when the angel Gabriel appeared to Mary, telling her she would be the mother of the Messiah.

When the angel greeted Mary in this passage, he called her "highly favored" and "blessed," two expressions that indicated God's special concern for her and his desire to give her great happiness in life.

Mary ranks as one of the greatest people in all of Scripture. She must have been one amazing girl for God to select her to be Jesus' mom. From the passage above, we see a number of things about Mary that make her great. She was probably in her early teens at the time (people married as early as thirteen in those days), but she displays a faith and commitment far beyond her young years.

In Bible times, guys and girls didn't date. Their families arranged marriages (though the children's wishes might have been considered). Girls were often married as soon as they were physically capable of having children, in their early teens.

Mary was betrothed to Joseph. Betrothal was like an engagement. However, it was a legal procedure. A couple would go through the legal processes of betrothal and then continue to live in their separate households as they prepared to be married.

Orders From Above

> LUKE 1:29–37 *Mary was greatly troubled at his words and wondered what kind of greeting this might be. But the angel said to her, "Do not be afraid, Mary, you have found favor with God. You will be with child and give birth to a son, and you are to give him the name Jesus. He will be great and will be called the Son of the Most High. The Lord God will give him the throne of his father David, and he will reign over the house of Jacob forever; his kingdom will never end." "How will this be," Mary asked the angel, "since I am a virgin?" The angel answered, "The Holy Spirit will come upon you, and the power of the Most High will overshadow you. So the holy one to be born will be called the Son of God. Even Elizabeth your relative is going to have a child in her old age, and*

she who was said to be barren is in her sixth month. For nothing is impossible with God."

When the angel Gabriel appeared to Mary, she was afraid and didn't know what to say. This was only the second time in more than **four hundred years** that God had appeared to someone and given them a message. Jews were not noted for telling "whoppers" about how God appeared to them. Such a statement was considered blasphemy, unless it was true, and you could be stoned for telling such stories.

check this out

second time
Luke 1:11–25

accused
John 8:41

four hundred years
time between the Old and New Testaments

Virgin Birth
conception and birth without prior sexual intercourse

Gabriel calmed Mary and told her she would conceive and have a son who would be called "the Son of God," and God would give him "the throne of his father David." This person was the long-awaited Messiah. Probably every Jewish girl in history wondered if she would be the mother of the Messiah. Maybe even Mary herself dreamed of it. But this was not how she had thought it would happen. Why? Look at her very next words. She asks Gabriel how she could have a baby, since she has never slept with a man. Gabriel gave her some technical terms about how God would create the baby inside her womb, but basically it meant that Jesus would be born of a virgin, called in theology the **Virgin Birth**.

How Others See It

Josh McDowell

The main problem that people have with the virgin birth is that it is a miracle. Scripture does not treat this event as an ordinary occurrence but rather as a supernatural act of God. The miracle of the virgin birth should not pose any special problem if one grants the possibility of miracles.[1]

You're the Boss!

Luke 1:38 *"I am the Lord's servant," Mary answered. "May it be to me as you have said." Then the angel left her.*

After Gabriel answered Mary's questions, she responded with submission, honor, and respect for God. What obedience! What great faith! Is that the kind of faith you have? Remember, Mary probably understood that this situation wouldn't be easy to explain. Joseph, her fiancé, could easily accuse her of adultery (to be betrothed was legally the same thing as being married in those days). If he did accept her story, how could she explain it to others? Her child, the Messiah, could easily be accused of being illegitimate. But God did not let Mary down. He explained the whole thing

Joseph
Matthew 1:18–25

Zechariah
Luke 1:18–25

prophesied
Isaiah 7:14

mute
unable to speak

to Joseph through a visit to Joseph from an angel. He confirmed the situation to Mary—that yes, she was going to give birth to the Messiah—through her cousin Elizabeth, who was also miraculously pregnant (though not as a virgin). The lesson is: When you serve God, even though the situations in life might look tough or even impossible, he never lets you down.

Here's one other thought about Mary. Contrast her teen faith with that of her older cousin-in-law Zechariah, Elizabeth's husband. When an angel told Zechariah that his wife, who was too old to have children, was finally going to have a baby, Zechariah did not believe the angel's announcement. Because he wouldn't believe, he was struck **mute** until his son, John, was born. Why did Mary, who was only a teen girl, believe, when the older man, who was a priest and had served in the temple many years, couldn't believe? This shows that teens can often have faith as strong, if not stronger, than that of people much older than they are. Don't let anyone tell you your dreams of faith are foolish, worthless, or dumb. Don't let anyone write you off because you're "just a teen." If you have great faith, don't be surprised if God does great things through you, just as he did with Mary. And don't hesitate to attempt great things in God's name.

How Others See It

Michael W. Smith

I think it kind of comes down to accountability—somebody that you invite into your life. My wife's the best one who does that for me. I also have a great prayer group of guys. We've been together for about eight years so they have pretty much been invited into my life to speak the truth and to just really be honest with me. And if they feel like I'm wandering off the path, then they're gonna have the honesty to tell me. I think you gotta have that, especially when you have people that continually tell you how great you are and lift you up all the time, and if you don't watch it, you start believing it. And I really know who I am. I'm a weak man who needs God desperately in my life.[2]

Notice something about Mary in the above passages: She wasn't naïve. The idea of having a baby without a husband was not acceptable in her culture, even though it had been prophesied in the Old Testament exactly that way. A woman who had sex outside of marriage was in danger of being stoned to death. And of course, it's impossible for a girl to have a baby without the contribution of a male. Mary stopped Gabriel and asked the natural question. That's a good lesson: Don't just accept anything anyone says. Get the facts. God is not afraid of your questions, so don't hesitate to ask them.

John Mark, a Deserter Who Made Good

> ACTS 15:36–40 *Some time later Paul said to Barnabas, "Let us go back and visit the brothers in all the towns where we preached the word of the Lord and see how they are doing." Barnabas wanted to take John, also called Mark, with them, but Paul did not think it wise to take him, because he had deserted them in Pamphylia and had not continued with them in the work. They had such a sharp disagreement that they parted company. Barnabas took Mark and sailed for Cyprus, but Paul chose Silas and left, commended by the brothers to the grace of the Lord.*

JOHN MARK: We don't know much about him. He doesn't take up a lot of room in Scripture. Even though he wrote the book of Mark, we still don't know many other details. From Acts 12:12, we know that Mary (not Jesus' mom) was Mark's mother. They lived in Jerusalem and were believers. They opened their home to other believers, even in the midst of persecution (see appendix A).

check this out

John Mark
Acts 13:4–5; 13:13
dispute
Acts 15:37–40

Barnabas
apostle, name means "son of encouragement"
Cyprus
island in the Mediterranean Sea

Mistakes Happen!

John Mark is an elusive figure, but in this passage we find him at the center of a dispute between Paul and Barnabas. John Mark had accompanied Paul and **Barnabas** on their first missionary trip to **Cyprus**, but later he deserted them at Perga (see Illustration #5). We don't know why Mark deserted them. Maybe he became afraid of being associated with the Christians. Maybe he got tired of traveling. But he disappointed the others. When it came time to go on a second trip, Paul did not want to take John Mark, feeling he was untrustworthy. Barnabas, though, was John Mark's cousin, and he decided to take the young man in a different direction.

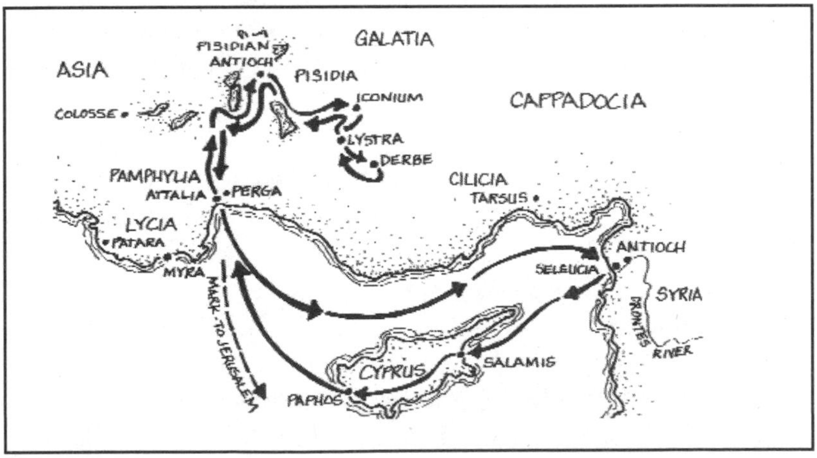

Illustration #5
Paul's Missionary Journey with John Mark—Mark accompanied from Antioch in Asia all the way to Perga, but there he deserted Paul and Barnabas for reasons we don't know.

think about it

How do you act when you've made a major mistake? Do you grin, bear it, and pretend it didn't happen? Do you hide, feeling forever humiliated? Or do you confess it and go on, confident that in Christ you are a new person? In 1 John 1:9 it says if we "confess our sins, he is faithful and just and will forgive us our sins and purify us from all unrighteousness." Those are powerful words and are a great hope to anyone who has failed.

After his failure at Perga, Paul almost wrote Mark off. But Barnabas didn't. He invited Mark to come along with him on the next journey. If you have failed in some way in your Christian life, do not shrink back if some older believer offers to "mentor" or "disciple" you. God has brought this opportunity to you because he cares. A mentor or discipler can do much to get you back on the right track. Pray that God will bring someone you can lean on like that, if you feel you need it. And who doesn't?

Mark's Change of Heart

> 2 TIMOTHY 4:11 ***Only Luke is with me. Get Mark and bring him with you, because he is helpful to me in my ministry.***

Mark was such a valued friend and comrade that Paul spoke highly of him to the **Colossians** and to **Timothy**, as above. Later, Peter spoke highly of him as his son, meaning that Mark was such a close disciple and friend that Peter considered him family. What could have happened? Obviously, Mark proved himself on his journey with Barnabas. Perhaps he was young and skittish earlier and just wasn't prepared for the rigors of a hard journey. That's understandable. The poor decisions of youth can be made right as we grow. John Mark shows us that there's always a second chance for those who will repent, follow God, and give their best for him. When Mark decided to write the book of Mark, it's believed that Peter gave him the information to put in it. John was a good writer, and perhaps that was his greatest calling. He could gather facts and stories and put them together in a logical order. Maybe Peter found that task daunting, or perhaps at that point he was too old to write a gospel. Mark rose to the task. God used him in this way, and he proves finally that God forgives us when we fail or sin and gives us many opportunities to come back and find our niche.

check this out

valued friend
Colossians 4:10; 2 Timothy 4:11

son
1 Peter 5:13

Colossians
people who live in Colossae, city of Asia

Timothy
Greek disciple of Paul's

How Others See It

Mike Jackson

No matter what I do, I know tomorrow is going to be a new day and the Lord will lift me up. To me, winners are the guys who, after they fail, come back battling. If I take that focus to the mound, then the Lord will receive the glory.[3]

Plainly, Mark had some hard times and some good times. He was a deserter at one point, and then a writer of a significant New Testament book. How do we measure such a life? Obviously, not the same way most people would. Mark is what you might call a "regular guy." He wasn't spectacular, but after some hard knocks he learned to be the kind of person who pleases God. No matter why he had deserted Paul and Barnabas earlier, it was forgiven and forgotten. Paul later gave Mark high marks for being a "useful servant."

think about it

A Great Coach

for real

The 1929 Rose Bowl between the University of California and Georgia Tech was slated to be a great contest. A young man named Roy Riegels went down in history as he played that game. Shortly before the end of the first half, Riegels recovered a fumble. He ran for all he was worth toward the goal line, not realizing it was the wrong goal line. Spectators watched astonished as Riegels almost scored for Georgia Tech. One of his teammates tackled him within yards of the goal. UC played out their downs and was caught behind the goal for a safety. Two points, the ultimate margin of victory in the game.

During halftime, the locker room was quiet except for Riegels's sobbing as he sat in front of his locker. Nibbs Price, the UC coach, didn't say much until the bell rang and he announced, "The same team that started the first half will start the second." That included Riegels. Everyone ran out, but Roy didn't move. Price walked over to him. "Did you hear what I said, Roy?" Roy nodded but added that he couldn't go out there. He had disgraced everyone. Price didn't bat an eye but just said, "Go out and play, Roy. The game is only half over."

Roy's coach was great—but he was nothing compared to our coach, God. God himself is the ultimate author of the second chance, letting us make mistakes and then pushing us back into the game, saying, "Keep on. It's only half over."

The only mistake in failure is to stay down. If you get up again, you haven't really failed.

Timothy, the Teen Who Became a Pastor

check this out

lineage
Acts 16:1–3

Lystra
Roman city of Galatia
Galatia
Roman province

> 2 TIMOTHY 1:3–7 *I thank God, whom I serve, as my forefathers did, with a clear conscience, as night and day I constantly remember you in my prayers. Recalling your tears, I long to see you, so that I may be filled with joy. I have been reminded of your sincere faith, which first lived in your grandmother Lois and in your mother Eunice and, I am persuaded, now lives in you also. For this reason I remind you to fan into flame the gift of God, which is in you through the laying on of my hands. For God did not give us a spirit of timidity, but a spirit of power, of love and of self-discipline.*

TIMOTHY: Timothy was a young Greek when he met the apostle Paul. His family (mother and grandmother) had become believers and passed on their faith to Timothy. The young man became committed enough to go with Paul on his journeys and to become Paul's main disciple. Paul wrote two letters of the New Testament directly to Timothy, and from them we learn how to run a church (see appendix A).

A Young Leader

Here we meet one of the great youth pastors of the Bible. He started out as a disciple of the apostle Paul. He learned from Paul as they traveled across the world. Yet he was a man who had great fears. Timothy was encouraged by Paul to stick to the mission God had given him. Paul obviously wanted to buck up his friend and disciple. Timothy responded by continuing to pastor the church at Ephesus and continuing to labor and use his gifts.

Timothy, a young man of Greek-Jewish lineage, followed the apostle Paul and learned directly from him how to do ministry. Two letters in the New Testament were written directly to Timothy as he pastored a church in Ephesus. Timothy's name means "one who honors God," and truly he was such a man. He was the son of Eunice, a Jewess. His father, a Greek, was not named. Both his grandmother Lois and his mother were believers who taught Timothy the Old Testament from his birth. He lived in **Lystra**, a city in **Galatia**, a northern Roman province, now part of modern Turkey.

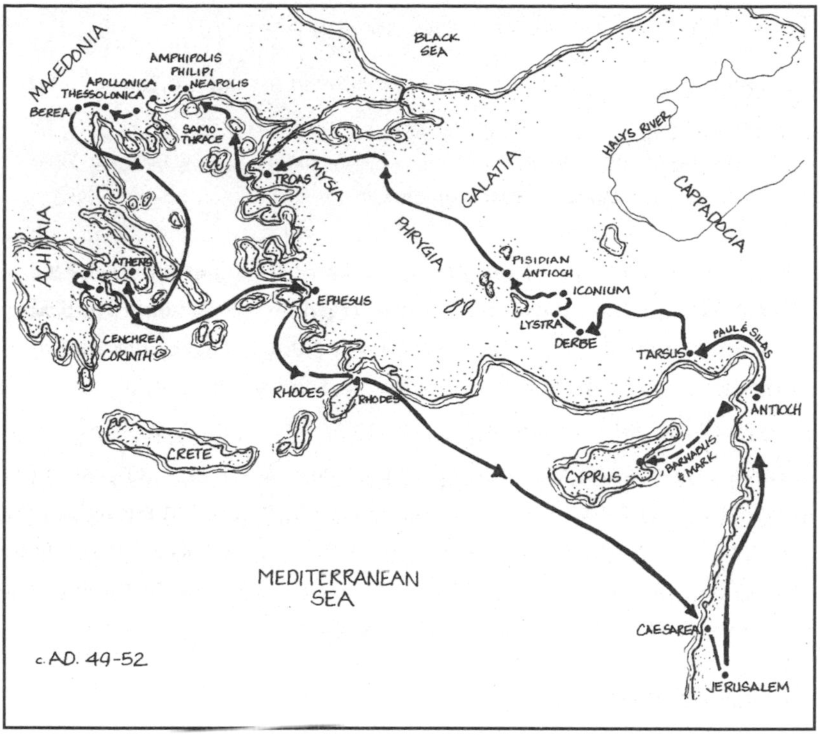

Illustration #6
Paul's Missionary Journey With Timothy—Timothy accompanied Paul on the second missionary journey. He became Paul's number one disciple and learned first-hand from the places they visited how Paul ministered to God's people.

Paul led Timothy to Christ while on his first missionary journey (see Illustration #5). When he stopped by Lystra on the second missionary journey (see Illustration #6), he invited Timothy to come with him as he visited the churches he'd planted. Timothy at that time was probably in his late teens. He ministered with Paul in **Berea**, **Athens**, and **Corinth**, and accompanied him on a trip to Jerusalem. During Paul's first Roman imprisonment, Timothy stayed with Paul, and then they both went to **Philippi** to encourage the believers there. Paul considered Timothy a "kindred spirit" who could be trusted to love the people he served.

What lessons does Timothy teach us? One of the greatest lessons comes from Timothy's timidity. Apparently, Timothy was all too aware of his youthfulness and realized older men and women might not listen to him. He shied away from making the powerful pronouncements Paul made so easily. Paul had to encourage him, as in the passage at the beginning of this section. He reminded Timothy of his personal love for the young man. Then he told him that he knew Timothy's faith was real. Paul reminded Timothy to "kindle afresh" the spiritual gift he had, which was probably preaching and teaching. Then he gave the great statement in 2 Timothy 1:7, which is a common memory verse.

check this out

ministered
Acts 17:14–15; 18:5; Philippians 2:19–23

youthfulness
I Timothy 4:12–16; 5:1–2

Berea
city of Greece

Athens
capital of Greece

Corinth
very sinful city of Greece

Philippi
mission city of Greece

think about it

How Others See It

Rebecca St. James

My first tour was when I was thirteen years old, and it was really kind of scary. I remember falling on my face in prayer before I went on stage, asking God for strength to carry me through.[4]

Perhaps Timothy feared failing in the wake of the great apostle's success in starting churches all over the Roman world. After all, who would want to compete with Paul for Christian service? But he never regarded it as competition. He followed Paul's orders and found strength in the words of God that filled his mind daily.

If there's one mark that stands out in Timothy's life, it was his willingness to listen to and follow his leader's ideas. He didn't waver; he even went to prison for his faith. But he stuck with the program. He was one determined disciple. Never be afraid of anyone if you're on God's side. The only thing to be afraid of is not being on God's side.

An Adventure Begins

I stood looking over the lake as the sun rose, its yellow light glinting off the water like a billion tiny jewels. I had never experienced anything like this before, yet I knew it was the most important thing that had ever happened to me.

Two days previous I had confessed to a friend that I believed Jesus was the Son of God.

The next twenty-four hours were a roller coaster. A gushing joy, an exuberant love, a deep sense of peace and tranquillity blew through me like a cool breeze on a hot night. Everything became a moment of discovery. I picked up a stone, and its weight and heft were astounding. I walked barefoot through dewy grass, and I knew I had been catapulted into a fresh new experience. Prayer was real. When I opened the Bible, it made sense.

Unable to contain it, I began spilling out my newfound faith to all my friends. They thought I was nuts. We had driven three hours to the Pocono Mountains of Pennsylvania to my grandparents' lake cabin. All weekend we skied, sailed, swam, and sunned. Meanwhile, my mind was in the clouds, worshiping God and drinking in a feeling of being loved and understood, which I had never sensed before. I had to tell them. I couldn't contain it.

"I just met God—he's real!" I told my best friend, Jon.

"It's eternal life!" I informed Jim and Art.

"Anybody can have it. It's for free! All you have to do is believe!" I said to Bob and Chris and Jeff.

They mostly laughed. "Littleton, you're weird." "Littleton's gone off the deep end this time."

I shrugged it off. They'd see, I was sure.

When it came time to go home, I rode with my parents. I wanted to tell them what had happened.

As Dad drove, I talked. "Dad, anybody can have it. All you have to do is believe." My mother commented, "Mark, I grew up with people who were into this. It was foolish. They wasted their lives. You have good things going for you. Don't blow it now on some little feeling."

"Mom, it's not a feeling. It's the most real thing I've ever seen."

"There are other things in life that are important too."

"But, Mom, what's more important than knowing God, having eternal life, and knowing what happens when you die?"

"I don't think you can know those things just like that," Mom answered. "Pretty soon you'll want me to storm to the altar, weeping about my ridiculous sins!"

I felt as if I were drowning. Didn't anyone understand that knowing Jesus Christ was the greatest thing that could happen? I said, "But I'm not afraid anymore. Not afraid of death. Not afraid of the future. I've always been afraid."

"That's all well and good," my mom said, "just don't push it on everybody else."

I wasn't listening. "Really, my whole life is changed. A week ago I believed in drugs, premarital sex, drinking, the theory of evolution, the Bible as just another book, and Jesus as kind of a good person who gave us a lot of neat quotes. But all of that has changed—in just a few days!"

The argument continued for the full three hours of our journey. The nearer we got to home, the more desperate I felt.

As my parents lectured me about reality and parried my bursts of religious enthusiasm, I began to think in altogether different terms. I would leave home. I would join a group of Christians who were living for Jesus. We would travel around the world telling people the Good News.

When Dad pulled into our driveway, I got out and said, "Dad, I'm leaving."

"What?"

Mom stared at me, furious.

"I can't deal with this anymore. I have to find people who believe in Jesus. I'm leaving home."

"Now? At ten o'clock at night?"

I decided not to argue anymore. I started up the street. My father followed me.

"What are you doing? What is this all about?"

"Dad, I don't think you know what life is all about."

He argued with me, coaxed me, begged me. I fought off every plea. We reached a corner, and a couple walked by, staring at us. I said to my father, "Right now, the way you look at me, you look like Satan!"

He shook his head with frustration. "Then you won't come home?"

"No." I turned to go. Dad watched me, and then I heard him turn back for home.

I wandered around, praying that God would do some miracle to show my parents the truth. Eventually, it came to me that I should visit my friends, the Pezzis, who had originally talked to me about Jesus.

I walked the two miles to their house. It was past midnight when I got there, but they were still up. Mrs. Pezzi invited me in, and I told them all that had happened. They were glad to know I'd converted, but they didn't know what to tell me about leaving home. Finally, Mrs. Pezzi called her friend Betsy Martin and asked her to come by and counsel me.

Betsy went through the plan of salvation using a little pamphlet. As she laid it out, I kept saying, "Right. That's what I believe. That's what I've done."

Finally she came to what had happened that night with my parents. She looked me in the eye and said, "Mark, do you know the Ten Commandments?"

"Sort of."

She opened her Bible to Exodus 20 and read them to me. When she reached the fifth one, she read it several times. "Honor your father and your mother." Then she asked, "Do you think that's what you did tonight?"

I bowed my head. I knew the answer and I said, "No, I guess I didn't."

She told me I should go back home and ask for forgiveness. That was the only way I could demonstrate I truly had believed.

I gulped, thinking that Mom and Dad might not even let me in the house.

We prayed together and I agreed to let Mr. Pezzi drive me home. At precisely 3:00 a.m., we pulled up in front of my house.

"Well, here goes nothing," I said.

Mr. Pezzi grasped my hand. "You've got a lot to learn, Mark, but Jesus is with you. Hang in there."

I nodded and opened the car door.

To my surprise, the back door to the house wasn't locked. I went straight up to my parents' bedroom on the third floor. When I opened the door, Dad jumped out of bed. "Thank God you're home!" he said, hugging me hard.

I stammered out my apology. He said, his arm over my shoulder, "Don't worry about it. These things happen."

Mom got up and they both led me back to my bedroom. She said, "We love you, honey. Don't ever forget that."

I asked that we take a second and pray. They agreed, and I said, "Lord, help me to honor my parents, and help them to understand what has happened. Thanks. Amen."

Dad hugged me again. "Get some sleep. You've got a big day tomorrow." I did. I was supposed to start a summer job.

That night I lay in bed marveling. How had all these things happened in so short a time? I didn't know. I felt frightened, actually. Satan was really trying to mess up my life.

Deep down inside, though, I knew that Jesus was with me and would show me the way step by step. I fell asleep with a deepening sense that an adventure had begun that would never end.

A good verse of Scripture to rely on comes from one of the teens in this chapter, whom Paul worked with. He said to Timothy, "For God did not give us a spirit of timidity, but a spirit of power, of love and of self-discipline" (2 Timothy 1:7).

That became a verse I relied on in those hard days after my conversion. I had to rediscover how to love, give, and show I was a true Christian by living a godly life. It was difficult. But God was with me, like he was with Mary, John Mark, Timothy, and the other teens in this book. You can be sure he'll be with you too—to fix broken relationships and help you learn to speak with truth in a way that gets people's attention.

It's a long, hard journey, but one well worth taking. I know. I've walked with Jesus for almost thirty years now, and I've never found him to be anything but loyal, loving, and willing to lead.

Are you ever timid? Do you ever feel as if no one will listen to you, even if you have something intelligent to say? Do you ever sense that you're competing with people in the church for a hearing? If so, you're in a good league with Timothy. Listen to these words: "So do not be ashamed to testify about our Lord, or ashamed of me his prisoner. But join with me in suffering for the gospel, by the power of God, who has saved us and called us to a holy life—not because of anything we have done but because of his own purpose and grace. This grace was given us in Christ Jesus before the beginning of time, but it has now been revealed through the appearing of our Savior, Christ Jesus, who has destroyed death and has brought life and immortality to light through the gospel. And of this gospel I was appointed a herald and an apostle and a teacher. That is why I am suffering as I am. Yet I am not ashamed, because I know whom I have believed, and am convinced that he is able to guard what I have entrusted to him for that day" (2 Timothy 1:8–12). These words provide power for those who feel shy or daunted because of their age. Jesus himself was only thirty years old when he began his ministry. Many were amazed that a young man should have such wisdom. But it's possible to those who will walk closely with God.

Rebecca St. James started singing when she was around thirteen years old. But what kind of ministry can a teen have? Rebecca's father wondered about whether to let her sing—could she really make an impact, or would she just face the hardships singers face?

The turning point that showed Rebecca and her father that God could use her even though she was so young came when she was fifteen years old. Rebecca was singing a concert at a maximum-security prison in Macon, Georgia. Naturally, the whole family was a bit nervous about a young teen being locked up with a bunch of murderers—after all, hostage situations happen!

"Yet it turned out to be one of the most incredible times of worship I have ever experienced," Rebecca recalls. "Those men just poured out their hearts to the Lord. But God was not only moving in the hearts of those prisoners that day; he also spoke very clearly to my father and me: This was the ministry God wanted me to pursue."[5]

Rhoda, the Teen They Should Have Taken Seriously

ACTS 12:7–17 ***Suddenly an angel of the Lord appeared and a light shone in the cell. He struck Peter on the side and woke him up. "Quick, get up!" he said, and the chains fell off Peter's wrists. Then the angel said to him, "Put on your clothes and sandals." And Peter did so. "Wrap your cloak around you and follow me," the angel told him. Peter followed him out of the prison, but he had no idea that what the angel was doing was really happening; he thought he was seeing a vision. They passed the first and second guards and came to the iron gate leading to the city. It opened for them by itself, and they went through it. When they had walked the length of one street, suddenly the angel left him. Then Peter came to himself and said, "Now I know without a doubt that the Lord sent his angel and rescued me from Herod's clutches and from everything the Jewish people were anticipating." When this had dawned on him, he went to the house of Mary the mother of John, also called Mark, where many people had gathered and were praying. Peter knocked at the outer entrance, and a servant girl named Rhoda came to answer the door. When she recognized Peter's voice, she was so overjoyed she ran back without opening it and exclaimed, "Peter is at the door!" "You're out of your mind," they told her. When she kept insisting that it was so, they said, "It must be his angel." But Peter kept on knocking, and when they opened the door and saw him, they were astonished. Peter motioned with his hand for them to be quiet and described how the Lord had brought him out of prison. "Tell James and the brothers about this," he said, and then he left for another place.***

RHODA: We know virtually nothing about this young girl except what she did in the book of Acts. As a servant, she probably performed menial tasks, including answering the door. She probably attended to a rich household, though we don't know that for sure.

check this out

Peter
Acts 12:1–25

Here's an amazing story. Peter had been taken to prison. While he was there, an angel appeared and led him out, past the sleeping guards. When he went to Mary's house, the young girl, Rhoda, didn't answer the door at first because Christians were being persecuted, and she was probably afraid. She asked who was there and Peter answered.

The group had just been praying for Peter. Rhoda was so excited that she didn't even open the door. She ran to the others and shouted, "Peter is at the door."

God had answered their prayers! But no one believed Rhoda. After all, she was just a young girl, and a servant at that. But Rhoda insisted. Finally someone let Peter in and found out that Rhoda had been telling the truth. God had miraculously rescued Peter, just as they had asked him to.

How Others See It

Michael W. Smith

I was extremely fired up. I wore a big wooden cross around my neck and carried a Scofield Bible. In Kenova, a town of five thousand people, we were extremely sheltered, but there were seventy-five to eighty people in our youth choir. For a small town, we were way ahead of our time.[6]

What would you have done? I'd have given everyone a lecture about not trusting our teens. But that's what happens, isn't it? In a group of adults, sometimes it seems teens aren't taken seriously. David wasn't when he offered to face Goliath. Samuel wasn't when he first heard God speaking to him. John Mark wasn't after his failure at Perga.

If you identify with Rhoda, what should you do? Though we know nothing else about her, she was clearly a teen of faith. She came to the prayer meeting. She probably prayed. She cared about the church and about the people. And God loved her. If that's you, let me say one thing to you: God loves you. He will use you in great ways if you let him. Don't let your youth be looked down upon. If you have a word from God, speak it loud and clear. If you have a mission from God, do it.

When Jesus was young, he was already showing how wise he was. When he was only twelve years old, as we'll discuss more in the next chapter, he was astounding church leaders who were way older than he was.

Probably a lot of people wouldn't listen to Jesus because of his age. But that didn't make any difference to him. He kept serving God wholeheartedly and learning more about God. We can do the same.

Few Christians who regularly read the Bible probably even remember Rhoda's name. But God knows it. That's the key to everything. God knows your name, who you are, what you've done, what you're doing, and that you have genuine faith. You are known by the only Person worth being known by. Everything else in the world will fade. But being known by God is what will last forever. Don't think of yourself as insignificant; God plus one is a majority.

When you have a chance next time to speak up about something important to you, why hold back? Why not stand in your tracks and shout out your best words for all to hear? Rhoda didn't have great courage. She didn't exhibit monumental faith. She just spoke up when it was needed. Sometimes that's what we all need to do.

You Can Serve God Now

You don't have to wait until you're an adult to start serving God. I discovered that when I was a teen. My church let teens lead services through "youth nights." So teens who had skills were able to use them to glorify God in the services. I didn't participate much in those, but they helped me see that teens could minister.

Where I did start learning how to serve God was through an organization called Kansas City Youth for Christ (now named YouthFront). Through this organization I learned how to use the Bible to lead people to Christ. I learned how to help start and lead a Bible club at my high school. I learned how to share my faith with my friends. I had a lot of outlets to serve God, which helped me grow a lot spiritually when I was very young.

Maybe your church doesn't do youth nights, and you don't have a Youth for Christ to teach you how to be a spiritual leader. But you can still serve God where you are. Look for opportunities to serve God (whether it's through leading a Bible study for your friends or just raking leaves for a busy neighbor), and ask him to open doors for you.

Teens do have a voice in our world. You can serve God with such a fervency that you'll be a good example to the adults around you! Like Nicole, my sixteen-year-old daughter. This year, Nicole has made a commitment to live for Jesus. As a result, I've seen a change in her life. Nicole loves to go to church and youth group, which she wasn't so crazy about before. She also reads her Bible and prays a lot. She asks God to help her control her temper and her attitudes and her patience with her younger sister and brother. And I see that difference in Nicole's life. She's obviously learning to love Jesus and serve him.

As I watch Nicole, I realize that I've come a long way since I was serving God as a teenager. Watching Nicole's zest for serving God is challenging me to make sure I'm serving him with all of my abilities.

Isn't that an interesting thought—to realize you might even be able to influence your parents and other adults with your faith? You don't need to be an adult to serve Jesus. God can use you right where you are!

Final Thoughts

- Mary shows us how to deal with a terrific problem through courage and faith.
- John Mark gave up the first time, but he came through the second time, and that is what we remember him for.
- Timothy turned out to be a great pastor because he had a great mentor. Everyone needs to find that one person who can help them grow in faith.
- Rhoda was a little fish in a big sea, but the one episode recorded in Scripture about her is a positive one. Can you think of any great epitaph?

Questions to Deepen Your Understanding

1. What about Mary's story is the most important to you? What principles from her life could you use in your own?
2. Have you ever given up on a task or a program? Have you ever wished you could go back and do it over? What does John Mark teach you about a second chance?
3. Who, like Timothy, do you look up to as a discipler? As a leader? How can you get closer to that person so you can learn from them even more?
4. Do you ever think of yourself as a mere Rhoda? What could you do to gain a hearing in your world?

read on

Some of Mark and Jeanette's favorite books about becoming acquainted with New Testament Teens:

- *1 & 2 Thessalonians, 1 & 2 Timothy, Titus, Philemon* (New Testament Commentary), Max Anders, ed., Broadman & Holman
- *Freshman: The College Student's Guide to Developing Wisdom,* Mark Matlock, NavPress
- *The Illustrated Bible Dictionary* (vols. 1–3), Tyndale
- *Men of the Bible,* Larry Miller, Thomas Nelson
- *Men of the Bible: A One-Year Devotional,* Ann Spangler and Robert Wolgemuth, Zondervan
- *Two From Galilee,* Marjorie Holmes, Bantam

Part Three

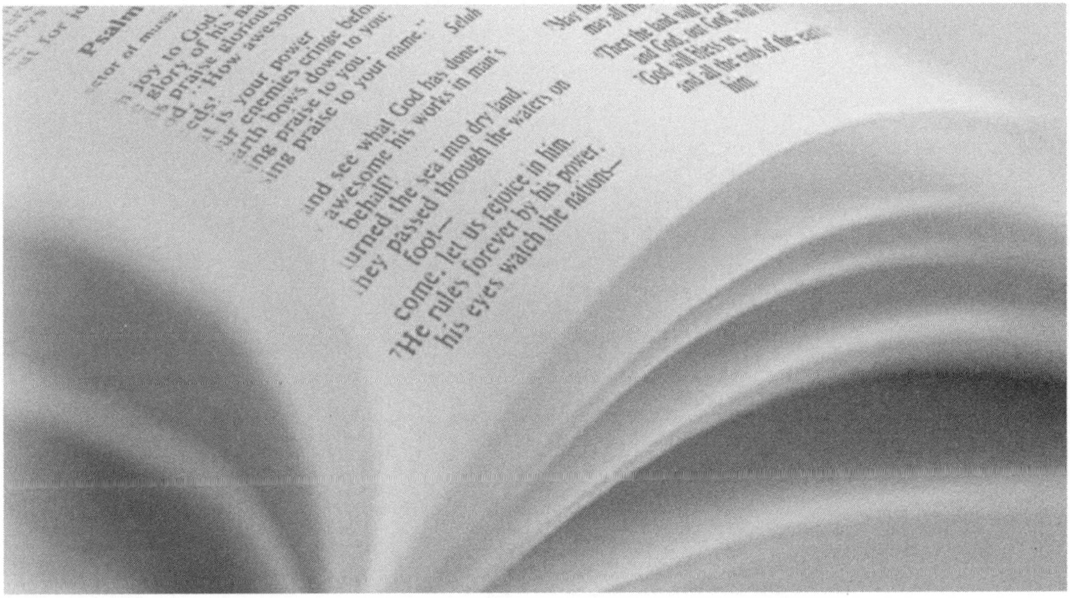

Living It Up

Chapter 5: Jesus Christ: The Perfect Example

Learning From Jesus' Example in Real Life

What's in This Chapter

- Jesus Was a Teen Too
- A Match for the Teachers
- Did Jesus Pump Iron?
- A Guy Who Pleased God
- Everyone's Friend?

Here We Go

Jesus. You've heard about him. You've known some of the things he did. Miracles. Famous words. Died on a cross. Rose from the dead.

But who was he really? And what was he like as a teen? In this chapter we want to explore Jesus as a teen. The Bible says very little about Jesus' teen years. In fact, we have only one real reference, and that happened when he was twelve. Beyond that, we know little. But from the later life of Jesus, we can define a number of character traits that made him distinct. In fact, one very short but powerful text of Scripture tells us a lot. We'll be looking at that in a moment.

Think about Jesus as a teen. What would it have been like to spend a relaxed day with him? What games might he have liked? Sports? What was he like in school? Was he friendly? Was he exclusive? Was he perfect?

Let's have a look.

Jesus Was a Teen Too

> LUKE 2:41–45 ***Every year his parents went to Jerusalem for the Feast of the Passover. When he was twelve years old, they went up to the Feast, according to the custom. After the Feast was over, while his parents were returning home, the boy Jesus stayed behind in Jerusalem, but they were unaware of it. Thinking he was in their company, they traveled on for a day. Then they began looking for him among their relatives and friends. When they did not find him, they went back to Jerusalem to look for him.***

Every year, Jesus' parents went to Jerusalem for the Feast of the Passover. This was a traditional time for Jewish people to visit Jerusalem. Passover was the primary feast of Israel, representing their escape from Egypt many centuries before. Jerusalem was considered the great city of God. Each year the visit to Jerusalem proceeded normally until the year that Jesus was twelve years old. Jesus must have been excited. It might have been the first time he'd seen the great city of Jerusalem, though that was unlikely. However, Jesus probably would have been excited to see the city in which so many famous events of Hebrew history took place. He would have enjoyed seeing many of the great teachers of Israel.

After the feast was over, while his parents were returning home, the boy Jesus stayed behind in Jerusalem, but they were unaware of it, probably because they traveled with a crowd, and possibly just figured Jesus was somewhere in the group with one of his friends.

Thinking he was in their company, they traveled for a day. Then they began looking for him among their relatives and friends. When they did not find him, they went back to Jerusalem to look for him.

think about it

You might ask, was Jesus being disobedient to his parents to not be with them when they were returning home? We know Jesus never committed any sin, so he could not have blankly disobeyed his parents. He was nearly old enough to be a man in his culture (thirteen) and to make his own decisions. More important, nothing in the text tells us of any exchange he had with his parents about staying in Jerusalem to talk to teachers or anyone else. The important thing is that Jesus understood the special relationship he had with his Father. His parents should also have understood that. But what follows after his parents come to get him is complete obedience to their wishes, even though he had a right to be doing what he was doing.

How Others See It

Rebecca St. James

As humans, I'm not sure that we will ever fully attain Jesus' humility, but it's something I am definitely seeking in my life.[1]

A Match for the Teachers

LUKE 2:46–51 ***After three days they found him in the temple courts, sitting among the teachers, listening to them and asking them questions.***

Everyone who heard him was amazed at his understanding and his answers. When his parents saw him, they were astonished. His mother said to him, "Son, why have you treated us like this? Your father and I have been anxiously searching for you." "Why were you searching for me?" he asked. "Didn't you know I had to be in my Father's house?" But they did not understand what he was saying to them. Then he went down to Nazareth with them and was obedient to them. But his mother treasured all these things in her heart.

The passage above tells us a little more about Jesus at age twelve. During a trip to Jerusalem with his family, while they were in the process of going home, Jesus remained. He conversed with the teachers and rabbis in the temple. He astonished them with his knowledge, and many gathered around to hear this young man ask questions and talk.

What kinds of questions did he ask? Undoubtedly, he spoke to them about the Messiah. How the Messiah would come. What he would be like. What he would do. He may have referred them to various texts in Isaiah and Jeremiah and the Law of Moses, citing Scriptures as proof of what he was saying. The men were mystified. Jesus undoubtedly spoke of a suffering Messiah, one who would die for the sins of his people, and not the great king they expected.

What Scriptures might Jesus have referred to? Here are some examples and questions he might have asked:

What the Old Testament Says About the Messiah

Scripture	Question(s)
Isaiah 53	Who is the suffering servant here? Why does the Messiah have to suffer?
Psalm 22	What is David referring to here in this form of execution? Why would David write such a psalm?
Psalm 110	How is the Messiah a priest like Melchizedek?
Genesis 3:15	Who is the one who will bruise Satan on the head?
Isaiah 7:14	How can a man be born of a virgin?
Isaiah 9:6–7	Who is the Prince of Peace, the Everlasting Father?

When Jesus spoke with the rabbis, perhaps they responded that they expected the Messiah to be a person who would reign over Israel and the rest of the world, rebuild the temple, and establish an everlasting kingdom with all the Jews at the top. The passages above, though, point to a very different Messiah, precisely the kind that Jesus was: suffering, humble, a Savior. The Jews weren't looking for a spiritual Savior but a political one. This later became a source of the greatest conflict between Jesus and the leadership of Israel. It was ultimately what they crucified him over, because he did not live up to their expectations.

check this out

Father's business
Luke 4:22, 32

wisdom
Isaiah 11:2–3

Father
God the Father

rabbis
Hebrew religious teachers

How Others See It

Steve Wiggins

Our human tendency is to look for a rule rather than a principle because it simplifies the decision-making process. . . . We want a clear system of right and wrong, but most choices don't fit into those compartments that neatly.

I think that was what caused the Pharisees in Jesus' day to make up a mountain of rules to live under. They took the simple laws that God had given and subdivided them, adding to them and changing them to the point that they became a burden. . . .

Then Jesus came along and said, "If you want to know what the Law of God is, I can sum it up in these two simple principles: 'Love the Lord your God with all your heart, soul and mind and . . . love your neighbor as yourself.'" . . . In the Bible, we have a complete record of not only what Jesus said, but also how he applied these two principles himself. As you turn every page, you see that his life was a perfect example. He loves his Father completely and he gave his own life for you and me.[2]

This passage contains a powerful clue to what Jesus must have been doing as a teen: his **Father's business**. Whatever the Father wanted, that was what Jesus did. He performed God's will to the letter. As a teen, Jesus must have been a good, decent, loving person. He never joked with dirty words. He never swore. He never stole from anyone or lied or had sexual relations with one of the girls in town. He was perfect.

Forget the SATs!

LUKE 2:52a *And Jesus grew in wisdom.*

What did Jesus do during all those "hidden" years we don't know about? It says that he "grew in wisdom and stature, and in favor with God and men." That points out four areas of growth in Jesus' life. First, wisdom. That's the intellectual and mental life. Jesus read. He memorized Scriptures. He learned from the **rabbis**. He asked questions. He gave answers when called upon. He went to school. He was a good student—not getting good grades because he was God incarnate but because he studied and took his studies seriously. He also learned about the world.

When travelers came through **Nazareth**, perhaps Jesus stopped them and asked them about their part of the world. When he walked through the fields, he consulted with the farmers as to how they planted, what kinds of crops grew in what soil, and how to cultivate the land.

check this out

temptations
James 1:2–4, 12–15

We know from Jesus' later life that he knew a lot about fishing, farming, plants, trees, crops, banking, money, service, tax-gathering, wine-making, and so on. He was probably a good questioner and one who learned quickly. But he didn't know it all just because he was God. He had to learn. He had set aside his omniscience to become completely human. That meant he had to work, study, and learn just like the rest of us. He must have had an incredible curiosity. He must have wanted to know everything about everything. He must have been amazed by his Father's world, studying birds and beasts, insects and reptiles with equal fascination.

Nazareth
Galilee village

temptations
when you want to do things you know you shouldn't do

tried
tested in a spiritual way

Did Jesus Pump Iron?

LUKE 2:52 *And Jesus grew in . . . stature.*

This verse tells us a second thing about Jesus: He grew in stature. That's physically. He grew up. He developed into a man. How did Jesus grow physically? He grew in all the ways a normal man grows: stronger arms, harder physique, better coordination.

heart to heart

Jesus must have had **temptations** during this time just as teenagers do today. The desire to sleep late. The desire to throw his homework out with the garbage. The desire to spend money frivolously. Even the desire to lust. You name anything you're facing and you can be sure Jesus also knew about it, though he never gave in to sin. That ultimately means that Jesus as a teen can help you as a teen when you face temptations. Jesus faced everything you'll ever face, and he knows how to show you the way around it. He also was **tried** during this time. The Father tried him in many arenas of life, to make sure he could withstand the problems during his ministry. The Father prepared Jesus to be ready for anything.

Jesus' earthly dad was a carpenter. Traditionally, at that time, a son usually followed in his father's career footsteps. So as Jesus grew up, he learned how to be a carpenter.

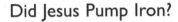

Carpentry was not easy work. Remember, electricity wasn't around yet, so there weren't electric drills and electric saws. Carpenters had to do all this with their own strength and sweat. As a result, carpenters probably tended to be pretty strong—from the arm muscles necessary for their skills to the muscles necessary for working with heavy wood. So Jesus was probably a pretty muscular guy.

Archaeological research shows us that the carpenters' tools were probably a marking tool, a compass or divider, an adze, an awl, a saw, a maul or hammer, nails, a chisel, and a bow drill.

That Older Brother

for real

I (Jeanette) have one older brother. When we were growing up, he was musically talented, great-looking, and an athletic star. Besides having roles in the school musical, my brother was a class officer. And he was terrific at any sport he tried.

I, on the other hand, was short and dumpy and wore thick glasses. I was lousy at all sports. When people found out I was Thurman's little sister, they expected me to be talented, popular, and athletic. They soon found out my brother and I weren't much alike. It was always disappointing to see that surprised look on their faces when they found out my brother and I were poles apart.

Imagine what it would have been like to be Jesus' little brother or sister. On one hand, I imagine it would have been tough. After all, they were the only ones on earth who truly had a perfect big brother! Mary, Jesus' mom, would have been less than human if she'd never scolded, "Why can't you be like your big brother, Jesus?" So it was probably tough being Jesus' sibling.

But on the other hand, I think it was probably pretty wonderful too. Since Jesus was perfect and had perfect love, he probably was so close to his brothers and sisters that he knew just how to be the perfect brother to them—someone they could truly look up to and respect and love.

Jesus wants to have that same kind of relationship with us. We don't need to fear growing close to him because he's perfect and we're not. Instead, we can share every area of our lives with him and enjoy his companionship. That's what being a Christian is all about—knowing Jesus.

A Guy Who Pleased God

LUKE 2:52 ***And Jesus grew in . . . favor with God.***

Growing "in **favor** with God." That's spiritual growth. God was pleased with Jesus. And Jesus learned to worship his Father. He studied the Scriptures and mined out of them the grand truths that help anyone face dark days and long nights. He went to synagogue and listened to the rabbi expound the Word of God. His desire was to know and serve God his Father.

Jesus also grew in ways that only God could know about. Jesus grew in the depths of his heart. He raised his voice to God in his soul and sang songs in the night. His thoughts became attuned to the voice of his Father, and he carried on conversations with the Lord of the universe day and night. He learned to relate to God as a man relates to his father. He learned to bring his fears and his deepest desires and lay them at the Father's feet. In effect, Jesus learned to love his Father. It's something we all must come to. Jesus led the way, but every teen and adult must develop in his relationship with God. That calls for submission, love, understanding, seeking, and obeying the great commandments. In every way, we learn to relate to the Father as a young man or woman in his universe, and we offer him worship and love as our Creator. When we do this, we truly learn what it means to walk with God.

check this out

worship
John 4:24

great commandments
Matthew 22:37–39

favor
approval

worship
to show reverence for, to adore

All Things for Good

for real

Kris was an attractive, lissome brunette with a sweet smile and a saber wit. And she didn't like me (Mark).

Not that I didn't deserve it to some extent. Her boyfriend, Joel, and I often talked as we washed dishes at the lodge-restaurant we worked at together. I wanted to help Joel find the Lord, and I knew I had to confront him about his relationship with Kris. He was living with her in one of the rooms at the lodge. He listened. I laid out the scriptural guidelines. Premarital sex was sinful. His relationship was headed for oblivion. He had to get it right with Kris or face the wrath of God. I was very direct.

The next day, Kris was very direct with me. She held a knife in her hand as she talked. "You leave Joel alone, or I swear I'll sneak into your room one night when you're asleep and cut you open like a Christmas turkey."

I stammered out something, I forget what.

Joel and I continued to talk. But we steered away from the subject of Kris.

Still, the anger and rejection grew. Kris lined up several of her friends at the lodge to let me know what they thought of me, my faith, and my attitude. It wasn't pretty. I still shudder sometimes when I think of it.

Romans 8:28 is a powerful anecdote for those who suffer rejection: "And we know that in all things God works for the good of those who love him, who have been called according to his purpose." God works in the midst of pain and suffering to bring forth good results. You may not see them right away. You may not see them ever. But God's promise is that he does work all things for good for the believer.

I saw this in my relationship with Kris. Our relationship remained difficult for some months. One day, though, she walked into the kitchen upset. I listened to her spill out a sad tale of a former boyfriend who had just been hired by the lodge. He had beaten her frequently, and she was terrified of him doing so again, even though they were no longer linked.

Gently, I began sharing with her what helped me to live through such fear. We talked for more than an hour. Suddenly, in the middle of preparing a sandwich, I said, "Would you like to accept Jesus?" She said, "I already did, while you were talking."

I was amazed. What was even more amazing, though, was that she and I became good friends after that and she stopped cohabiting with Joel.

Rejection hurts. But as we apply the right principles to the situation, relief and hope are at hand. Trust God to do what you cannot do. Remember Jesus. Nearly everyone rejected him. Even his disciples deserted him in his last moments. But he saw what was ahead. He saw what his Father planned to do once he rose from the dead. Rejection is only for a moment. Eternity is for an eternity. Trust God to deal with those who reject you, and be amazed when he does the impossible!

Many years ago, a Bible teacher was talking with a young lady about going to heaven. The teenage girl felt that she lived a good, moral life and was going to pretty much walk into heaven without having to make any kind of atonement for her sins or any kind of confession. The teacher, in his wisdom, sat down and talked with her. "Rachel, do you think you sin at all?" "Well," Rachel said, "I guess I do occasionally, but I don't think it's so much that God would care." "Okay, Rachel, do you think that you sin at least once a day?" "Oh, I don't know about that, teacher. I don't think so."

The teacher asked, "Do you think that you sin by saying something wrong once a day?" "Yes, now that you say that, I probably do say one bad thing a day."

"Then that would be a sin, Rachel." "Yes, I agree with you. I do sin once a day." The teacher went on: "And do you think you might sin by doing something wrong once a day in an action either by taking something or by going somewhere you shouldn't, by acting in the wrong manner by being angry? Do you think you have done something wrong one time a day in that way?"

"Yes, sir, I will agree to that once a day." The teacher then said, "Okay, so let's say that you sin three times a day. You are fourteen years old. If you sin three times a day and there are 365 days in a year, and you have lived fourteen years, that means you have committed over fifteen thousand sins. Do you think God would want you in heaven with fifteen thousand sins?"

Fifteen thousand sins.

The girl went to bed that night shaken by the thought of carrying the load of fifteen thousand sins on her back and possibly into judgment. Fifteen thousand sins! Rachel then realized that she needed someone. She needed someone special to be her Savior and to erase those sins. And so she came to Jesus, made it plain and simple, and she found out in a simple way that she needed the Savior for salvation. She accepted Jesus into her life to take away those sins.

Everyone's Friend?

LUKE 2:52 ***Jesus grew . . . in favor with . . . men.***

In this last part of the passage, we find that Jesus grew in "favor with men." That's social growth. Jesus knew how to get along with people. He knew how to talk, converse, ask questions, give subtle answers, and avoid bad people.

As Jesus grew in "favor with men," he probably had a group of guys he hung around with. He must have had friends who tried to get him into trouble now and then. He knew how to be polite and how to use manners at the dinner table. He knew how to have a good time. In fact, one of the things Jesus was accused of in later life was being a "**glutton** and **drunkard**." That means he liked to eat and drink. Certainly, Jesus never got drunk or ate to excess. He kept everything in balance. But he did enjoy the good things of life, and he knew how to have fun.

glutton
Matthew 11:19

glutton
overeater

drunkard
a person who drinks too much wine

How Others See It

Michael W. Smith

Everyone needs a solitary place to meet with God, whether it's a desk in the corner of your basement, a rusty old swing on your back porch, or ten minutes in the shower every morning away from the phone. The solitary place prepares you for what lies ahead. On the last night of His earthly life, Jesus escaped to the garden called Gethsemane. Sweating drops of blood as He began to understand more completely the terrible price He had to pay, He got alone with the Father and prayed for each of us.[3]

Jesus grew in all these areas as a teen. He's our model, one whom we can follow without reservation. What do you think of him? Is he someone you can lean on, someone you can trust? Could you tell him your secrets, your secret sins, your secret hopes? Could you give to him 10 percent of all the money you make without hesitation? Jesus knows what it's like to be you. Believe that, because it's true. For that reason, you can trust him as the exemplary teen worth imitating. We don't need a lot of stories and details about Jesus' teen life. We know from this passage that he had guts, a heart, commitment, intelligence, and determination. That should be enough for any teen to think he's well worthy of our best.

Final Thoughts

- Like any teen, Jesus liked to be independent. That explains part of why he left his parents' caravan and stayed in Jerusalem.
- As Jesus conversed with the teachers, he stunned them with his wisdom and questions—questions they couldn't answer, but he could.
- Jesus grew in four ways: In wisdom (mentally), in stature (physically), in favor with God (spiritually), and in favor with men (socially).

Questions to Deepen Your Understanding

1. What can you learn from Jesus' foray into the temple? What questions would you ask a teacher if you had the chance?
2. Are you growing in wisdom? In what ways?
3. Has your physical development frustrated you? How can you be thankful for the way God made you?
4. How might you grow spiritually this week and so please your Father in heaven?
5. What are some ways you can grow socially and so please the adults in your life?

read on

Some of Mark and Jeanette's favorite books about learning from Jesus' example in real life:

- *And the Angels Were Silent: The Final Week of Jesus,* Max Lucado, Questar
- *It's Not About Me, Teen Edition,* Max Lucado, Integrity
- *The Jesus I Never Knew,* Philip Yancey, Zondervan
- *13 Crucial Questions Jesus Wants to Ask You,* Tom Carter, Kregel
- *Three From Galilee: The Young Man From Nazareth,* Marjorie Holmes, Harper & Row
- *What's So Amazing About Grace?,* Philip Yancey, Zondervan
- *When God Whispers Your Name,* Max Lucado, Word

Chapter 6: A Jet Tour Through Theology

Looking at Basic Truths of the Bible

What's in This Chapter

- The Study of God
- Three in One? Egg-Zactly
- God 101
- God's Personal Spirit
- The Future of Planet Earth

Here We Go

Theology is the "study of God." It comes from two Greek words, *theos*, which means "God," and *logos*, which means "word" or "study." In fact, Jesus is often called the *logos* or the "word" of God.

Theology seems like a big, scary concept, but it's not. As we go to church, we learn more about theology. As we study our Bibles and understand more about Jesus and God, we're studying theology. As you read this book, you're studying theology. Theology is simply getting to know God better and learning more about who he is and what he's like.

check this out

treasure
Psalm 119:9, 11

The Study of God

> JOHN 1:14 ***The Word became flesh and made his dwelling among us. We have seen his glory, the glory of the One and Only, who came from the Father, full of grace and truth.***

Although in one sense theology has a simple definition, you can see from this verse that the very idea of theology also carries some heavy-duty ideas. Who is God? What is he like? Where is he? What does he have to do with us? These are questions people have asked since the beginning of time. In some ways, the idea of God is our greatest obsession. Why? Perhaps because he's the one who calls us all to account. He's the one who rules. He's the one who makes things happen. If we neglect him, we neglect the most important person in our life to our own peril.

It is important for us to study theology because without knowing the basic facts and truths of our faith, we are only disasters waiting to happen. God wants us to "treasure" his Word in our hearts. In this way, we can be assured of God's blessing and leadership in our lives.

check this out

treasure
Joshua 1:8

> ### How Others See It
>
> **Jennifer Knapp**
>
> I've seen people around me who lost their fire and passion for God, even though they're still in church. So that's one of the things I try to communicate, having an honesty with God, because that's what He wants. . . . Even though we are Christians we need grace.[1]

heart to heart

If you understand basic theology, your faith will be able to grow. Then your faith won't get shaken when things go wrong in your life. When we have treasure, the Word and truth of God in our hearts, we can stand up to anything this life throws at us.

Get a good study Bible, such as the *Student's Life Application Bible*, and read the points of theology that you find in the back pages. If you or your parents don't have a good study Bible, check your church library or ask your youth pastor or pastor.

Three in One? Egg-Zactly

> 2 CORINTHIANS 13:14 ***May the grace of the Lord Jesus Christ, and the love of God, and the fellowship of the Holy Spirit be with you all.***

The idea of God's being a "trinity" is pictured in this text. Here we have the "grace of Christ," "the love of God," and the "fellowship of the Holy Spirit." The word *trinity* is not used, but it's implied in the text.

Even the Old Testament contains one place where we see all three persons of the Trinity in one verse. Look at this: "Come near me and listen to this: 'From the first announcement I have not spoken in secret; at the time it happens, I am there.' And now the Sovereign Lord has sent me, with his Spirit" (Isaiah 48:16).

In this verse, we find three words that refer to members of the Trinity: "the sovereign Lord," who is God the Father; "me," who is Jesus the Son; and "his Spirit," who is the Holy Spirit. Throughout the Old Testament and the New, God is a name associated with three persons: the Father, the Son, and the Spirit. What do we make of this? That God exists as three distinct persons, yet all three are one God or one "essence." One substance. God works in the world through three different personalities, each of whom is distinct, individual, and divine (see Illustration #7).

Holy Wholeness

By this we see that God as a trinity is whole and complete in himself. He has equal and individual beings who return to him love and intellectual stimulation. He can make plans, talk through ideas, and study an issue with two partners who are equal to him in mental, emotional, and physical capacity. This is an important principle to grasp, for it means that God ultimately did not need to create us for companionship or friendship or even love. He had all of that safely in the confines of his own being. No, he created us because he is a creator, and he wanted to use his gifts and powers for a good thing: creation. But does he need us? Does he depend on us? If he lost us all, would he grieve? No, he wouldn't need to, though of course the reality is that he loves us and would not want to see such a thing happen. In fact, he loves us so much that he plans to spend eternity with us.

check this out

he loves us
John 3:16

John the Baptist
Matthew 3:13–17

John the Baptist
prophet and cousin of Jesus

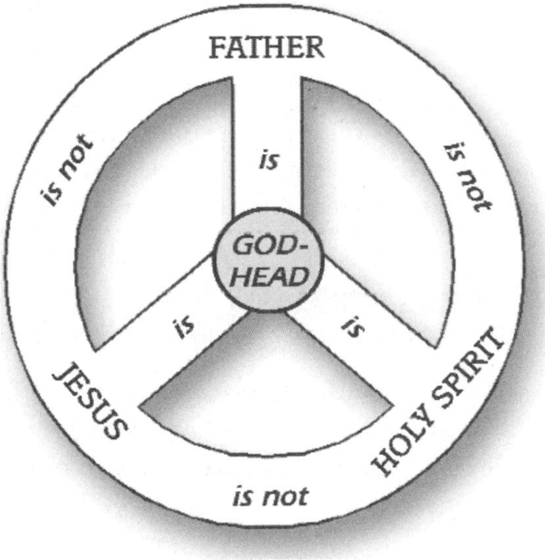

Illustration #7
The Trinity—This illustration puts God at the center as the one essence, but he appears in three persons, each of whom is God, but who is not the other two. They are three distinct persons.

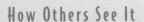

How Others See It

Curtis McDougall

The Bible contains much that is relevant today, like Noah taking 40 days to find a place to park.[2]

When the Father thought of his Son, Jesus, he was very proud, as most any father is of a son. In fact, when Jesus was baptized by **John the Baptist**, the first thing that happened as he came out of the water was the opening

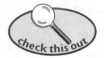

check this out

Father
Ephesians 4:1–6

head
leader or ruler

of the heavens and a voice saying, "This is my Son, whom I love; with him I am well pleased." At that moment, Matthew says that the Holy Spirit descended as a dove and came upon Jesus (see Illustration #8). The Trinity is right there in the baptism of Jesus, at the very beginning of his ministry. All three of the persons of the Godhead participated in the launching of the most important person who ever walked planet Earth. They were also there at the end when Jesus went up into heaven. He ascended to the Father and sent his Spirit into the world to fill the lives of those who followed him.

Sometimes it's hard to grasp the concept of God's being three people. One way I explain it to my daughters is that God is like an egg. An egg has three parts: a shell, a yolk, and the egg white. Although an egg has three distinctly different parts, it is still one egg. The Trinity is like that. God has three parts, each person in the Trinity has his own role to play and purpose, but the three still make one God.

Illustration #8
The Descending Dove—Matthew 3:16 reads, "As soon as Jesus was baptized, he went up out of the water. At that moment heaven was opened, and he saw the Spirit of God descending like a dove and lighting on him."

The Supreme Commander

> 1 Corinthians 11:3 *Now I want you to realize that the head of every man is Christ, and the head of the woman is man, and the head of Christ is God.*

Here we see the "**head**" of Christ, or the One over him, is God the Father. In other passages we see that the Spirit does the bidding of Jesus. Whatever Jesus wants him to do, he does.

God the Father is the Supreme Commander of the Trinity. He is the One at whose desk the buck stops. Jesus answers to him, and the Spirit answers to Jesus. This does not mean the Holy Spirit and Jesus have less power or dignity or importance than the Father. It shows that there's a chain of command even in heaven. To make things run well, God organized even himself as a person with authority, submission, and dependence.

Buddhist
follower of Buddha

Hindu
worshiper of India's many gods

When you consider the Trinity, don't think of three individual gods. There is one God, but he exists as three persons. This is hard to understand. It's not easy to sit down and think through the implications of God's being three-in-one. How do they operate? How do they get along? How do they make things run well? This is the key, here. Jesus submits to the Father. The Spirit submits to Jesus. This is how things stay in balance in heaven. Christ is your head. Are you letting him be the head, or are you trying to make the tail wag the body?

How Others See It

Bob George

If you deny the Trinity, you'll lose your soul. If you try to understand the Trinity, you'll lose your mind.[3]

Eugenia Price

God the Father is God for us. His intentions are all toward us. God the Son is God with us, and in him is the same nature as the Father. The same intentions. The Holy Spirit is God in us, enabling us to respond to himself. The Holy Spirit, of course, has the same nature as the Father and the Son.[4]

He's Still Going . . .

REVELATION 4:8 ***Each of the four living creatures had six wings and was covered with eyes all around, even under his wings. Day and night they never stop saying: "Holy, holy, holy is the Lord God Almighty, who was, and is, and is to come."***

This verse refers to God's eternity. God has always been around—from even before the beginning of time as we know it. He exists now. And he'll always exist. There is no gap in the reality of God. He is the One who lives forever.

When we speak of God, we need to understand what he is like. If you ask a **Buddhist** what God is like, he will probably respond, "I do not think of God. I am God. You are God. All of us are God and all return to him when we attain perfection." If you ask a **Hindu**, he might say, "Which god? We

check this out

attributes
Psalms 103:8–14; 145:1–21

Muslim
follower of **Muhammad**

Muhammad
writer of the Muslim bible, the Koran

Allah
name of Muslim god

Yahweh
name of God, meaning "I am"

infinite
without physical or spiritual limits

immanent
in the world

sovereign
supreme commander or leader

believe in millions of gods." If you ask a **Muslim**, he would refer to **Allah** and give you a litany of things about Allah, which would be different from the Bible's idea of God. If you ask a Jew about God, he would reply, "God is the Master of the universe, **Yahweh**, the One who is, who was, and who is to come."

The Bible presents a clear picture of what God is like. Many attributes of God are presented in Scripture, including the fact that he is loving, all-powerful, all-knowing, **infinite**, **immanent**, **sovereign**, holy, righteous, and just. Look at the following chart to gain a better understanding of a full picture of God's attributes.

God's Attributes

Attribute	Meaning	Scripture
Unity	God is one	Deuteronomy 6:4
Infinity	Without limit	Revelation 1:8
Eternity	Beyond time	Psalm 90:2
Immutability	Unchangeable	James 1:17
Omnipresence	God is everywhere	Psalm 139:7–12
Sovereignty	God is supreme ruler	Ephesians 1
Omniscience	All-knowing	Psalm 139:1–7
Omnipotence	All-powerful	Revelation 19:6
Justice	Perfectly just	Acts 17:31
Love	Infinitely loving	Ephesians 2:4, 5
Truth	Truthful in all ways	John 14:6
Freedom	Independent from world	Isaiah 40:13–14
Holiness	Righteous and good	1 John 1:5
Grace	Giving and sacrificial	John 1:14

Adding It All Up

Psalm 103:8–14 ***The Lord is compassionate and gracious, slow to anger, abounding in love. He will not always accuse, nor will he harbor his anger forever; he does not treat us as our sins deserve or repay us according to our iniquities. For as high as the heavens are above the earth, so great is his love for those who fear him; as far as the east is from the west, so far has he removed our transgressions from us. As a father has compassion on his children, so the Lord has compassion on those who***

fear him; for he knows how we are formed, he remembers that we are dust.

This Scripture passage gives us more specific thoughts of who God is and how he acts. When you add all this up, you find a God who is very powerful, infinitely loving, willing to give and sacrifice for his children, and who can be trusted without question. If we were to sum up God as a person, we would say at least four things about him:

1. God exists. He is there. He is here. He is everywhere. He knows everything about us, is ultimately ruler over us, and in the end we answer to him for what we've done with our lives.
2. God loves us. "God is love," John said (1 John 4:16). He loves us whether we love him or not. He loves us infinitely, more than we can imagine, and he was willing to pay the ultimate price for our freedom and our happiness.
3. *God has a plan* for our lives. Before we even existed, the Bible teaches, God planned out everything that would ever happen. He included our lives, our personalities, and our choices in his plan. No one can stop his plan from happening.
4. *God wants us to know him*. A well-known **catechism** of the faith asks the question: "What is the chief end of man?" Answer: "To know God and enjoy him forever." Imagine! God wants us to know him personally, be his friend, be his child, be his heir, and he wants us to enjoy that relationship forever.

check this out

God exists
Genesis 1:1;
John 1:1

God loves us
1 John 4:8;
John 3:16

plan
Ephesians 1:19–20;
Mark 1:17

know him
Isaiah 1:18;
Matthew 11:28–30

catechism
a question-and-answer formal teaching format that some churches use

How Others See It

Michelle Akers

My inheritance in Christ is rich beyond measure. The very God who rules all, is above all, and knows all, desires to draw me close, to love me intimately, and to protect me forever.[5]

If we seek God, he promises to make himself known to us. Multitudes of Scriptures confirm this. God wants us to seek him, to long for him, to search. He promises that he will guide us directly to him if we're sincere and we take the necessary steps.[6]

words to live by

God wants us to enjoy him. Have you ever thought of what that statement means? Worship him? Sure. Follow him? Of course. Obey him? Certainly. But enjoy him? Somehow it sounds so simple, so fun! But that's it. God

check this out

find him
John 1:12

image
picture or representation

wants us to have a little fun in this world. He's not a cosmic killjoy, standing in heaven watching for reasons to club us to death! No, he's seeking a friendship with us that will be the most enjoyable relationship we could have in this world. The relationship he longs for is one of worship, love, and joy. Above all, he wants us to enjoy his presence, his guidance, his conversations, his leadership. If we respond to his love, draw near to him, listen for his voice, we soon find he draws even nearer to us. After all, what is a real relationship? Isn't it give and take, speak up and listen to, take a walk down the road together, and share secrets, hopes, and dreams? That's what God wants to have with us. What do we really want in a relationship with God—just going to church, putting some money in the plate, and then running off to do what we really want to do? No, God wants much more than that. Why, because he's lonely or needs our love? Not really. It's more because he knows we can only be complete and whole as we learn to relate to him intimately and deeply. Is that what you want with God? If so, then seek him. His promise is that you will certainly find him.

Jesus the Son

> JOHN 3:16 ***For God so loved the world that he gave his one and only Son, that whoever believes in him shall not perish but have eternal life.***

Jesus is the One and only, the unique Son of God. No one else is like him. Clearly, we're talking about a supernatural person here, not someone average or normal or purely human.

But what does it mean that Jesus is the Son of God? Did God the Father give birth to him? Then who was his mother? Has he always been the Son? Why is he called the Son? Why not the "companion" or "friend" of God the Father? Wouldn't that be more appropriate?

Perhaps another passage will help, this one from Colossians.

God 101

> COLOSSIANS 1:15–18 ***He is the image of the invisible God, the firstborn over all creation. For by him all things were created: things in heaven and on earth, visible and invisible, whether thrones or powers or rulers or authorities; all things were created by him and for him. He is before all things, and in him all things hold together. And he is the head of the body, the church; he is the beginning and the firstborn from among the dead, so that in everything he might have the supremacy.***

From this passage, we get the idea that Jesus is the ultimate object lesson of what God the Father is like. In other passages, Jesus said if you've seen him, you've seen the Father. Another way Jesus often put it was to say the Father was in him and he was in the Father. He is equal to God the Father, but he has chosen to be under the Father's authority. That means Jesus has submitted himself to whatever orders the Father gives.

check this out

Son
John 14:6–11

So Jesus is the Son in the sense that he is under God's authority. It's not because God the Father gave birth to him, but it's a term God uses to help us understand the different people in the Trinity. All the attributes that apply to the Father also apply to Jesus. He is all the things God is, including all-powerful, all-knowing, infinite, and sovereign. But he still puts himself under his Father's authority.

How Others See It

Branley Smith

There's nothing in this world that can match the riches that come from a relationship with Christ. For that reason alone, I would have quit Hootie a thousand times over.[7]

If Jesus, being God, was willing to put himself under his father's authority, how much more should we obey our earthly father's authority? Yes, some fathers demand too much, are abusive, or fail to live up to standards that call for obedience. But statistically, most fathers are decent, loving, and hardworking men who want to do the best for their sons and daughters.

Just Like Jesus

PHILIPPIANS 2:5–8 ***Your attitude should be the same as that of Christ Jesus: Who, being in very nature God, did not consider equality with God something to be grasped, but made himself nothing, taking the very nature of a servant, being made in human likeness. And being found in appearance as a man, he humbled himself and became obedient to death—even death on a cross!***

God wants us to become more like Christ every day. Philippians 2:5–8 speaks of our attitude as Christians. What is it to be? The same as the attitude Jesus had—to be completely obedient to God the Father.

This kind of obedience is tough. How can anyone do that? Only one way: By letting Jesus make it happen in your life as you walk with him. You

check this out

tempted
Hebrews 2:10

human
1 Timothy 2:5

tempted
to be enticed to do evil

throne of grace
God's throne, his presence, open to anyone who will come

sinless
without sin

blasphemy
to speak sinfully of God

God incarnate
God in human form

can't do it alone. Jesus has to make this happen in your heart through the Holy Spirit's work. He doesn't expect you to somehow develop the right feelings. He wants you to trust him to help you have the right feelings.

> **How Others See It**
>
> **C. S. Lewis**
>
> A man who was merely a man and said the sort of things Jesus said wouldn't be a great moral teacher. He would either be a lunatic on the level of a man who says he's a poached egg—or else he would be the devil of hell; you must make your choice. Either this was, and is, the Son of God, or else a mad man or something worse. You can shut him up for a demon, or you can fall at his feet and call him Lord and God. But don't come up with any patronizing nonsense about his being a great moral teacher. He hasn't left that alternative open to us.[8]

Just Like Me?

> HEBREWS 4:15–16 ***For we do not have a high priest who is unable to sympathize with our weaknesses, but we have one who has been tempted in every way, just as we are—yet was without sin. Let us then approach the throne of grace with confidence, so that we may receive mercy and find grace to help us in our time of need.***

Although Jesus was God, he was also completely human in every sense of the word. Jesus was just like us. He had feelings. He got tired. He ached. He became angry at times. He had a normal human body just like ours—nothing supernatural about it. His Father didn't protect him from the normal aches and pains of life either. He experienced everything we all encounter as the daily problems of life.

You'd think God on earth would spend time with royalty—with the kings and presidents and actors and other socially important people. But he didn't. He spent time with everyday people like you and me. He also spent time with people our moms certainly wouldn't want us to hang out with—people who were criminals or were involved in shady deals. He didn't flinch from helping any person.

There is only one way Jesus was not like us. Jesus was **sinless**. He never committed a single sin, nor could anyone accuse him of sin. The Jewish leaders of his time accused him of **blasphemy**, but that's because they refused to acknowledge that he was, in fact, **God incarnate**. If Jesus was persecuted and hated, how much do you think we who follow him also will be persecuted and hated by those who hate him?

> **How Others See It**
>
> **Bill Spiers**
>
> Jesus was crucified for my sins, and knowing that Christ is my Savior gives me a sense of peace and tranquility. He is by my side, during the bad and the good times.[9]

died
I Peter 3:18;
Romans 5:8–9

One of the great truths that come with Jesus being fully human is that he can understand anything we're going through. He knows what it's like to be tempted and tested. He has felt extreme hunger (see Matthew 4:1–11), the desire to be famous, and the need not to listen to the Father's will but to go his own way. He felt all those things, yet he never sinned. He has gone the length and width and breadth and depth of temptation without giving in.

Consider the fact that Jesus has been tempted in every way we have been tempted, yet he never sinned. If Jesus never sinned, how does he know what it's like to give in to temptation? He knows what it's like to experience the consequences of sin. Where? On the cross. When Jesus died, the sins of the world were placed on him, and he experienced all we do in terms of guilt, embarrassment, pain, suffering, and anguish.

Think of it this way. Imagine a marathoner who has trained to run the marathon over many years. In the course of his training, he learned what it was to run a quarter mile, then a mile, then several miles. He experienced everything that comes at those levels. But then he goes the ultimate distance. Jesus has gone the complete distance of temptation like that runner without ever giving in to sin. That means he can help you in your temptation situation, no matter what it is.

A Worthy Sacrifice

ROMANS 5:8 ***But God demonstrates his own love for us in this: While we were still sinners, Christ died for us.***

We always say, "Jesus died for our sins." But what does that mean? What is sin?

For most of us, *sin* is an old word for "doing wrong things." Like what? Getting drunk. Lying. Stealing. Cursing. But are those things really that bad?

propitiation
payment
hell
the final place of the condemned

The truth is, God made us to be perfect. But when our first parents broke God's rule in the Garden of Eden, they plunged all of us into a terrible situation: We became imperfect. We all went whatever way we desired, and in the end, we all broke God's laws left and right. Breaking God's laws, however small they may seem to us, is very big to God. Why? Because when we lie, when we steal, when we curse each other out, when we cheat and use drugs and get drunk, we inevitably not only hurt others, but we also hurt ourselves. Isn't the whole problem in the world that everyone does things that hurt others? To be sure, some commit worse crimes than most of us. Certainly, few of us will ever commit murder. But think about what happens when you do a little thing like cheat on a test. You may cheat once, but the second time it becomes even easier. Soon cheating is a way of life. If you go through your days cheating many times, sooner or later you will be caught. Then you will pay a heavy price, perhaps having to go to prison or worse. Even short of that, you destroy your character in the eyes of others. People recognize you as a cheat and don't trust you.

Committing sin is like throwing a rock into a lake. It produces ripples and waves that go out in every direction. That sin touches many people. And that's just the beginning. Look at our world today. Everywhere you look, you see people blaming, hurting, fighting, and destroying. That's the result of sin.

What has God done about it? Jesus came to pay the penalty for all the sins of every person who has ever lived. That's the whole reason God sent Jesus to earth. Jesus came to die, to pay the penalty for our sins. Every sin that every person has ever committed was laid on Jesus Christ as he suffered on the cross. Jesus paid the complete penalty of suffering and death. What he did was accepted by God the Father as a **propitiation** for mankind's sin. We could illustrate it this way. Imagine that you commit a crime, are tried in court, and are sentenced to death by lethal injection. Seconds before you are to be executed, someone steps up and says he will be lethally injected in your place. Why? Because he loves you.

In the same way, every person who has ever lived will be tried in God's court for everything he has ever done wrong. God will listen to all your reasons and excuses and other defenses, and then he will pronounce the sentence: guilty. Banishment to eternal **hell**.

Imagine. Just as you are about to be whisked away by an angel, Jesus steps up and says, "Father, I have paid this person's sentence by dying on the cross." Because Jesus is perfect and sinless, he doesn't have to pay for his own sins. He can, however, pay for yours and mine. God accepts Jesus' payment, and you go free.

We owe God the Father a huge debt because of our sins. We all have a multitude of them—thoughts, words, and deeds—and they amount to a big sentence. Imagine if every time you did something wrong in thought, word, or deed, God gave you a fine like a policeman gives a ticket to a speeder. For a hateful thought, you get a fifty-dollar fine. For a swearword or for taking God's name in vain, it's a hundred dollars. And for gossiping about someone else or taking revenge on someone, even mildly, it could be thousands of dollars. Now imagine all those fines piled up over years and years. Each of us owes God billions! How do we pay? We can't, so we're sentenced to spend our eternities in hell. But Jesus comes along and he pays the fines himself, with his life on the cross. God accepts what Jesus did and we now don't owe God anything—that is, if we accept what Jesus did for us.

check this out

payment
1 Corinthians 15:2–4

rose
Romans 1:1–4;
1 Corinthians 15

Stay Underground? No Way!

> 1 CORINTHIANS 15:3–8 ***For what I received I passed on to you as of first importance: that Christ died for our sins according to the Scriptures, that he was buried, that he was raised on the third day according to the Scriptures, and that he appeared to Peter, and then to the Twelve. After that, he appeared to more than five hundred of the brothers at the same time, most of whom are still living, though some have fallen asleep. Then he appeared to James, then to all the apostles, and last of all he appeared to me also, as to one abnormally born.***

In this Scripture passage, Paul writes to the Corinthians that Jesus rose again from the dead to prove that God accepted his sacrifice on the cross. This is crucial. If Jesus had died on the cross, was buried, and then was revered for a while but largely forgotten, his death would have meant nothing. All his lofty words about seeking the lost and saving them would be meaningless. But God did something to show that Jesus' death paid the penalty and that we could all have life anew: He raised Jesus from the dead. Because the debt was paid, God could give us the thing he wanted to give us all along: eternal life. Jesus' resurrection proves it.

words to live by

Buddha, Confucius, Muhammad, Gandhi . . . what do these people have in common? They were all leaders who were followed far and wide and revered by people. You could probably add more names to the list.

check this out

transform
John 7:37–39

saint
holy one

But although Jesus was followed by many and revolutionized the world, we can't put him on the same list. Why not? Because when they died, the remains of all these people stayed on earth. They led while they were alive, but when they died, their bodies remained behind. But we have no grave for Jesus. If you go to Jerusalem, you can see the tomb where tradition tells us Jesus was placed. But you can also look inside it and see that it's empty!

Only Jesus, of all the powerful leaders in the world, had the power to overcome death. Because he died, he lives. And because his power can even overcome death, you can be sure that he has the power to handle whatever you are facing in life. Don't be afraid to ask for his death-revolting, life-changing power to help you today!

Jesus' Apartment Address Is "Your Heart 1A"

> **JOHN 1:12–13** ***Yet to all who received him, to those who believed in his name, he gave the right to become children of God—children born not of natural descent, nor of human decision or a husband's will, but born of God.***

What are we to do about the things Jesus did for us on the cross and in rising from the dead? He asks one simple thing: to believe in him. But what does it mean to believe? It's more than intellectually saying, "Yes, I think these things are true." It's more than telling someone else you think they're true, though that is a good thing to do. Belief in Jesus means trusting Jesus personally. Tell him in prayer that you believe the facts about him and that you put yourself in his hands. Ask him to forgive you for the sins in your life. Ask him to work in your life, to transform you from being a sinner to being a **saint**, to make you ready for heaven. When you trust him like that, he says he makes you a "child of God."

everyday insights

Branley Smith, the former drummer for Hootie and the Blowfish, became a Christian and quit the band before it became one of the biggest acts in rock music. He is now a youth pastor. Of his choice to follow Christ, he says, "I have peace about the past and trust that this is where God wants me to be. As long as I have Christ, there won't be any regrets."[10]

We can experience that same certainty in our lives.

Our New Daddy

Jesus will make the one who believes in him a child of God. We'll talk more about what that means later in this book. But for now, remember that God wants to make you his child. He wants you to believe in his Son, he wants to give you eternal life, and day by day he wants to change you personally into a person whose character is like his own: perfect, good, loving, gracious, and wise.

check this out

Holy Spirit
John 14:25–27

> **How Others See It**
>
> ### Will McGinniss
>
> I came from a broken family. I didn't have a father figure in my life. I really took hold of God being my "Abba" Father. My walk with him is really like hangin' with a best friend. You know that you can crawl up in his lap when things are not going good.[11]

heart to heart

Becoming a Christian is the most important step anyone can take in his journey on this earth. The whole reason we exist is because God wants us to believe and follow his Son. Where are you in this process? Have you believed? Do you trust him? If so, you are on the way to a remarkable journey that will end in heaven forever.

Spirit Is More Than a Pep Rally

> JOHN 16:13 ***But when he, the Spirit of truth, comes, he will guide you into all truth. He will not speak on his own; he will speak only what he hears, and he will tell you what is yet to come.***

We now move on to perhaps the most controversial person of the Trinity. The Holy Spirit is a much misunderstood character in the holy trio of the Godhead. Some well-meaning Christians have turned him into a spiritual genie who heals on command and makes people do crazy things like speak in weird languages, fall on the ground and laugh hysterically, or make animal noises. While many such people are sincere, the only one of these experiences found in Scripture is speaking in weird languages, or "speaking in tongues," which, according to the Bible, was the power to speak in an actual language you didn't know.

The Holy Spirit is more than a giver of spiritual gifts and spiritual leading. He is the key to much of spiritual living. Without him we would always fail in our desire to please God. Who, then, is the Holy Spirit, and what is his work about?

hierarchy
divided into levels of authority

How Others See It

Jed Jansen

It's easy to get caught up in the emotional roller coaster. We feed off the inner strength from the Holy Spirit. It's certainly easier dealing with the pressure with the presence of Christ.[12]

God's Personal Spirit

ACTS 5:3 ***Then Peter said, "Ananias, how is it that Satan has so filled your heart that you have lied to the Holy Spirit and have kept for yourself some of the money you received for the land?"***

Here we see that the Spirit of God is a person. Peter tells Ananias that he has "lied" to the Holy Spirit. This lie cost Ananias his life. The Holy Spirit is a person with a real personality, real concerns, real desires, and real love for each of us. He is called the Spirit, but it is just a name God has given us for him. He is no different from the Father or the Son in his personhood. If you imagine the Father and Son as members of a family, perhaps the Spirit is the wife or daughter. That's not to say he's feminine—God is not masculine or feminine, he is Spirit—but he would function much like a wife functions in a marriage. She is a partner, a companion, a helpmate to the Father and the Son. So is the Spirit. The Spirit submits himself to Jesus' leadership, even as Jesus submits himself to the Father's. You see here a "chain of command" within the Trinity. Jesus does what the Father says; the Spirit does what Jesus says. That does not make them any less equal or powerful or divine. All three are equal, but in order to function as a Trinity, there is a **hierarchy** of responsibility.

---

everyday insights

The music group Delirious enjoys seeing the Holy Spirit work through their ministry. Often, rather than performing for their audiences, they end up leading the people in worship. Watching the Holy Spirit work and people's lives being touched is "a mark of what we do," says guitarist Stuart Gerrard. When the audience breaks into spontaneous worship, Gerrard says, "I think we're still hearing the Holy Spirit and flowing with Him."

The guys in Delirious feel the Holy Spirit can flow through all aspects of their music that they work so hard on, even the preplanned technol-

ogy. "We believe that technology has just as much a way of evoking a spiritual reaction and is just as soaked in the Holy Spirit as what we are doing," explains Stewart Smith. "They're not two separate things. Hopefully it's all working as one."[13]

indwells
Romans 8:9;
I Corinthians 6:19–20

salvation
being preserved by God from hell and death

The Holy Spirit's Job Application

> JOHN 16:8–11 ***When he comes, he will convict the world of guilt in regard to sin and righteousness and judgment: in regard to sin, because men do not believe in me; in regard to righteousness, because I am going to the Father, where you can see me no longer; and in regard to judgment, because the prince of this world now stands condemned.***

What does the Spirit of God do? In this text, we see several things he does: He convicts the world of sin and righteousness and judgment. This means he tells us when we're sinning; he guides us to practice the truth, and he warns us of impending judgment. But there are many other things he does too.

The Spirit indwells us. He comes to live inside of us when we accept Jesus as Savior and Lord in our lives. This indwelling happens at the moment of **salvation**, not after. All believers have the Spirit dwelling in them.

If God is in you, are you letting him have his say, or are you fighting him all the way?

> **How Others See It**
>
> **Steve Crawford**
>
> We have the responsibility to make people aware that first of all, the Holy Spirit has the ability to convict and direct and instruct.[14]

Imagine you're a house. You've invited Jesus to come into your house and be a resident. That's salvation. But now Jesus is going through the house, looking into the various rooms, and suddenly he comes to a room with a locked door. This is the room in your spiritual house where you do some things you know Jesus wouldn't approve of: drugs, smoking, illicit sex, obsession with sports, gambling, etc. Jesus wants to go into that room. Why? Because he wants to embarrass you? No. Because he wants to confront you? Maybe. But mostly because he wants to clean that room up and make it habitable. You can't have rooms in your spiritual house that are closed off to Jesus. If you do, he will speak to your heart and make you open the door so he can see what's inside. And then he will begin cleaning house.

Exercise for a New Kind of Body

> 1 Corinthians 12:7–11 *Now to each one the manifestation of the Spirit is given for the common good. To one there is given through the Spirit the message of wisdom, to another the message of knowledge by means of the same Spirit, to another faith by the same Spirit, to another gifts of healing by that one Spirit, to another miraculous powers, to another prophecy, to another distinguishing between spirits, to another speaking in different kinds of tongues, and to still another the interpretation of tongues. All these are the work of one and the same Spirit, and he gives them to each one, just as he determines.*

check this out

baptized
1 Corinthians 12:13

body of Christ
the church universal

giftedness
your special mix of spiritual gifts

When we come to Christ, we are all baptized into the body of Christ. The word *baptize* means to "dip or immerse." In that sense, you were dipped or immersed into the **body of Christ**. You became part of Christ's body—perhaps a hand or foot or heart or lung—and you must function within that body according to your special place and **giftedness**. Think of it this way: You were transplanted, the same way an organ is transplanted from one body to another, into Christ's body. He took you in and made you a part of his body. The body of Christ is the whole church. We all together function as extensions of Christ. He uses some of us in very public, amazing ways—like Billy Graham and others. He uses others in "behind-the-scenes" ways; they'll never be famous, but when they get to heaven, they'll have a tremendous reward.

That's what it means to have the Spirit of God dwell in you. He is inside your body, mind, soul, and heart, just as you are inside Christ's body. It's a spiritual reality. When you understand this truth, you become a powerful tool in the hands of God. He can now lead you into the great work in which he intends to employ you.

The Spirit of God gives us spiritual gifts. This is the primary ministry of the Spirit. He gives us a mixture of several gifts of the Spirit that will enable us to serve Jesus effectively and fulfillingly. What are the gifts of the Spirit? The following chart shows twenty of them. Some of them, many scholars believe, are no longer available or used today.

Gifts of the Spirit

Name of Gift	Scripture	Use
Wisdom	1 Corinthians 12:8	To give sound advice
Knowledge	1 Corinthians 12:8	To know truth
Faith	1 Corinthians 12:9	To exercise faith
Healing	1 Corinthians 12:9	To heal
Miracles	1 Corinthians 12:10	To perform miracles
Prophecy	1 Corinthians 12:10	To tell the future
Distinguish spirits	1 Corinthians 12:10	To recognize demons
Tongues	1 Corinthians 12:10	To speak languages
Interpretation	1 Corinthians 12:10	To understand languages
Apostle	Ephesians 4:11	People who start the church
Prophet	Ephesians 4:11	Someone who speaks God's word and truth
Evangelist	Ephesians 4:11	One who preaches and starts new churches
Pastor/teacher	Ephesians 4:11	One who nurtures believers
Encouraging	Romans 12:7	Lifting others up, giving them hope
Leadership	Romans 12:8	Being in charge of others
Giving	Romans 12:8	Sharing
Serving	Romans 12:7	Meeting others' needs
Showing mercy	Romans 12:8	To comfort
Helps	1 Corinthians 12:28	To aid others
Administration	1 Corinthians 12:28	To organize

How do you know what gifts you have from God? There are several ways to determine this. First, consider your abilities. What are you already good at? What things do you excel in that involve spiritual activities? For instance, if you're a great piano player, test to see whether you can play music so that it builds up believers. If so, you may have the gift of teaching, exhorting, or serving. A musical gift can be any combination of those three.

Second, what do you enjoy doing? What builds you up? Chances are, the thing you enjoy is the thing God wants you to do.

check this out

fills
Colossians 3:16

Third, what do others say you are good at? If you think you have the gift of preaching, but every time you preach people say, "You should try something else," you might need to do some more work. Should you go to school? Should you begin practicing more? Should you work at getting opportunities to preach more? Something like that takes much effort. It doesn't come to you as a perfect ability. You have to refine it. So if you have a strong desire, whether it's music, teaching, sports, or something else, seek God and ask for his guidance. At the same time, keep working at it till either you find you'll just never succeed in that kind of work, or you're led in a new direction.

Get Your Fill, It's God's Treat

> EPHESIANS 5:18–21 ***Do not get drunk on wine, which leads to debauchery. Instead, be filled with the Spirit. Speak to one another with psalms, hymns and spiritual songs. Sing and make music in your heart to the Lord, always giving thanks to God the Father for everything, in the name of our Lord Jesus Christ. Submit to one another out of reverence for Christ.***

The Spirit of God *fills* us. What does that mean? To be filled is to be animated, led, and empowered by the Spirit. Think of a glove. Without the Spirit in your life, you are like an empty glove. Looks good, but that's it. You can't do anything to please or serve God. But put a hand inside that glove, and suddenly it comes to life. It can grab, gesture, play a piano, whatever. That's the Spirit of God. Without him, you're little more than a limp, empty glove. With him, you can snag home-run balls in Yankee Stadium.

words to live by

What happens when you're filled with the Spirit? Paul provides some insight in the passage above. Notice four things that happen when you're filled with the Spirit. One, you speak the word of God to others. Two, you sing and make "music" with your heart to God. That means you're filled with joy and a sense of beauty about life. Three, you begin giving thanks. No more complaining. No more worrying. No more nasty attitudes. Instead, you're thankful for the many blessings you're receiving daily. Four, you submit yourself to others. You care about others and seek to serve them. You obey your parents and listen to them. You follow the guidance of God in all circumstances. Imagine what can happen in a life when it's filled with the Spirit like that!

Abba
Aramaic word for "Daddy"

How Others See It

A. W. Tozer

The doctrine of the Spirit as it relates to the believer over the last half-century has been shrouded in a mist such as lies upon a mountain in stormy weather. A world of confusion has surrounded this truth. This confusion has not come by accident. An enemy has done this. Satan knows that Spiritless evangelicalism is as deadly as Modernism or heresy, and he has done everything in his power to prevent us from enjoying our true Christian heritage.[15]

Imagine you're standing on a basketball court with the Chicago Bulls and the Los Angeles Lakers. You're the star forward for the Bulls. Only one problem: You don't know how to dribble, shoot, drive, or rebound. What do you do? You could go out there, bumble around, make a fool of yourself, and then quit. But imagine that Michael Jordan has offered to come live inside your body and play basketball through you. How do you think you might do now?

That's what happens when the Spirit of God indwells and fills you. He develops you like a coach. He leads you like a friend. He strengthens you like an internal battery pack. You'll soon be playing basketball like a pro. Why? Because Michael Jordan, the greatest basketball player in human history, is inside you. As a Christian, that goes even further. Michael Jordan might be a great basketball player. But God invented basketball. God gave Michael Jordan his moves. And God is inside you in the person of the Holy Spirit!

Touring Life With God

> ROMANS 8:13–16 *For if you live according to the sinful nature, you will die; but if by the Spirit you put to death the misdeeds of the body, you will live, because those who are led by the Spirit of God are sons of God. For you did not receive a spirit that makes you a slave again to fear, but you received the Spirit of sonship. And by him we cry, "**Abba**, Father." The Spirit himself testifies with our spirit that we are God's children.*

From these verses we learn that the Spirit (1) stops us from doing evil things, (2) leads us because we're sons and daughters of God, (3) enables us not to fear anything in this world, (4) guides us to call God "Daddy," and (5) assures us we are really God's children. That's all part of his leading.

think about it

The Spirit of God guides and leads us through the circumstances of life. The Spirit's purpose is to help us see the truth and then apply it to our lives. He also guides us through difficult circumstances, speaking to our hearts when we're confused or unsure of what to do.

The Spirit teaches us the truth. The Spirit works in your life to open your mind and heart to truth, to the things God wants you to learn. He gives you insight into Scripture and shows you how the Bible applies to your life. He helps you understand Jesus' parables and the mysteries of faith. He leads you in comprehending what the future holds and what God is doing in the world. Why do you think unbelievers cannot understand a lot of scriptural truths?

When unbelievers come to doctrines like salvation by faith, God's grace, and the idea of angels and demons, they often laugh. They think these ideas are old-fashioned. But the believer knows that these are words of great truth. Why? Because the Spirit of God has opened his or her mind. Until God's Spirit opens the unbelievers' eyes, they will never come to Christ. They will continue to think of Jesus as a great teacher, an impostor, or even a devil. But we have the Spirit of God inside us to teach us and to lead us—in the major areas of our lives, and in the minor areas.

---

everyday insights

A while ago I took my daughter out to buy a winter jacket. Cold had come to Des Moines, Iowa, and snow lay on the ground. It was after the Christmas holidays, and it seemed everyone was sold out of winter jackets.

As we drove toward the main mall in town, I prayed that God would help us find a jacket my daughter would love. I asked her what she really wanted, and she said, "A Chicago Bulls jacket," so I prayed for that. As we drove toward the mall, I had a sudden notion to try the local discount store on the way. We went inside and found the only rack of winter jackets left in the place. Lo and behold, there was a Chicago Bulls jacket, perfect for winter weather and a perfect fit for my daughter. Things don't always happen that quickly or clearly, but that's guidance. The Holy Spirit will put you where you need to be.

God's Gotcha Covered

1 John 5:13 ***I write these things to you who believe in the name of the Son of God so that you may know that you have eternal life.***

Paul wrote these words so believers in the early church would be assured of their salvation. The Spirit gives assurance of salvation too. He communicates with us Spirit-to-spirit and tells us, "Yes, you are God's child. You have eternal life. You're a member of God's family." How does he do this? It's an almost mystical-sounding truth, but he speaks to our hearts. Only a real Christian can experience this. There's a supernatural, spiritual communion between you and the Father. He's real. He's in your life. He's making good things happen in your life and his blessing rests upon you. That's assurance.

Many teens have trouble with assurance. They've accepted Christ, but they don't "feel" saved. How can you get a sense that you really are God's child, that he has become a part of your life and is your leader and friend?

words to live by

Assurance comes through many means. Sometimes a truth from the Bible will hit your heart in such a way that you know it's God speaking to you. Suddenly, for the first time, he seems "real" to you. That's the beginning of assurance. Romans 8:15–16 tells us that one of the things we acquire sooner or later in our spiritual lives is the sense that God is our "daddy." In those verses, the apostle Paul tells us that we call God "Abba, Father." *Abba* is the Middle Eastern word for "Daddy." There comes a time when you recognize God's presence and you start to think of him as your heavenly Daddy. That's assurance too.

In those same verses, Paul says that the Spirit "testifies" that we "are children of God." That's the Spirit of God speaking to us in our hearts. Again, this is a strong form of assurance: God speaks to us deep in our hearts, and we recognize his voice because we are his children.

Other ways to gain assurance are through simply exercising faith. If you believe in Jesus and you have trusted him with your life, the Bible says you "have eternal life," according to 1 John 5:13. You may not "feel" anything. But over time, as you exercise faith again and again, you will find that God's presence and company begin to seem more and more real.

Don't despair if you sometimes wonder if you're really a Christian. All Christians struggle with the issue at one time or another. One of the best things to do is simply to pray about it. Ask God, "God, please help me to know for certain that you are my God. Open my eyes and ears to your

intercedes
prays for someone

voice and the truth." God will answer your prayer, perhaps not right away, but in time.

Don't let your feelings get out ahead of you. Feelings change. Facts never change. But faith grows.

More Than Words Can Say

> ROMANS 8:26–27 *In the same way, the Spirit helps us in our weakness. We do not know what we ought to pray for, but the Spirit himself intercedes for us with groans that words cannot express. And he who searches our hearts knows the mind of the Spirit, because the Spirit* ***intercedes*** *for the saints in accordance with God's will.*

The Spirit teaches us to pray and even intercedes for us. One important principle of Scripture is that we're to "pray in the Spirit" (Ephesians 6:18). When we pray that way, we are assured of praying in God's will, which means God will surely grant the request we've made.

What's this verse all about? Undoubtedly, there have been times in your prayer life (or will be, if you haven't had this happen yet) when you are so emotionally moved by a situation—a friend's illness, a death, the possible loss of something important—that you can hardly find the words to speak. At that time, you may simply "groan in your spirit." You may come before God but have no words to say. That's the Spirit of God working in your life. He takes over at that point and expresses all that's in your heart, all that you can't seem to put into words, and he makes clear to the Father what is needed.

> **How Others See It**
>
> **George W. Bush**
>
> Prayer has comforted us in sorrow and will help strengthen us for the journey ahead.[16]

The Basics

We now move into another theological area that I call "the basics." These are bedrock truths that will anchor your attitude in the right place as you understand the nature of people and things in this world. Let's turn our attention to four basic areas of theology that every Christian needs to understand.

What Is Salvation?

> Ephesians 1:4b–8 *In love he predestined us to be adopted as his sons through Jesus Christ, in accordance with his pleasure and will—to the praise of his glorious grace, which he has freely given us in the One he loves. In him we have redemption through his blood, the forgiveness of sins, in accordance with the riches of God's grace that he lavished on us with all wisdom and understanding.*

check this out

trusted
John 3:17–18

forgiven
1 John 2:1

second death
Revelation 2:11

bondage
Galatians 5:16, 25–26

new family
Galatians 4:6–7

Once you understand the truth about God the Father, Son, and Spirit, you're ready to plumb the depths of the issue we call **salvation**. What is salvation, and why is it so important for life in this world? To be saved is rather simple, really. You believe that Jesus was God, that he died for your sins, and that he lives now to work in your life and make you a new person inside and out. Anyone who believes those basic truths about Christ can be saved. But what does it mean to be saved? Several things.

salvation
freed from the consequences of sin

second death
eternal or spiritual death, separation from God forever

1. ***We are saved from eternal death.*** When you trusted Christ, the first thing you received was eternal life. In other words, you're going to heaven!
2. ***We are freed from the consequences of sin.*** A second thing that happened was this: You were forgiven of all your sins, past, present, and future. You will not have to pay any eternal or spiritual penalty or suffer any punishment for any sin you ever committed. They're all forgiven because Christ took them away when he died on the cross. Though you will die physically, and though you may have to face consequences for your actions on this earth, you will never die permanently or experience the "**second death**." God has saved you from that.
3. ***We are liberated from bondage of sin.*** Not only did Christ free you from the consequences of sin, he freed you from the bondage of sin. Non-Christians have no choice but to sin, but Christ gives a choice. You can say no to any sin or addiction or problem. He will give you the power.
4. ***We are born into a new family.*** Ever wonder what it might be like to be born into the royal family? Well, if you're a Christian, you are. You're born into God's family and are his personal heir. He has made you a prince or a princess in a way that no royal family on earth could ever accomplish.

When you trust Christ, these and many other things happen in the eyes of God. Study your Bible to learn what all those things are. You'll come across them day by day as you learn the truth of your new family.

heart to heart

If God did all those things for you through your salvation, what should be your response? Indifference? Pride? Love? Gratitude? Obviously, a couple of those responses are wrong. And it's sad if you don't have a real spirit of love and gratitude toward God because of what he did for you. Ultimately, God deserves our love and respect regardless of what he has done for us in salvation, simply because he is God and our Creator. But when you realize all the amazing things he has done for us in Christ, God deserves our love and gratitude all the more. You can never love and thank him enough for his great gifts to us.

We All Have the Disease

> ROMANS 5:12 ***Therefore, just as sin entered the world through one man, and death through sin, and in this way death came to all men, because all sinned. . . .***

Here the author of Romans, Paul, tells us that death entered the world through sin. He's referring to Adam and Eve's sin in the Garden of Eden. He goes on to say that death—spiritual death—came to all people because of that sin. Because of this, all people are born in spiritual death.

Why do people start wars? Why do people hate each other? Why are there murderers and liars and rapists and gossipers and drunkards and everything else that is bad on our planet? Not because some people are bad and others are good. But because all of us have a problem called a sin nature. That means we have a natural disposition or tendency to commit sin. It is born in us.

Don't get me wrong. I'm not saying people can't do decent, good, and kindly things for one another. But everyone everywhere has a nature that tempts them to commit sins. For some it's gambling and drugs, for others it's illicit sex and hatred. It doesn't matter what sins you choose. The truth is you will choose some, and they will snare you forever.

check this out

sin nature
Romans 7:18–19

nature
Genesis 3:1–7

choose
Romans 7:1–25

A couple of chapters later, Paul points out that even when we want to do good, we still do what's wrong because of our sin nature. Even when we want to do what's right, we can't.

What does that mean? It means you and I know what's good. We know the right thing in many circumstances. But we choose to do the wrong thing anyway. What a wretched existence! You know what's right but can't do it. You know what's wrong and you don't want to do it, but you do it anyway! That's the sin nature.

Why do we have a sin nature? Because of something called **original sin**. When Adam and Eve were first created by God, they were told not to eat the fruit of a certain tree. God told them if they did eat from it, they would die. What did they do? They ate, and they died. First, they immediately died spiritually. They hid from God. They didn't want anything to do with him. That's spiritual death. In time, they would die physically. And ultimately, they would die eternally in hell, if God didn't save them (which he did). When Adam and Eve died spiritually, something happened inside them so that all their children and every person born thereafter would have the same "mark" upon them.

died
Genesis 3:8–21; 4:1–7

original sin
Adam and Eve's sin

How Others See It

Billy Graham

Young people talk a lot about love. Most of their songs are about love. "The supreme happiness of life," Victor Hugo said long ago, "is the conviction that we are loved."

"Love is the first requirement for mental health," declared Sigmund Freud. The Bible teaches that "God is love" and that God loves you. To realize that is of paramount importance. Nothing else matters so much. And loving you, God has wonderful plans for your life. Who else could plan and guide your life so well?[17]

Out of the Pit

Have you ever felt like you were in a pit of despair that you just couldn't get out of? Perhaps this story will help you understand the real pit every one of us is in when we live without Jesus in our lives.

How Holmes had gotten into the pit he didn't know. He'd been there ever since he could remember. Jagged crags jutted up above him, and when the sun shone down from above, it sometimes was unbearably hot. He'd tried to climb out many times, but it was impossible. The sides of the pit cut his hands and feet. Where he could get a fingerhold, he was as likely to lose a fingertip as to hold on. Climbing out wasn't the way.

But Holmes wanted out. He hated the pit. It was desolate, lonely. Something within him cried that life had to be better than this.

Then one day a man appeared at the edge, looked down, and spied Holmes instantly. "So you're in the pit," he said.

"What's it look like?" answered Holmes cheerlessly. "You know a way out?" The man nodded. "The truths of the Buddha will help you get out." Holmes became excited. "What do I do? Tell me."

The man said, "You must overcome all desire. Follow the eightfold path and you will break the endless cycle of karma. Your soul will be set free and you'll be out of the pit, even though your body will still be in it."

Holmes squinted at the stranger. "My soul set free but my body still here? What kind of nonsense is that?"

"No nonsense. Just meditate. Then your suffering will end." The man turned to leave. Holmes snorted. "I guess I can't lose anything trying this." He plopped himself down and tried to clear his mind. "I will think of nothing, do nothing, be nothing," he said. He concentrated. But as he did, it seemed his desire to escape the pit only magnified. After several hours of struggle and failure, he gave up. At that moment, he spotted another man passing by the edge of the pit.

"Hey!" yelled Holmes. "You have any ideas how to get out of the pit?"

This fellow was wearing a yellow robe and appeared to be bald. "Of course. All you have to do is chant, 'Hare Krishna, Hare Krishna, Hare Rama, Hare Rama.' Just say it about three thousand times a day."

"Why?"

"It'll make you happy."

Holmes slumped. "I don't want to be happy. I want to be out of the pit."

The fellow yawned. "Sorry. Our book doesn't say anything about pits. Just about how to be happy." He wandered off and Holmes once again was alone.

"Creep!" he shouted. "Creep!"

Suddenly a bearded man with a notebook stopped and gazed at the hapless Holmes. "Can I offer you my services?"

"Who are you?"

"A scientist," he said. "And a doctor of engineering."

"Fantastic!" said Holmes. "Can you engineer a way for me to get out

of the pit?" The scientist looked around. "I think so. I've built such contraptions before. Let me see what I can do."

The scientist brought in a team of students who began putting together a marvelous piece of machinery. In no time the scientist had dropped it in by parachute with a full manual and list of instructions.

"How do I work it?" shouted Holmes.

"Read the directions," said the scientist, and headed off down the road.

Holmes read. And read. And read. He tried this button and that lever. But nothing happened. Then he found the electrical cable.

"There's nowhere down here to plug it in!" he cried.

Holmes shouted again, but his voice only echoed. "Great!" he said. "Now I'm not only not out of the pit, but things are more cluttered up than ever."

He sat down and banged his fist on the ground. "I'll never get out of here." Then another man appeared on the edge of the pit. He peered down. Holmes was about to speak, but then the man simply clambered over the edge of the pit and began climbing down. Holmes watched with fascination.

The man found handholds and footholds where there was sheer rock before. As he drew nearer, Holmes noticed his back, bent and torn. And his hands and feet had great scars on them.

"He must be used to climbing into pits," Holmes said to himself.

It was only minutes until the man alighted and stood before him. "Get on my back," he said.

Holmes was about to protest, but the man's face was so utterly sincere that the hesitation and fear left him. He jumped onto his back.

The man began climbing. Holmes marveled as he watched him pick his way upward. He climbed smoothly, effortlessly from Holmes's point of view, but many times the man cried out in pain. When they reached the top, his fingertips were bloody.

Holmes hopped off and said, "Can I bandage your wounds?" The man held out his hands and Holmes made a dressing from some fresh grass and leaves. When he finished, the joy of being out of the pit struck him. He sucked in the cool air. "I can't believe it. I'm out. It was that simple. How can I ever thank you?"

"Just say it," he said.

Holmes laughed. "That's all? Just say thank you?" The man smiled and nodded.

Holmes bowed. "Thank you." He paused. "But how can I ever repay you?" The man smiled again. "You can't."

He was shocked at this blunt honesty. But suddenly he understood. "That's strange to say. But you're right. I can't repay you. I can only thank you."

Holmes gazed at the man, perplexed. It had been so simple, so matter-of-fact. He said, "But why did you do this? Why did you come down to get me?"

The man blinked. "Because I love you."

Holmes shook his head. "I don't understand."

"You will." The man got up and began walking away. Holmes ran after him. "Wait, where are you going?"

"There are other pits, other people."

"But what should I do?"

The man turned, his eyes piercing Holmes to the heart. "Follow me."

When he said it, Holmes's heart jumped. He stood there, momentarily staring back at the pit and the vast landscape before him. "I could just go my own way," he muttered. "Why should I follow him?"

But something within told him there was much more to this than just being free. "I've got to find out more about this man," Holmes said to himself. He joined the man at his side. "What's your name?"

"I am who I am," he said. "But you may call me 'Lord.'"

Holmes nodded and began gazing about at the countryside around him. He looked into the Lord's eyes and his mind seemed to fill with enormous thoughts, too great to contain. His heart swelled within him.

"This can't be," he said. "I must be half crazy. I'm beginning to think you're much more than a person who climbs down into pits."

"I am."

"But who are you?"

"I am the Bread of Life, the Resurrection, the Way, and the Truth. But you can't understand all this now. You have to grow."

Holmes bowed before him. "I will follow you. But what do I do?" Suddenly a cry pierced the air. "Help, I'm in the pit!"

Holmes thought a moment. Suddenly, he leaped. "That's it, Lord! I'll look for people in pits and you can come to rescue them."

The Lord laughed and motioned with his arm. "Do it."

Holmes ran in the direction of the voice. In only moments he found a man in a pit much like his own. He shouted down to the man that help was coming. Then he looked toward the Lord and cried, "Over here, Lord. This guy is really desperate."

sin nature
Romans 5:12

This story points out the truth of a great verse of Scripture where Jesus tells his disciples, "For the Son of Man came to seek and to save what was lost" (Luke 19:10).

You can know all kinds of theology and memorize many Scriptures. But if you miss the truth that Jesus seeks and saves those who are lost, you've missed the whole point of everything. Jesus wants to use each of us to speak to our friends and acquaintances, tell them about Jesus and his mission, and lead them to the Savior. That's what theology is all about. That's what life in this world is all about.

The only question is: Are you taking that mission seriously? Are you going out with Jesus and seeking to save those who are lost?

Scripture teaches that when Adam and Eve faced the test of the fruit, all of us were, in a sense, casting our vote with them. They were representatives for us, but if we had been them, we would have done the same thing. If we hadn't, why do we all continue sinning when we know it's wrong? Adam and Eve passed along a defective gene called a sin nature, which we all now have.

Have you ever seen a sign on a wall or a piece of furniture: "Do not touch. Wet paint!" What do we inevitably do? We touch it to see if it's really wet. Why? Is there something inside us that compels us to do that? Yes. Original sin. A sin nature. We don't like anyone telling us it's off-limits. As soon as we see the Stay Away sign, we immediately run to it. That's the sin nature. All of us have it, and we'll never be rid of it completely until we get to heaven.

Here Comes the Judge

REVELATION 20:11–15 ***Then I saw a great white throne and him who was seated on it. Earth and sky fled from his presence, and there was no place for them. And I saw the dead, great and small, standing before the***

check this out

judgment
2 Corinthians 5:10; Matthew 25:31–46

judged
1 Corinthians 3:11–15; Romans 2:4–10

throne, and books were opened. Another book was opened, which is the book of life. The dead were judged according to what they had done as recorded in the books. The sea gave up the dead that were in it, and death and Hades gave up the dead that were in them, and each person was judged according to what he had done. Then death and Hades were thrown into the lake of fire. The lake of fire is the second death. If anyone's name was not found written in the book of life, he was thrown into the lake of fire.

There's something else we need to know about when it comes to the basics. It's the principle of judgment. God is righteous. God is holy. God is just. That means he can't simply sit back and say, "Oh well, boys will be boys," about sin. No, he has to get involved. First, he has to stop sin. Second, he has to judge it. And third, once judged, he has to put it somewhere where it can't hurt anyone else.

Judgment is a scary thing. "You mean, I'm going to stand before God and answer for everything I've done in my life?"

If you're not a believer, yes, you will do exactly that. God will look at all your sins and then he will make a final judgment about how you will be punished. Make no mistake about it. All of us will face a day when we stand before God and answer to him for all we've done. If we don't have Christ to pay for our sins and forgive us, we're going to have to pay for them ourselves. That's not a very pretty thought.

Christians will not be judged for their sins—they have all been forgiven through Christ—and they will not be in danger of being sent to hell—they have already been promised heaven. No, Jesus will reward believers for what they did for him in this life on earth. Amazing, isn't it? God plans to give us each astonishing rewards, favors, prizes, and gifts just because of what we did with our lives after we became Christians.

words to live by

Judgment scares us. But the real Christian doesn't need to fear the judgment of God. God assures us the reason for judgment is because God wants to bless us, to enable us to enter into his kingdom with real joy and hope. He wants us to start heaven on a good note that will never die. Think of it! Right now God is preparing you for that moment. He's putting in your life and your path all sorts of wondrous things. Good deeds. Loving acts. Kind words. They'll all be rewarded. No one may have noticed what you did in this world. But God did. And one day he'll show before all of creation the great deeds you did in his name. So look forward to the judgment with expectation. God is going to bless your socks off.

How Others See It

Tony Evans

There's only one way we can know the difference between good and evil. There must be a standard. Otherwise, we're lost, because what is good and right to one person may not be good to another person. We need a guideline and a standard that will govern everybody.[18]

check this out

first creation
Job 38:7

ministering spirits
1 Kings 19:1–8

Carrying Out God's Business

HEBREWS 1:14 ***Are not all angels ministering spirits sent to serve those who will inherit salvation?***

Another basic area of interest for Christians is that of angels. Angels are real, supernatural beings. They never die. They were God's first creation. When God first chose to create, he created angels.

There are many types of angels, and some have names. There's Gabriel, for example, the angel who came to the Virgin Mary and told her she would be the mother of Jesus; and Michael, the archangel who often fights against Satan (who was once an angel himself).

Angels are ministering spirits. Their primary purpose is to minister to humans, to help them out of temptation, to get them through trials, to carry messages, and to carry out many other ministries. An angel once helped a prophet named Elijah, who was very depressed, by cooking him meals and giving him sleep (1 Kings 19).

Shining Warriors

for real

A missionary lived in an area of Africa where natives fought and killed. He had come to bring the Gospel to the tribes in that region, but the tribal chief didn't like him. One night the missionary felt a sense of danger and hid with his family in the house, praying. Looking out the windows, he knew many warriors were hiding in the jungle around the house. But as the night wore on, nothing happened.

Some time later, that missionary was able to lead the chief of the tribe and many of his people to the Lord. One day the chief mentioned that night when he and his men stood in the bushes waiting to attack. He said to the missionary, "Who were the shining ones standing around your house?"

The missionary didn't know. He had seen no one. "Yes," said the chief, "there were many shining warriors standing guard. We didn't attack because we were afraid of them." The missionary reflected on this and realized these "warriors" must have been angels sent to protect him and his family.

check this out

study
Hebrews 13:2

Lucifer
shining one

You're a Walking, Talking Textbook

EPHESIANS 3:10 ***His intent was that now, through the church, the manifold wisdom of God should be made known to the rulers and authorities in the heavenly realms.***

Angels study us. One of the most remarkable things about angels is not only do they minister to us, they study us too. They want to understand the depth of God that he illustrates through our lives.

Angels study us to learn about God. Why do they study us? Because at one time there was a rebellion of the original angels, led by **Lucifer**—one of the greatest angels—who became Satan. These rebellious angels believed that God was not worthy of love and respect. They wanted to follow Satan, so they staged a rebellion. How was God to deal with that? He could have destroyed all the rebels, but perhaps another group of rebels would arise from the remaining angels. He could have given them their own world. But that was not right, because greater angels there would prey on lesser angels, and God always does what is just and right. So God decided to do something else: He decided to start a grand experiment. He created earth and the universe, and he said, "In this place we'll try out my ideas and we'll try out Satan's, and we'll see whose are the best."

How Others See It

Billy Graham

Angels are God's secret agents.[19]

The Criminals of Eternity

ISAIAH 14:13–14 ***You said in your heart, "I will ascend to heaven; I will raise my throne above the stars of God; I will sit enthroned on the mount of assembly, on the utmost heights of the sacred mountain. I will ascend above the tops of the clouds; I will make myself like the Most High."***

From the very beginning, God revealed there was a real **devil** and a horde of **demons** who follow him. Where did this devil come from and who is he? The devil is Satan (whose name means "adversary"), who once was Lucifer, the highest archangel God ever created. Lucifer had a multi-jeweled covering and was probably a walking light show. His job was to protect God's glory and instruct the angels of heaven in all the truth of God the Father. However, according to Ezekiel 28, Satan became proud and corrupted his wisdom. (If you look up Ezekiel 28, you should know that many believe the "king of Tyre" to be Satan.) He began to lie and connive and plot with other angels against God. Finally, one day, perhaps after negotiations and threats directed to God, and with many dire warnings from God, we find that Satan decided to start a campaign against the Almighty. Here's a breakdown of what he said:

1. "I will raise my throne above the stars of God." Satan would take a position—God's position—as ruler over the stars of God, a reference to all the angels.
2. "I will sit enthroned on the mount of assembly." Normally, God convened his angels at times to talk things over. God sat on the throne, leading the assembly. But Satan threatened to steal that place too.
3. "I will ascend above the tops of the clouds." The tops of the clouds touched the bottom of God's most private, personal, intimate place where no one else could come.
4. "I will make myself like the Most High." He would take the place of God in every way, making himself a replica of God in power, knowledge, and authority.

That was quite a threat. And quite a boast. At this point Satan was rebuffed in his attack, along with a third of the angels who had rebelled with him. God sent him plummeting from heaven. But now what to do? As we said earlier, it was at this point that God began grand experiment B, the creation of the universe, planet Earth, and mankind. There, as in a **biosphere**, God would let Satan fantasize, while God himself worked out his plan. At the end of time, all would see whose ideas and plans were better, Satan's or God's.

check this out

convened
Job 1–2

take the place
Ezekiel 28:11–19

devil
accuser

demons
evil angels

biosphere
a dome in which there's a perfect biological environment

check this out

tempt
James 1:12–16;
1 Corinthians 10:13

How Others See It

Jeffrey Bryant

Satan's most effective warriors are in the mainstream: Misguided, apathetic Joe and Jane Schmos who . . . live "normal" lives. But their minds are deceived and their lives are permeated by subtle, socially acceptable, ungodly attitudes. Such "innocent Satanists" have the greatest influence in our world. Is it possible that some of Satan's strongest influence comes even through members of Christ's church?[20]

Satan's Playbook

1 John 4:4 ***You, dear children, are from God and have overcome them, because the one who is in you is greater than the one who is in the world.***

What, then, does Satan, "the one who is in the world," do to us? How does he work to mess up God's plan and keep us from finding it out and aligning with God? Remember, the main thing Satan wants to do is keep you from believing in and obeying Christ. Short of that, he'll be satisfied with merely making you a mediocre Christian who is only halfway committed to Christ. If he can't keep you there, he'll try to derail you with a terrible spiritual blowout—gambling, an addiction, sex, drugs, drinking, or maybe something less dramatic but equally guilt-causing—and if he can't do that, he'll spread lies and rumors about you so the world hates you and fights you.

Satan uses four basic tactics to fell us: temptation, deception, accusation, and consumption.

TEMPTATION The first tactic is temptation. Satan's demons will tempt you with whatever is your most vulnerable weakness. If you are a sports fanatic, they'll tempt you with being even more obsessed. If you're lazy, they'll get you with even deeper laziness. They'll constantly try out new things on you too. They're always studying and observing you to learn your weaknesses and strengths and where an attack will be most successful. They'll go with the flow too, setting up impromptu situations to fell you. But their greatest strategy is to start small and get bigger.

How is Satan likely to tempt you? Say you're interested in a girl or a guy and that person starts "making moves" on you. First, it will be subtle, innocent things: holding hands, an arm around your shoulders. But gradually, your personal tempter will step up the heat and gradually—slowly and at your pace—they'll have you snared in big-time sin. It all starts small and easy and moves on to bigger things. You can see this strategy in nearly any "normal" pastime out there. You just have to know where to draw the line. You have to be sure you know what's right and wrong and that you won't cross over into wrong—no matter what!

Tricks of the Devil

for real

A few years ago, former sports hero Frank Gifford was the subject of a plot developed by a popular tabloid magazine. While Gifford was on a road trip away from his wife, the magazine hired a woman to pretend she was attracted to Gifford. She laid the compliments on strong. She flirted and teased and finally got Gifford, who'd never had a reputation for playing the sexual field, into bed with her. Gifford never imagined she was being paid to seduce him. The hotel room was equipped with hidden cameras, so the magazine got plenty of pictures. Their scheme worked, as their headlines proclaimed.

That's the same way Satan works things. He plots and schemes to get us. He goes all out to make us fall!

If the devil were to write his own **beatitudes**, they might go something like this (author unknown):

- Blessed are those Christians who are too tired, too busy, too distracted to spend time with their fellow Christians in church—they are my best candidates to backslide.
- Blessed are those Christians who wait to be asked and expect to be thanked—I can use them to slow things down.
- Blessed are those Christians who are touchy; with a bit of luck, they may stop going to church and get others to quit—they are my missionaries.
- Blessed are those Christians who are very religious but get on everyone's nerves—they are my most effective stumbling blocks.
- Blessed are those Christians who are troublemakers—they are my best wrecking crew.
- Blessed are those Christians who have no time to pray—they are easy prey for me.
- Blessed are those Christians who are complainers—they are my best discouragers.

check this out

beatitudes
Matthew 5:3–12

beatitudes
declarations made by Jesus in the Sermon on the Mount beginning "Blessed are . . ."

- Blessed are you when you read this and think it is about other people and not yourself—I've got you.

deception
John 8:44

Satan is out to get you. But praise be to God, he can't touch us unless he gets God's permission. And how often do you think God gives permission?

Liar, Liar—Whoa! His Pants Really Are on Fire!

> JOHN 8:44 ***You belong to your father, the devil, and you want to carry out your father's desire. He was a murderer from the beginning, not holding to the truth, for there is no truth in him. When he lies, he speaks his native language, for he is a liar and the father of lies.***

In this passage, Jesus tells us Satan is a liar. Satan tells you lies in your mind and in your heart. He is called the "father of lies" because he is the original liar. He invented lying.

DECEPTION Thus, a tactic of Satan and his demons is deception. The enemy will trick you about anything and everything, but usually he blends truth with error so that it doesn't seem like error. For instance, he won't tell you, "There's no God, so don't worry about it." No, he'll more likely say, "Sure, there's a God. But all he does is give rules. Who wants to keep rules all the time?" Or, "Yes, God's there. But why would he care about you?" Or, "Of course there's a God. But believe me, you don't want to get involved with him. He'll probably make you become a missionary!" Ever had those lies foisted on you? That's deception, one of Satan's best tactics.

A minister visited a Scottish sheepherder one day and found the man very troubled in spirit. The minister asked what was wrong. The sheepherder said, "I lost sixty-five of my best lambs last night. Wolves got in." The minister expressed sympathy, then said, "And how many sheep did they kill besides?" The shepherd shook his head. "None. Don't you know that a wolf will never take an old sheep so long as he can get a lamb?" The most vulnerable time of life for a Christian is either when he first believes, like a little lamb, or when he's been in the faith so long he's forgotten to cling to the master.

> **How Others See It**
>
> ### Michael W. Smith
>
> I think I just got deceived and believed in a lie that I was missing out on the good times. . . . All of a sudden I'm in the party scene . . . it's like you're trapped and can't even think.[21]

Play #357: Accuse

REVELATION 12:10 ***Then I heard a loud voice in heaven say: "Now have come the salvation and the power and the kingdom of our God, and the authority of his Christ. For the accuser of our brothers, who accuses them before our God day and night, has been hurled down."***

ACCUSATION The third tactic Satan uses is to accuse us of wrongdoing, mistakes, errors, and even things that are good, like being too aggressive in witnessing. According to John 8:44, as an accuser Satan tattles to God about the things we've done wrong and expects God to make us pay for our infractions.

He accuses us of sins galore. When we're tempted to commit a sin, he accuses us of being wimps, scaredy-cats, jerks, and all other kinds of nerdish names. Once we have sinned, he then turns around and accuses us of being too bad to go back to God. He tells us before we sin, "Go ahead, don't be afraid," and if we balk, he says, "You wimp. What're you scared of?" Once we've given in, he says, "God'll never forgive you for this one," and, "You're the worst Christian I've ever seen. You have no right to call yourself by that name." That's accusing. Satan loves it and he's a master at it.

> **How Others See It**
>
> ### A. C. Green
>
> Christians mainly fight spiritually against an unseen foe. . . . He's the reason we can't leave cracks in the foundation. He tries to make us hang on to some little thing to get the advantage later when he jumps on it and torments us with it. It might be lust, jealousy, pride, a bad temper, or something else. He uses anything as a foothold. He springs his attacks after something really great or in the midst of problems.[22]

This Guy Gives a New Meaning to the Word *Demolition*

> 1 Peter 5:8–9 ***Be self-controlled and alert. Your enemy the devil prowls around like a roaring lion looking for someone to devour. Resist him, standing firm in the faith, because you know that your brothers throughout the world are undergoing the same kind of sufferings.***

CONSUMPTION The fourth tactic of Satan is simply to eat us up! With guilt, worry, fear, or anything else he can use to keep us on the sidelines. Satan burns to destroy every Christian who ever lived. He cares nothing for people who don't believe, except to keep them unbelieving. But he wants to totally terminate every Christian. Even if we're not at war with the devil, it doesn't matter. He's at war with us!

How do we stop the devil in his tracks? How do we keep ourselves from falling from his ever-present attacks? Check out our guidance in James 4:7: "Submit yourselves, then, to God. Resist the devil, and he will flee from you."

Submit to God. Resist the devil. How? By obeying, quoting Scripture, praying, fleeing from the scene of temptation, falling at the feet of Christ and asking for his help, and spitting in Satan's eye and telling him to go away because you'll have nothing to do with this sin. Oh, he'll come back, but you'll be ready for him then too.

> **How Others See It**
>
> **Saint Cyril**
>
> The devil has power to suggest evil, but he was not given the power to compel you against your will.[23]

The Church Needs a Full-Body Workout

> Colossians 1:18–20 ***And he is the head of the body, the church; he is the beginning and the firstborn from among the dead, so that in everything he might have the supremacy. For God was pleased to have all his fullness dwell in him, and through him to reconcile to himself all things, whether things on earth or things in heaven, by making peace through his blood, shed on the cross.***

Paul writes in this passage that Christ is the "head of the body," which is the church. As the body of Christ, we are parts of Christ, members, joined to him mystically.

This brings us to another important area of theology, the church. We are the church, which is Christ's body. What does that mean? In some mystical sense, the church is the extended picture of Christ in the world. We are Christ's hands, feet, ears, and eyes. He works in the world through us. If you've ever wondered about the issue of significance—Am I significant? Do I count?—the metaphor of the body dispels that problem. You are significant because you are the picture of Christ to the world. When anyone looks at you, as you do good, speak kind words, and offer hope, they will see Christ in you. We are to be Christ to the world and love the people of God the way Jesus laid it out in the passage above. Collectively, we make up his whole being.

Generally, scholars divide the idea of "church" into two categories: the local church and the universal church. The **local church** is any small body meeting in houses or a building, composed of believers from a single community. The **universal church** is all believers from all time who will make up Christ's complete body in heaven. There is also a third form of the church: the apostate church. These are people who attend church but aren't Christians. The apostate church is composed of people who have internally rejected the reality of Christ and are only playing "church" for gain, notoriety, popularity, prestige, or other reasons.

Jesus told a parable to illustrate the apostate church. It's called the parable of the wheat and tares. In it, Jesus tells a story of a man who has a field where his wheat crop grows beautifully. But at night an enemy comes and plants tares among the wheat. What are tares? Tares are weeds that look just like wheat until the wheat ripens. Then the tares distinguish themselves by having no kernels of grain. Jesus warned his disciples not to try to "weed out" unbelievers from the church (the wheat). Only God knows who is real and who isn't, and we'll all have to wait till the end when God will separate the wheat from the tares at the judgment.

check this out

wheat and tares
Matthew 13:24–30

local church
any community of believers in the world

universal church
all believers from the time of Christ onward

How Others See It

Eli

You walk into a thrift store and all of a sudden life becomes very real, you never know what you're going to find . . . but the one thing [all thrift store items] have in common is that somewhere along the way, someone didn't want them anymore, they were thrown out and discarded. Now they're being given a second chance. And if that's not a parallel of the gospel and what the church should be, I don't know what is.[24]

everyday insights

A man said to the great nineteenth-century evangelist Dwight Moody, "I do not know why I cannot be just as good a Christian outside the church as within it." Moody said nothing but walked over to the fireplace, took a blazing coal from the fire in a pair of tongs, and set it aside. As the two men watched, the coal burned itself out. The man decided to go to church the next Sunday.

Ambassadors for Christ

EPHESIANS 1:22–23 ***And God placed all things under [Christ's] feet and appointed him to be head over everything for the church, which is his body, the fullness of him who fills everything in every way.***

The church is Christ's body. Through the church, Christ influences and affects the world. Without the church, Christ would have no one to represent him on earth.

So how should we "do" church? Scripture advises us to do several things. First, we should assemble and gather with other believers to build each other up. This gathering involves worship, singing, praying, preaching of the Word, giving, and serving. All Christians are supposed to get involved with the church in this way.

Second, we are to discover and use our spiritual gifts so that we can serve and help one another. No teen will ever find fulfillment as a Christian until he or she begins serving the Lord.

Third, we are to engage in real fellowship. What is fellowship? The Greek word for fellowship, *koinonia*, means to associate or bind together. Jesus spoke of the disciples engaging in fellowship to build a close union and camaraderie. He wanted them to love each other. A good way of looking at fellowship is to consider the "one another" principles found in Scripture. The term "one another" is found about sixty times in the New Testament. Paul uses it forty times.

The "one another" principles show us how to relate to one another in the church and what we should be doing to make real fellowship possible. Look at the following chart to get a feel for what fellowship involves.

check this out

gather
Hebrews 10:24–25

How Christians Should Treat One Another

Scripture	Concept	Purpose
Romans 12:5	Members of one another	To make us a body
Romans 12:10	Devoted to one another	To build unity

How Christians Should Treat One Another (cont'd)

Scripture	Concept	Purpose
Romans 12:10	Honor one another	To strengthen love
Romans 15:5	Be of the same mind	To find agreement
Romans 15:7	Accept one another	To not leave anyone out
Romans 15:14	Admonish one another	To deal with sin
Romans 16:16	Greet one another	To show love
Galatians 5:13	Serve one another	To help each other
Galatians 6:2	Bear one another's burdens	To lift up the hurting
Ephesians 4:2	Bear with one another	To not give up on anyone
Ephesians 5:21	Submit to one another	To learn to obey
1Thessalonians 5:11	Encourage one another	To cheer on

You can see from this chart that anyone who takes these things seriously and any church that begins doing these things will build a courageous, loving, and powerful body. They will become very effective tools in God's hands. And they will have a church whose members really love one another. That's the goal.

A young teen on crutches with a broken foot was trying to get on a subway. His hands were loaded with packages for the Christmas holidays. As the subway stopped, people rushed for the doors, knocking over the boy, sending his crutches flying and his packages every which way. As the platform emptied, a man stopped, helped the boy to his feet, then gathered his crutches and his packages, guiding him onto the train. As the man and boy stepped aboard, the young man looked gratefully into the man's eyes and said, "Sir, are you Jesus?"

To live above with the saints we love—that will be glory. To live below with the saints we know—now that's another story. Noah's ark is sometimes like the church: If it weren't for the storm outside, you couldn't stand the stench inside.

think about it

Why is the church so messed up? Because it's made up of sinners. We're all sinners saved by the grace of God. No one is perfect. Someone once said, "If you find a perfect church, don't join it. You'll ruin it!" The church is led by Jesus Christ, empowered by the Spirit, and loved by God the Father. But it's imperfect. Don't expect any church you attend to have all mature believers, equally committed to the mission of reaching the world and loving one another. It's impossible. There are going to be conflicts, problems, and sin in the church. But the great thing is that Jesus still intends to get us all into heaven, perfect and fully assured. If you love your brothers and sisters in Christ as Christ loves them, you will always be able to see beyond the faults to the saint within.

A Recipe for Church

> ACTS 2:42–47 ***They devoted themselves to the apostles' teaching and to the fellowship, to the breaking of bread and to prayer. Everyone was filled with awe, and many wonders and miraculous signs were done by the apostles. All the believers were together and had everything in common. Selling their possessions and goods, they gave to anyone as he had need. Every day they continued to meet together in the temple courts. They broke bread in their homes and ate together with glad and sincere hearts, praising God and enjoying the favor of all the people. And the Lord added to their number daily those who were being saved.***

There is no better example of what the early church looked like than that found in the above passage from Acts. The marks of a true church are:

1. Devotion to the Word of God.
2. Devotion to fellowship and the "one another" principles.
3. Sharing of bread and wine with one another (**Communion** and fellowship).
4. Devotion to prayer.
5. A sense of awe about what God is doing.
6. Helping people in need, even to the point of selling possessions.
7. Meeting together to talk, pray, and share meals.
8. People coming to Christ and becoming believers.

think about it

If you want to find a solid church, look for these eight marks. But perhaps the main mark you should look for in a church is whether you feel free, happy, and excited to invite your friends to it. The chief purpose of the church is to lead people out of darkness and into the light of Christ, and to help those who convert to grow and become more like Christ. Don't play church. Be in a real church in a real way with real heart and real courage. Then you will have a real church, not a play one.

Dunk, Pour, or Sprinkle?

> JOHN 3:1–5 ***Now there was a man of the Pharisees named Nicodemus, a***

member of the Jewish ruling council. He came to Jesus at night and said, "Rabbi, we know you are a teacher who has come from God. For no one could perform the miraculous signs you are doing if God were not with him." In reply Jesus declared, "I tell you the truth, no one can see the kingdom of God unless he is born again." "How can a man be born when he is old?" Nicodemus asked. "Surely he cannot enter a second time into his mother's womb to be born!" Jesus answered, "I tell you the truth, no one can enter the kingdom of God unless he is born of water and the Spirit."

check this out

sprinkling
I Peter 1:2
effusion
Acts 10:44

Here Jesus tells us that we must be born of "water and the Spirit." Some scholars interpret being born of water to be baptism. This is an important rite of the church. Jesus' disciples baptized believers in the Lord. God wants us to be born of water as much as of the Spirit.

One of the first issues new believers will face is baptism. What should they do about being baptized? What if they were baptized as infants, or even baptized at an earlier age when they didn't fully understand the Gospel?

These are difficult questions, and many churches have fought bitterly over the answers. *Baptism* comes from a Greek word that means to "dip" or "immerse." The reason many translators of the Bible coined the English word *baptism* is because they didn't want to deal with the "dip" issue. At the time of the earliest translations of the Bible into English (the King James Version was done in 1611), the church practiced infant baptism by sprinkling in most cases. Apparently, the translators didn't want to stir things up any more than necessary. So they settled on taking the Greek term *baptizo* and making it into an English word.

There are several different ways that churches baptize people today. Each represents a different theological interpretation of its meaning. Study the following chart to see what the differences are:

Different Methods of Baptism

Kind	Scriptural Idea	Meaning
Sprinkling (minister sprinkles water on person's head)	Set apart for God's blessing	For babies, God protects and loves the child until they make an act of faith when they first understand the Gospel; for adult believers, this represents cleansing from sin through faith.
Effusion (minister pours cup of water onto person's head)	Giving of Spirit	Represents receiving the Spirit into your heart.

Different Methods of Baptism (cont'd)

Kind	Scriptural Idea	Meaning
Immersion (minister immerses person in pool of water)	Death and resurrection	Going under water represents death, coming out of water represents new life spiritually.

To baptize someone meant more than simply to dip him or her. One Greek poet and physician who lived about 200 BC named Nicander once supplied some insight into this through a recipe for making a pickle. He said first that the cucumber had to be dipped (*bapto*) into boiling water and cooked. After that, it was immersed (*baptizo*) in vinegar. What was the difference? The boiling water merely cooked the pickle. But the vinegar changed its nature. And that's the essence of baptism, a good reason it couldn't be simply translated by the word *immerse*. When you are baptized, it represents a fundamental internal change within you. That change is conversion.

If you are a believer in Christ, you should be baptized by whatever means you decide is right. You should study Scripture to make that determination. Being baptized does not make you a believer. Accepting Christ into your life and trusting him for your salvation is what makes you a believer. But baptism is like an engagement ring. It symbolizes something God has done in your relationship with him. When a young man loves a woman and wants to marry her, he gives her an engagement ring. That ring doesn't make her married; it's only the promise that they will be married soon. In baptism, you are showing the world that you are now engaged to Christ, and when you go to heaven, you, along with the rest of the church, will be Christ's bride.

Bread and Wine

1 Corinthians 11:23–25 *For I received from the Lord what I also passed on to you: The Lord Jesus, on the night he was betrayed, took bread, and when he had given thanks, he broke it and said, "This is my body, which is for you; do this in remembrance of me." In the same way, after supper he took the cup, saying, "This cup is the new covenant in my blood; do this, whenever you drink it, in remembrance of me."*

The other well-established **rite** of the church is the Lord's Supper, which Paul describes to the Corinthian church above. The last night of Jesus' life on earth before his crucifixion, he took his disciples into the upper room

immersion
Romans 6:4

rite
ritual

of a house and celebrated the **Passover** meal with them. This became the basis of the Lord's Supper, also called Communion or the Eucharist.

check this out

Lord's Supper
Matthew 26:26–29; Mark 14:22–25; Luke 22:17–20

The Lord's Supper has also gone through much controversy over the years. In the Roman Catholic Church, people are taught that the bread and wine used in the Lord's Supper actually become the body and blood of Christ in some mystical way. This is called the doctrine of **transubstantiation** and means that the bread and wine are transformed during the Mass. Most Protestant churches do not follow this teaching, but believe that the Lord's Supper is a "remembrance," a kind of object lesson to remember the death of Christ on the cross and what he did for each of us.

Passover
Jewish holiday

transubstantiation
the belief that the bread and wine actually become the body and blood of Christ

The Important Stuff

> 1 Corinthians 11:27–32 ***Therefore, whoever eats the bread or drinks the cup of the Lord in an unworthy manner will be guilty of sinning against the body and blood of the Lord. A man ought to examine himself before he eats of the bread and drinks of the cup. For anyone who eats and drinks without recognizing the body of the Lord eats and drinks judgment on himself. That is why many among you are weak and sick, and a number of you have fallen asleep. But if we judged ourselves, we would not come under judgment. When we are judged by the Lord, we are being disciplined so that we will not be condemned with the world.***

What matters here is that you partake of the Lord's Supper on a regular basis, at least several times a year. What are you to do when you take the Lord's Supper? *First, confess all known sin before you partake.* Eating the bread and wine or grape juice with known sin hanging over your soul is dangerous and can lead to many bad things including personal judgment by God. God is not pleased when we take the Lord's Supper with sin in our lives.

words to live by

Second, we should remember Christ's death for us and show gratitude. Many churches, when they celebrate the Lord's Supper, also have a time of praise and thanksgiving unto God. This is a way to remember his work in our lives and to thank him for all his blessings.

Third, we are not to let unbelievers participate, for this brings them under the judgment of God, as Paul explains to the Corinthian church above. We are not even to encourage unbelievers to take the Lord's Supper out of respect for the church or the minister or anyone else. God judges those who do it with uncleansed hearts.

Grape Juice or Wine?

Do you wonder why some people drink grape juice at Communion instead of wine? Here's the story.

In the 1860s, a man named Dr. Thomas Welch, a dentist, was Communion steward for the First Methodist Church in Vineland, New Jersey. One weekend, a friend of the family visited the Welches. He had a problem with alcohol, but was trying to quit. When he took Communion at the church that Sunday, he went on a drinking binge. Dr. Welch decided something had to be done. He didn't drink wine except at Communion and wondered why it was necessary. In 1869, he and his wife and son picked about forty pounds of ripe grapes, squeezed out the juice, pasteurized it, and bottled it. Then they waited to see if the juice fermented and exploded the bottles. Nothing happened, so finally he went to his pastor with the unfermented grape juice and offered it as a substitute. He soon began selling it to other churches, and in 1890 created a brand name called "Dr. Welch's Grape Juice." The rest is history.

The Future of Planet Earth

MATTHEW 24:36 ***No one knows about that day or hour, not even the angels in heaven, nor the Son, but only the Father.***

Everyone wants to know what's in the future. Actually, God has revealed to us a number of things that are definitely in the future. Heaven. Hell. Judgment. Eternity. Eternal life for the saints. Eternal death for the unbelieving wicked. Rewards for the believing. Bliss. Joy. No more tears.

The future holds great promise for believers from all the ages. It holds unimaginable horror for those who reject God and want to go their own way. How do we know what the future holds? By a little warning system that God calls **prophecy**. All through history God has sent people to tell the common folks and kings what will happen. He did this for several reasons:

1. Because he wanted to warn people of danger when they sinned.
2. Because he wanted to give his people hope when they were in tough circumstances.
3. Because he wanted to confirm the validity of the person giving the message (so other messages would also be believed).

prophecy
a prediction of something to come

4. Because he wants all people to know that he is God and knows the end from the beginning.

Tribulation
seven-year period at end time

Rapture
catching up of church in air

Antichrist
Satan's version of Christ

Examples of prophecies include specific statements about subjects ranging from Jesus (his life, death, and resurrection) to certain cities and countries in the Middle East to the time of the end shortly before Christ returns. All these kinds of prophecies fit into one of the four purposes above.

Kinds of Prophecies

Scripture	Subject	Meaning
Isaiah 7:14	Virgin Birth	That Jesus would be born of a virgin
Psalm 22:11–18	Crucifixion	That Jesus would die on a cross
Micah 5:2	Birthplace	Jesus born in Bethlehem
Joel 2:28–32	**Tribulation**	A time of trouble at the end of time
Isaiah 40:3	John the Baptist	The prophet who led the way for Jesus
Isaiah 35:1–10	Kingdom	Jesus' thousand-year kingdom
Matthew 24:1–31	End times	Earthquakes, etc., before coming of Christ
1 Thessalonians 4:13–18	**Rapture**	All believers taken off Earth
2 Thessalonians 2:1–9	**Antichrist**	Satan's puppet at end of time
Revelation	Wrap-up of Earth	Everything that will happen at end of time

As you can see from the chart above, prophecy covers a whole spectrum of issues and subjects. God wanted us to know all that would happen ahead of time, so when it happened, we would know he had done it. There are many disagreements about prophetic issues, especially about the immediate future. Some scholars have gone so far as to try to predict precisely when Jesus would return. This is impossible, though. God has made clear that not even Jesus, when he was with his disciples, knew when that date was.

What is in the future for the earth? There are several major considerations. One is the immediate end of the earth. That involves something called the Tribulation. This is God's special time of trouble in the book of Revelation. Of this time there is much argument, but the major question is: Will you and I go through the Tribulation? There are several theories about this, and it all concerns when the Rapture, or "catching up," of the church will occur. Look at the following chart.

Different Beliefs About the Rapture of the Church

Kind of Rapture	Meaning
Pretribulation	The Rapture happens before the Tribulation begins; the church does not go through the Tribulation.
Posttribulation	The Rapture happens at the end of the Tribulation; the church goes through the Tribulation.
Midtribulation	The Rapture happens in the middle of the Tribulation; the church escapes the horrible part of the Tribulation.
Partial Rapture	Only committed believers are raptured.

There are good and committed people behind each of these definitions. Which one you believe will depend on how much research you're willing to do and which one will seem most logical in your theological perspective. In reality, though, there is not much to worry about. God promises to protect and save his people no matter when the Rapture happens. God wants each of us to be committed to the truth we've learned and studied. You can't be committed to something you know little about.

What Is That Thousand Years About?

> REVELATION 20:1–3 ***And I saw an angel coming down out of heaven, having the key to the Abyss and holding in his hand a great chain. He seized the dragon, that ancient serpent, who is the devil, or Satan, and bound him for a thousand years. He threw him into the Abyss, and locked and sealed it over him, to keep him from deceiving the nations anymore until the thousand years were ended. After that, he must be set free for a short time.***

Here we find the statement that an angel chained Satan in the bottomless pit for a thousand years and the church reigned with Christ for a thousand years. Many people over the years have interpreted this various ways. It seems clear, though, that some period of a thousand years will happen at the end of time.

This brings us to the second major issue of prophecy, something called the "millennium," a thousand-year kingdom in which Christ reigns in the lives of people. You might ask, What does this have to do with me now? Plenty. It's a matter of where you will spend your eternity. Christ plans to return and reign no matter what scenario you choose, so you have to ask where you stand with him. If he's not in the picture, maybe you're out of focus.

Different Beliefs About the Millennium

Millennial View	Belief
Amillennialism	There is no Millennium, or it's happening now.
Postmillennialism	The Millennium happens after the church gains complete control of the world, and a great age of prosperity occurs without Christ's actually being on earth.
Premillennialism	Christ will reign for a thousand years on earth. It begins after Christ's **second coming**.

check this out

heaven
2 Corinthians 12:2–4; Revelation 21–22; Isaiah 11:1–10

second coming
when Christ returns to earth to reign

Our Welcome-Home Party

REVELATION 21:1–4 *Then I saw a new heaven and a new earth, for the first heaven and the first earth had passed away, and there was no longer any sea. I saw the Holy City, the new Jerusalem, coming down out of heaven from God, prepared as a bride beautifully dressed for her husband. And I heard a loud voice from the throne saying, "Now the dwelling of God is with men, and he will live with them. They will be his people, and God himself will be with them and be their God. He will wipe every tear from their eyes. There will be no more death or mourning or crying or pain, for the old order of things has passed away."*

Let's look at this brief quote from Revelation. Here's a short list of the things that will be true of heaven:

- Completely new
- No sea
- New Jerusalem
- God among us
- No more tears
- No more death or mourning
- No more crying or pain

Sound pretty good? And that's only the beginning. Consider what God did in the first Creation with climates, countries, creatures, and people. Do you think he couldn't do better after he's had all this time to think about it? He can and he will.

Heaven will be all you could ever dream of and more. But don't just listen to me. Study your Bible and see for yourself!

check this out

hell
Matthew 5:27–32;
Luke 16:23;
Revelation 20:11–15

How Others See It

John Newton

When I get to heaven, I shall see three wonders there: The first wonder will be to see many whom I did not expect to see; the second wonder will be to miss many people whom I did expect to see; the third and greatest of all will be to find myself there.[25]

Hell

> MATTHEW 13:37–43 *He answered, "The one who sowed the good seed is the Son of Man. The field is the world, and the good seed stands for the sons of the kingdom. The weeds are the sons of the evil one, and the enemy who sows them is the devil. The harvest is the end of the age, and the harvesters are angels. As the weeds are pulled up and burned in the fire, so it will be at the end of the age. The Son of Man will send out his angels, and they will weed out of his kingdom everything that causes sin and all who do evil. They will throw them into the fiery furnace, where there will be weeping and gnashing of teeth. Then the righteous will shine like the sun in the kingdom of their Father. He who has ears, let him hear."*

Here Jesus says that hell will be a place of weeping and gnashing of teeth. Clearly, it's a place where pain is placed at a maximum. It's a place of punishment, where God puts all evil people because of their unwillingness to obey or believe in him.

The reality of hell has long been a matter of debate among all religions. Is there a place where bad people are punished? In Hinduism and Buddhism, reincarnation is the answer. You keep returning to life in different forms, living out the law of karma (which says that you are punished in your next life for the wrong you did in this one; or you are rewarded in your next life for the good you did in the previous one). Eventually, you reach nirvana and return to the peace and bliss of nonexistence. Not very much fun!

Other religions have their own ideas, but Christianity and the Bible state clearly that there is a hell. "Gehenna" was the name given to it in the New Testament, and it referred to the town dump. In that dump, fires raged all day and night burning up the waste. Ugly, disgusting worms bred in the filth and fed on the waste. That's why Jesus said of Gehenna that it's a place where "their worm does not die, and the fire is not quenched" (Mark 9:48).

Hell will be a place of unspeakable horror. Darkness. Separation. Isolation. Absolute loneliness. Burning, perhaps because of the sensation of deprivation. No food. No sustenance. No pleasure. No diversions. Nothing to do. No one to talk to. You, yourself, alone forever. God forbid that it should happen to any of us.

> **How Others See It**
>
> **C. S. Lewis**
>
> We must picture hell as a state where everyone is perpetually concerned about his own dignity and advancement, where everyone has a grievance, and where everyone lives the deadly serious passions of envy, self-importance, and resentment.[26]

Billy Graham explains: "Hell was not prepared for man. God never meant that man would ever go to hell. Hell was prepared for the devil and his angels, but man rebelled against God and followed the devil. . . . Hell is essentially and basically banishment from the presence of God for deliberately rejecting Jesus Christ as Lord and Savior."[27]

Sometimes people ask how a good God could send people to hell, but Jesus never asked that question. He declared the reality of hell in bold red letters. He never flinched from telling people the dire circumstances in which they lived. One of his parables makes the point in Luke 16:19–31.

There he tells about a rich man and a poor man. Lazarus, the poor man, used to lie at the rich man's doorstep hoping for some crumbs to eat. Both died the same day. The rich man found himself in hell. He looked over a wide chasm and saw Lazarus being held by Abraham. He begged that Lazarus might reach over and place a droplet of water on his tongue. He was told Lazarus couldn't do that because a wide chasm separated them and was uncrossable. The rich man cried out, "Then I beg you, father, send Lazarus to my father's house, for I have five brothers. Let him warn them, so that they will not also come to this place of torment." Abraham replied, "They have Moses and the Prophets; let them listen to them." The rich man answered, "No . . . but if someone from the dead goes to them, they will repent." This is Abraham's stark and searing reply: "If they do not listen to Moses and the Prophets, they will not be convinced even if someone rises from the dead." That story is an exact illustration of what

think about it

happened with Jesus. He has risen from the dead, but many people still don't believe. It's a warning. Have you heeded it?

Are You Winded?

for real

Whew! Feeling out of breath? We covered a lot of territory in this chapter! But the good news is that we'll not be testing you on any of it.

Actually, in this chapter we've covered truths about the Christian faith that many older people don't even know. That's one of the neat things about being a Christian and reading the Bible: You can study the Bible and Christianity your whole life, and you'll learn more and more about God.

I (Jeanette) came to know Christ when I was twelve years old. That was, um, a few years ago. But I'm still learning about God. I'm still appreciating him more and more. And I still learn a lot each time I read the Bible, even though I've read all of it several times, and some parts dozens of times (a few verses might even rate hundreds of times!). We'll never know all there is to know about God and living for him until we get to heaven. In a way, that makes Christianity really fun. It's like a daily adventure. I've also learned to some degree that my relationship with God, like many things in life, is just what I make it. Christ made the initial step by dying for me and inviting me into his family. The way I make my relationship with God grow is the same way I make my relationship with my friends grow—by spending time together. As I make time in my schedule to talk to God through prayer and study his Word, I grow closer to him. And he ends up being a great friend!

Enjoy your journey into the Christian faith and take the effort to make the most of it!

Final Thoughts

- Theology is the study of God. Ultimately, God is the most fascinating, interesting, and compelling personality we can ever learn about.
- The Trinity is the way we refer to the Godhead, or the fact that God exists as three persons: Father, Son, and Holy Spirit.
- God the Father possesses many attributes that make him worthy of our worship, our love, and our obedience. Some of these attributes are love, grace, holiness, goodness, all-powerfulness, all-knowing, and many others.
- God the Son is the second person of the Trinity who came to earth as a man and walked among us. His mission was to communicate God to all people, show what God is like, and also to die for the sins of mankind. Ultimately, he would rise again from the dead, showing that God has power over death.
- God the Holy Spirit comes to dwell in us and to guide us into the life pattern that God has for us. As we listen to his guidance and leadership, we will grow in the knowledge of Jesus and the grace that makes us like him.
- Salvation is the most important event of our life. Without it, we will perish.
- The church functions as the place where we can have true fellowship.
- Baptism and the Lord's Supper are the two all-important "ordinances" of the church.
- The prophecies about the end times, heaven, and hell are important because we all want to know what's ahead in the future and where we're all going.

Questions to Deepen Your Understanding

1. What would you say is the most important teaching about God the Father?
2. What about Jesus is important for everyone to know?
3. What does the Holy Spirit do in our lives today?
4. Why is being involved in a church so important for the Christian life?

5. Have you been baptized? Why or why not?

6. As you look forward to the future of God's world, what most intrigues you?

read on

Some of Mark and Jeanette's favorite books about looking at basic truths of the Bible:

- *Basic Christianity,* John Stott, Eerdmans
- *Basic Theology: A Popular Systematic Guide to Understanding Biblical Truth,* Charles Ryrie, Moody
- *Christianity 101:Your Guide to Eight Basic Christian Beliefs,* Gilbert Bilezikian, Zondervan
- *Daily Grace for Teens: Devotional Reflections to Nourish Your Soul,* John C. Maxwell, Cook
- *For All God's Worth,* N. T. Wright, Eerdmans
- *30 Days to Understanding What Christians Believe in 15 Minutes a Day!* Max E. Anders, Thomas Nelson

Chapter 7: Everyday Christianity

Walking With Christ in Daily Experiences

What's in This Chapter

- Peace on Earth
- Show You Care With Prayer
- Faith: The Invisible Power
- When Common Sense Tells You Not To
- Relating to People: The Hard Stuff
- Sharing Your Faith
- Living a Life of Love

Here We Go

The Christian life is all about relationships. In Part Two, we examined the lives of teens of the Bible and saw how their relationships affected their lives. Sometimes the teens' interactions led to peace and faith, and other times they led to conflict and tragedy. From where we sit, it's easy to point out where the Bible's teens went wrong, but what about our own relationships? When we're in the driver's seat, sometimes we can't see too far down the road. How can we cultivate "healthy" relationships in an unhealthy world? In this chapter, we'll dive into the Bible and find out what it takes to live in harmony with God and others.

Peace on Earth

> ACTS 2:42–47 ***They devoted themselves to the apostles' teaching and to the fellowship, to the breaking of bread and to prayer. Everyone was filled with awe, and many wonders and miraculous signs were done by the apostles. All the believers were together and had everything in common. Selling their possessions and goods, they gave to anyone as he had need. Every day they continued to meet together in the temple courts. They broke bread in their homes and ate together with glad and sincere hearts, praising God and enjoying the favor of all the people. And the Lord added to their number daily those who were being saved.***

These verses from Acts paint the picture of a happy Christian community. Where did the peace and harmony come from? Relationships. A good relationship with God and with others produces teaching, fellowship, the breaking of bread (or Communion), prayer, and evangelism—basic elements of Christian living (see Illustration #9). In this chapter, we will look

check this out

be still
Psalm 46:10

speak
Jeremiah 33:3

at life practices that will enhance and strengthen our connections with others.

> **How Others See It**
>
> **Peter Furler**
>
> God cares about our loneliness, not just our fallenness. People are always looking to belong somewhere. Take the homosexual community. They are a family. Be it unholy. Be it what it is. They are there for each other. They are very united. Sometimes the church isn't that way.[1]

Building Your Relationship With God

JOHN 4:24 ***God is spirit, and his worshipers must worship in spirit and in truth.***

God seeks worshipers, people who will seek to know him and enjoy him. God looks throughout the world to find anyone who wants to walk with him. He wants them to worship him from the heart.

In many ways, our relationship with God is like our other relationships. If we want to be close to him, we have to devote time and energy to the task. We have to talk to him, learn about him, and share with him who we are. Close relationships require time and vulnerability. What tools do we have to cultivate a close relationship with our Father?

A quiet time is a time to be still before God and to hear him speak to your heart. Sometimes he speaks to us through his Word, at other times through prayer, and often he simply puts impressions in our hearts. When we are safely enclosed in a quiet moment, heart and mind serene before God, hearing his voice becomes easier.

Unfortunately, spending quiet time with God is often one of the most difficult habits for a Christian to develop. How can you have an effective quiet time? You may want to include several elements. There are basically three parts to a worthwhile quiet time:

- Getting quiet enough to hear God
- Reading and thinking about God's Word
- Praying about personal needs and the needs of others

Illustration #9
The Relationship Ring—Here is a handy illustration outlining the basic ways we relate to God and others. Note that God's Word and prayer are vertical elements—through them we listen to and communicate with God. Fellowship and evangelism are horizontal—through them we relate to the world.

These three elements can easily take up fifteen minutes, and before you know it, you'll want the quiet time to be longer.

When you first begin spending time with God, it's wise not to go overboard and plan to wake up at 4:30 a.m. and pray for two hours. Most of us, no matter how committed to Christ and enthusiastic about knowing him better, would fall right back to sleep. It's better to bite off a reasonable chunk of time and make it count. Otherwise, you'll end up feeling guilty and burned out. Fifteen minutes is a good starting place.

How Others See It

Rebecca St. James

Live radically for God. Read the Bible. Pray. Stand up for what you believe in and make a difference in your world.[2]

Book It!

2 Timothy 2:15 ***Do your best to present yourself to God as one approved, a workman who does not need to be ashamed and who correctly handles the word of truth.***

God desires that we study his Word, understanding his true meaning and intent. He wants us to "accurately handle" the Word of God. That is, to interpret it according to the original intent and idea that the writer had when he wrote it.

Start off with a few minutes of quiet. Let your mind and heart become still—replace your worries with a peaceful attitude. Then begin reading. It's good to start with easy texts. Try John, Luke, Ephesians, Philippians, James, or 1 Peter. As you read, ask yourself what God might be saying to you through the text. Is he pointing out a sin? Offering a promise? Presenting a challenge?

heart to heart

When you feel God has spoken, meditate on what he has said. Ask yourself how you can apply his message to your life. Studying the Bible, either in our personal quiet times or with other believers, enables us to understand who God is and who he wants us to be. What does it mean to study God's Word? When we listen to a sermon on Sunday, are we studying?

> **How Others See It**
>
> **Ruth Graham**
>
> Each morning when I went down to breakfast, my father—a busy missionary surgeon—would be sitting, reading his Bible. At night, her work behind her, my mother would be doing the same. Anything that could so capture the interest and devotion of those I admired and loved the most, I reasoned, must be worth investigating. So at an early age I began reading my Bible and found it to be, in the words of the old Scotsman, "Sweet pasturage."[3]

Give Me a Hand

What makes your hand work efficiently is that all five fingers work together. If you've ever broken a finger, you know that the use of one finger can sometimes be the difference between whether or not you're able to do simple things like brushing your teeth. When all five fingers work together, however, we can accomplish a lot. Just as your hand needs all five fingers to work effectively, there are five basic elements of Bible study. They aren't much good on their own, but used together they can help you understand Scripture and apply it to your life (see Illustration #10).

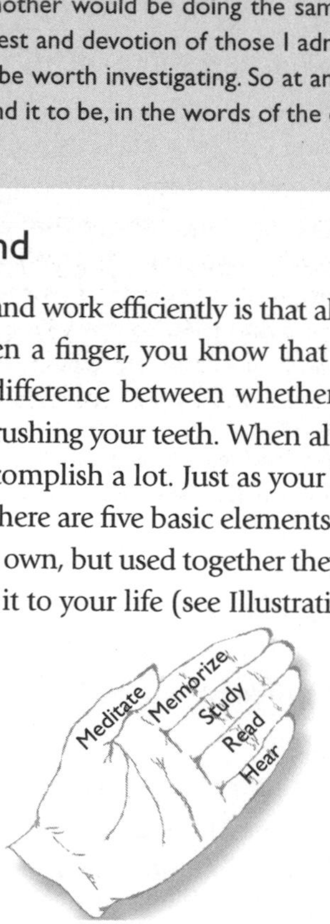

Illustration #10
The Hand Picture—Use this diagram and outline of the fingers to help you remember the five elements of Bible study.

Hear. Imagine trying to hold on to the Bible with your pinky finger. How easy would it be to lose your grip? We forget 98 percent of what we hear within seventy-two hours. When we only hear Scripture, our understanding and memory of the message are no stronger than our pinky finger.

check this out

purifying
Psalm 119:9

Read. If we hear and read the Bible, it's likely to stick a lot better, just as we can hold a Bible much more tightly with the ring and pinky fingers. But hearing and reading alone are still not enough to establish real comprehension.

meditate
to think about, study, concentrate on

Study. When we study the Bible, we usually ask the following questions: what, where, when, who, why, and how. When you ask and answer these questions, you're starting to really study the Bible.

Memorize. When you memorize Scripture, it becomes a part of you. It is stored in your brain and in your heart and has a purifying effect. Now, with four fingers grasping God's Word, you aren't likely to lose hold.

Meditate. When you meditate on Scripture, you ask God to speak directly to your heart through his Word. The Bible says that meditation on Scripture gives us wisdom.

How Others See It

Howard Hendricks

God wants to communicate with you in the twentieth century. He wrote his message in a Book. He asks you to come and study that Book for three compelling reasons: It's essential to growth; it's essential to maturity; it's essential for equipping you, training you, so that you might be an available, clean, sharp instrument in his hands to accomplish his purposes. So the question facing you now is: How can you afford to stay out of it?[4]

Get the Word of God into your heart, or Satan will fill your heart with his own words.

God Wants to Hear Us Talk!

PHILIPPIANS 4:6–7 *Do not be anxious about anything, but in everything, by prayer and petition, with thanksgiving, present your requests to God. And the peace of God, which transcends all understanding, will guard your hearts and your minds in Christ Jesus.*

check this out

morning
Mark 1:35

interceding
praying for others

heart to heart

Prayer is simply talking to God. We can tell him everything that's going on in our lives and everything in our hearts—good and bad. And best of all, he wants to listen!

As we talk to God about the stuff going on in our lives, we'll find that we have his peace filling our lives, reassuring us that God listens and cares. We don't ever need to be lonely when God is waiting to talk to us through his Word and listen to us through prayer! Some people like to make prayer lists to remember their needs and the needs of others. You might want to make a "top ten list" of people in your life who don't know Christ. As you pray through the list, ask God for opportunities to bear witness to those people. When you finish praying, think again about the application for today. What has God said to you?

It's that simple. As you grow, you can pray for longer periods of time. You might want to keep a journal and write down your thoughts and prayers. Remember: A quiet time is a meeting with God. In the morning, before bed, or whenever, it will build and strengthen your relationship with him.

The neatest thing about prayer is that you can talk to God anytime, anywhere!

How Others See It

Rebecca St. James

Prayer is such an important thing to me. It's something I just can't go without.[5]

Show You Care With Prayer

COLOSSIANS 1:9–12 *For this reason, since the day we heard about you, we have not stopped praying for you and asking God to fill you with the knowledge of his will through all spiritual wisdom and understanding. And we pray this in order that you may live a life worthy of the Lord and may please him in every way: bearing fruit in every good work, growing in the knowledge of God, being strengthened with all power according to his glorious might so that you may have great endurance and patience, and joyfully giving thanks to the Father, who has qualified you to share in the inheritance of the saints in the kingdom of light.*

Few people find it easy to pray. It's work. Truly **interceding** for people in need takes heart and passion, and that doesn't come automatically. The most common problem you'll probably encounter when you pray is staying focused. It's easy to let our minds wander when we try to pray. In fact, one of Satan's primary tactics when we try to pray is to get us off track, confusing us with stray thoughts, worries, fears, and a multitude of other problems. However, this can be easily combated with a little concentration and effort to focus on a list or a series of thoughts that you can follow and keep as your guide in a prayer time.

Years ago someone developed an acronym that has helped many people focus during prayer. Maybe this acronym will help you pray effectively. The acronym spells out the word *ACTS*. Each letter has a defining word. It goes like this:

A *Adoration*. Spend time praising and adoring God. Let him know what you appreciate about him. Think about all the reasons you love him. You can do this by praising him, by worshiping him, and by telling him something you really like about him today, something that might have happened that made you realize how great he really is. It isn't that God wants to be "buttered up." It's just that when we show appreciation for his work in our lives, we show him we're not only noticing that he's doing something for us, but also that we are enjoying seeing him work.

C *Confession*. Confess your sins to God. Think about your life over the last few days. What sins have tripped you? When you've evaluated and labeled your sins, admit them to God, **repent**, and ask for his forgiveness. If you need to look at a list of possible things you may have done wrong, consult such passages as 2 Timothy 3:1–7; 1 Corinthians 6:9–10; and Galatians 5:19–21. These passages might remind you of some things you have overlooked or brushed under the table.

T *Thanksgiving*. Thank God for the things that have blessed you today. It doesn't matter how big or small the blessings are, God loves to receive your thanks. You can even express gratitude for issues in your life that seem confusing, knowing that somewhere down the road God will work everything for your benefit.

S *Supplication*. This means making requests for yourself and others. Tell God what you really want and need in your life. Invite him to jump into your life, and believe he'll answer your requests. Be specific so that you know when he has answered. Don't just say, "Bless my family." But zero in on what is really needed: "Help Mary with that test. And lead John as he plays soccer today. Help my dad with that report at work." Like that.

check this out

adoration
Psalms 47; 103:1–4

confession
James 5:16;
Proverbs 28:13;
1 John 1:9

thanksgiving
Psalm 100:4–5;
1 Thessalonians 5:18

benefit
Romans 8:28

supplication
Philippians 4:6–7

repent
to change your mind and heart

transcendental meditation
a practice of meditation based on Indian religions

Real prayer is the most important thing we can do for ourselves and for others. Through prayer we get God involved in our lives and we ask him to work in the lives of others. What can be more gratifying than to learn of something good that happened to a friend because you prayed for him or her?

Never Give Up

> **Luke 18:1** ***Then Jesus told his disciples a parable to show them that they should always pray and not give up.***

At the beginning of Luke 18, Jesus tells his disciples a story to help them with their lack of faith. The parable Jesus told was about a cruel judge who refused to give an old woman justice. The woman kept coming back, demanding that the judge do something about her problem. Finally, he said, "I will see that she gets justice, so that she won't eventually wear me out with her coming!" He granted her request.

Jesus told his disciples, "Listen to what the unjust judge says. And will not God bring about justice for his chosen ones, who cry out to him day and night? Will he keep putting them off? I tell you, he will see that they get justice, and quickly" (Luke 18:6–8). Remember: Prayer is a conversation with God. You talk and God listens. Then you listen while God talks. When you pray, God will act.

How Others See It

James I. Packer

Praying to God is a problem for many today. Some go through the motions with no idea why; some have exchanged prayer for quiet thought or **transcendental meditation**; most, perhaps, have given prayer up entirely. Why the problem? The answer is clear. People feel a problem about prayer because of the muddle they are in about God. If you are uncertain whether God exists, or whether he is personal, or good, or in control of things, or concerned about ordinary folk like you and me, you are bound to conclude that praying is pretty pointless, not to say trivial, and then you won't do it.

But if you believe, as Christians do, that Jesus is the image of God—in other words, that Jesus is God-like in character—then you will have no such doubts, and you will recognize that for us to speak to the Father and the Son in prayer is as natural as it was for Jesus to talk to his Father in heaven, or for the disciples to talk to their Master during the days of his earthly ministry.[6]

Faith: The Invisible Power

> HEBREWS 11:1–3 *Now faith is being sure of what we hope for and certain of what we do not see. This is what the ancients were commended for. By faith we understand that the universe was formed at God's command, so that what is seen was not made out of what was visible.*

gives
Titus 3:5–7

Faith is an important ingredient of Christian living. But what is faith? This passage tells us it is "being sure of what we hope for and certain of what we do not see," but what does that mean?

faith
believing in and acting on the truth

saved
given the gift of salvation

grace
God's forgiveness given freely

What are we sure of? We're sure of our hopes and dreams. What, then, do we hope for? How about eternal life, a place in heaven, and a chance to see God? When we hope for these things, and we're convinced in our hearts that they exist and will come to pass, we have faith.

Faith is also being certain of "what we do not see." What don't we see here on earth? Again, the answer points us to heaven—God, Jesus, angels, demons. We can't see these things in the same way that we see Washington, D.C., or the president on the news, or our best friend's face. Only earthly things are visible. We can believe they exist because we can see and touch them. But what about things like love? How do we know love is real? After all, you can't physically touch an emotion. But we have faith that love exists. Think of faith as a sixth sense. With your eyes you see. With your ears you hear. With your tongue you taste. With faith, you perceive the things of God.

How do we get faith? It's a gift that God gives us. It's something God puts inside us to discover the moment we come to believe in him. Look at this verse: "For it is by grace you have been **saved**, through faith—and this not from yourselves, it is the gift of God—not by works, so that no one can boast" (Ephesians 2:8–9). Notice the process here. By **grace** you have been given salvation. What is grace? It's God's favor, love, and goodness given to us freely, without charge. All this comes "through faith." That is, the way you get saved is through faith. But where does faith come from? It's the "gift of God." It doesn't come by "works" or effort on our part. It's something God <u>gives</u> us.

When Common Sense Tells You Not To

I (Jeanette) love movies. Not just the new stuff, though. Sometimes I'm a real sucker for the tried-and-true faves. The old version of

transforming
Romans 12:2

faith
Luke 17:5–6;
Matthew 17:19–20

Miracle on 34th Street *with Natalie Wood and Maureen O'Hara is a traditional must-see in my life. My favorite line is, "Faith means believing when common sense tells you not to."*

In a sense, our whole Christian life is one long journey of believing when common sense tells us not to.

Common sense tells me God's gotta be mad at me when I sin and has a hard time forgiving me. Faith tells me that when I come to God truly sorry for stupid things I do and ask God to forgive me, it's not an issue anymore.

Common sense tells me God can't use me, I'm too much of a failure. Faith tells me that yes, God wants to use even me.

Common sense tells me that God doesn't care enough for me to make miracles happen. Faith tells me to keep trusting and praying.

Remember, whether you're a Miracle on 34th Street *fan or not: Faith means believing when common sense tells you not to!*

The Transforming Power of Faith

> **HEBREWS 11:6** ***And without faith it is impossible to please God, because anyone who comes to him must believe that he exists and that he rewards those who earnestly seek him.***

When we have real faith, we grow and learn. When we have faith in Christ, we should become more like him every day. He will work in our lives, transforming us by the power of the Holy Spirit.

The question is, do you have faith? Maybe you're saying, "Yes, I have some faith, but I need more." You can strengthen your faith by exercising what you have. Trust God about an issue or problem you believe he can really help with. As you see him work, you will develop your faith and begin to trust him about bigger things. That's how faith grows.

How Others See It

C. S. Lewis

I believe in Christianity as I believe that the sun has risen; not only because I can see it, but because by it I see everything else.[7]

Company for the Road

1 JOHN 1:6–7 *If we claim to have fellowship with him yet walk in the darkness, we lie and do not live by the truth. But if we walk in the light, as he is in the light, we have fellowship with one another, and the blood of Jesus, his Son, purifies us from all sin.*

Over and over, the Bible pictures the Christian life as a walk. Why is walking such an important principle?

Think about the fundamentals of walking. You put one foot in front of another. You make progress. Walking is one of the easiest things we ever learn to do. It's as simple as getting from A to Z in one hundred steps.

Now take it a step further. When you're walking with Christ, you have someone beside you. Step by step, day by day, you have a companion to share your troubles with; someone to help when you need a hand.

Walking with Christ is just like that. He's with you wherever you are. You can start or stop talking to him whenever you want. He's always listening. If you walk with Christ, you will never be without a friend who loves you enough to die for you.

To Eat or Not To Eat?

MATTHEW 6:16–18 *When you fast, do not look somber as the hypocrites do, for they disfigure their faces to show men they are fasting. I tell you the truth, they have received their reward in full. But when you fast, put oil on your head and wash your face, so that it will not be obvious to men that you are fasting, but only to your Father, who is unseen; and your Father, who sees what is done in secret, will reward you.*

Fasting is one of the most misunderstood and misused of all Christian spiritual practices. Some people see fasting as a tool that can convince God to act against his own will, or at least talk him into changing his plans.

Fasting *does* move God to action, but its purpose is to show our **dependence** on him. When we fast, we show we want to be totally in God's hands, voluntarily suspending our immediate needs to take our concerns to him.

Scripture tells us about a lot of occasions when people fasted. In three of these stories, people fasted for forty days and nights. It is possible to fast for a long time and remain healthy, but it's always wise to talk to a doctor

check this out

forty
Deuteronomy 9:9; I Kings 19:8; Matthew 4:1–2

fasting
refraining from food or water for a period of time

dependence
relying on someone

Mahatma Gandhi
Indian political leader

before going on a long fast. Fasting can put a strain on the heart and lungs, to say nothing of the taste buds!

Grandpa's Stroke

When my (Mark's) grandfather suffered a stroke, he was paralyzed on the left side of his body—including his face. He couldn't speak. We didn't know if he would live. He was put in a nursing home.

How do you deal with it when your grandfather may die? I immediately decided to fast and pray for my grandfather's health. I only fasted one day, but that one day really boosted my hope.

Months later, my grandfather was out of the nursing home, walking and driving, talking fine, and walking close to God. I wondered if this was the result of my fast, or if it would have happened anyway. In reality, I believe if I hadn't prayed, God might not have answered. God works through relationships and acts on the basis of our prayers. When we fail to pray, he has no obligation to do anything for us. Of course, there may have been others who prayed for Grandpa too. I just don't know. But that's the whole point: If you do fast, good things may happen; if you don't, who knows what will happen? God may work anyway, to be sure. He loves us, and our failures do not limit him. But he also assures us that we should pray and not give up because he will do things that will amaze us. Why? Because he loves us and wants to make our lives joyous and fulfilling.

How to Fast

MATTHEW 4:1–2 ***Then Jesus was led by the Spirit into the desert to be tempted by the devil. After fasting forty days and forty nights, he was hungry.***

Jesus fasted for forty days to prepare for his great test in the wilderness with Satan. The text says he became hungry after the forty days. Actually, Jesus was at the point of starvation, but he was well prepared for his test.

We can fast in one of many ways. Some people abstain from both food and water for a period of time—from one to several days. Others give up food but drink water and other beverages for up to forty days or even more. In recent times people have fasted (like **Mahatma Gandhi**) to get their governments to do something they feel is important. But in spiritual matters, fasting is strictly between you and God.

Other types of fasting include the sleep fast (refusing to sleep for a period of time in order to devote yourself to prayer), or a fast from any specific item for the purpose of using the same time for prayer and study (fast from TV, music, movies, etc.). These are all creative ways of fasting that show you depend upon and love God. God honors us when we sacrifice to show how much we trust him. Fasting is a powerful tool in your spiritual arsenal to defeat Satan and to grow in grace.

check this out

Israelites
Isaiah 58:3–5

The Israelites had many fasts, but they used the fasting as a spiritual activity in place of things like compassion, justice, and goodness. They thought that fasting would please God, even if they neglected the things that really mattered. Fasting does not make God more willing to do anything, and it will not please him if our hearts are not sincere. Fasting simply helps us to see our dependence on God and to show him our devotion in a tangible way.

Few people know that a day of fasting and prayer was observed on May 17, 1776, only weeks before the Declaration of Independence was signed on July 4, 1776. All of the colonies obeyed, and our nation came into being through fasting and prayer—something we seem to have forgotten in recent days.

How Others See It

Thomas à Kempis

Jesus has many who love his heavenly kingdom, but few who bear his cross. Many want consolation, but few desire adversity. Many are eager to share Jesus' table, but few will join him in fasting.[8]

Relating to People: The Hard Stuff

> GALATIANS 5:13 ***You, my brothers, were called to be free. But do not use your freedom to indulge the sinful nature; rather, serve one another in love.***

Relationships are one of the most difficult elements of life. How do you build and maintain good relationships? According to Galatians 5:13, we are to serve one another. Watching out for the needs of others is at the base of care, love, and fellowship. When we serve others, it's a reflection of our truly wanting to serve God.

fellowship
spending time with, enjoying, and relating with other Christians

Fellowship is crucial to Christian growth. For that reason, I've devoted a section of chapter 8 to this very topic, so I won't go into much detail here.

Take another look at the verses at the start of this chapter, Acts 2:42–47. The believers in the first Christian community shared love for each other and for God. They shared a common faith and common goals, which involved caring for the community and spreading the Gospel. They lived in harmony with one another, and more people became Christians as God blessed their efforts. This is the basis of the idea of fellowship. When we are truly contributing to the life of a community, we are living in fellowship. All Christians should make it their goal to become part of a body of believers. Your involvement with other Christians is an essential element in your walk with Christ. When people relate to one another with love, understanding, kindness, and gentleness, they will experience the beauty of true fellowship. Their relationships will become important, powerful, and life-enhancing. Isn't that what we all want anyway?

How Others See It

Andy Pettitte

There are a lot of Christian brothers on the team, and it makes it real special to be able to come to the ballpark and fellowship with other guys who believe the same way that you do.[9]

Sharing Your Faith

2 Timothy 4:2–5 *Preach the Word; be prepared in season and out of season; correct, rebuke and encourage—with great patience and careful instruction. For the time will come when men will not put up with sound doctrine. Instead, to suit their own desires, they will gather around them a great number of teachers to say what their itching ears want to hear. They will turn their ears away from the truth and turn aside to myths. But you, keep your head in all situations, endure hardship, do the work of an evangelist, discharge all the duties of your ministry.*

Another element of true Christian living is telling others about Jesus. This involves telling others the good news about who Jesus is and what he came to do. It's sharing the story of how you became a Christian. Strangely, a lot of Christians seem to forget to share about Jesus with others. Some surveys tell us that 95 percent of Christians never tell anyone about their faith. They never tell anyone about what Jesus Christ has done for them.

Pretty sad, huh? And pretty amazing, considering what Jesus did. We'll talk about anything—what Jill did in seventh hour today, who kissed whom in the lunchroom, what we did last weekend, what kind of car we hope to get on our next birthday, how badly our cat threw up the night before. But when it comes to the greatest thing anyone has ever done for us, we're silent.

check this out

disciples
Acts 10:39–42
witnesses
Acts 2:32

A big part of the problem is that we just don't know how to share our faith. Sometimes we just don't know what to say. Besides, it's scary to tell people about Jesus. Who knows how they might respond? Will they be offended? Will we get in trouble?

But if we really believe what happened two thousand years ago when Christ died on the cross, we can't take it for granted. Jesus did the most loving, remarkable thing in human history. How can we afford to keep our mouths shut like it's our little secret? Telling people about God is actually a responsibility—something we should do. In the New Testament, Jesus' disciples simply told others what they'd seen and heard and learned at the feet of Jesus. Like a witness in a courtroom, they just explained the facts as they had seen them unfold. In the same way, we are to function as witnesses. A witness simply tells a court or a group of people what he or she saw happen. To be a witness to the Gospel and tell the truth about Jesus, we simply tell others what Jesus has done in our lives. We've seen him work, and when we tell others about the things he's done, that's evangelism.

heart to heart

"So What Makes You So Hopeful?"

> 1 Peter 3:15 ***But in your hearts set apart Christ as Lord. Always be prepared to give an answer to everyone who asks you to give the reason for the hope that you have. But do this with gentleness and respect.***

How do you go out into your classes, sports events, and lunchrooms and tell others what you've learned and seen and heard as a Christian? First Peter 3:15 points out the best process—just tell others "the reason for the hope that you have." What is that hope? The hope, or actually knowledge, that we will have eternal life in heaven. Why do we believe we have eternal life? Who do we think Jesus was? We have reasons for all those things, and telling others about those reasons is the center of evangelism.

How, then, do we actually do it? Peter says, "But do this with gentleness and respect." These are the two great attitudes of a witness. Gentleness

Judea
Israelite nation

Samaria
half-Jewish nation north of Judea

Gospel
the message that Christ died so we can live eternally

means being kind, understanding, and willing to listen, instead of being pushy or mean. Respect means letting others tell you their opinions and showing consideration for their beliefs rather than criticizing their thoughts. When we build such attitudes into our lives, Peter assures us that others will want to know what has happened to us and why we believe what we believe.

> **How Others See It**
>
> **Paul Little**
>
> The Holy Spirit can't save saints or seats. If we don't know any non-Christians, how can we introduce them to the Savior?[10]

Keep It Simple

> ACTS 1:8 *But you will receive power when the Holy Spirit comes on you; and you will be my witnesses in Jerusalem, and in all* ***Judea*** *and* ***Samaria****, and to the ends of the earth.*

Being a witness and sharing the Gospel are the primary purposes for which we are on this earth. Yet, as we've pointed out, many Christians never tell another person about their beliefs and faith in Christ. Why? An enemy named Satan (the devil) will do anything to stop us from telling others about Christ, so he stokes fear in our hearts and scares us by filling us with worries about others making fun of us or not liking us anymore or being upset that we told them about Jesus. That's the main reason many people have a hard time making the Gospel message plain to non-Christians. The **Gospel** is the Good News we have for the world about what Jesus has done for us personally—and for them. The Gospel is simply the good news that Christ died for our sins so that we can live forever in heaven instead of going to hell.

One of the best ways to share the Gospel is by building relationships. If we can get to know someone, eventually we'll gain the chance to share personal stuff about ourselves, including the fact that we're Christians. Most people who become Christians learned about Jesus from a friend, relative, neighbor, schoolmate, or co-worker. After we tell a friend about our experiences with Jesus, we can take that friend to Bible passages that will help him or her.

The Romans Road

We can use many passages of the Bible to explain to a friend how Christ loves them and died for them. One of the best Scripture plans of the Gospel is called the Romans Road. It uses a number of verses from the book of Romans. Look at the chart on the following page and see how each part relates. This chart can help you witness more effectively. Memorize these verses of Scripture and God can use you to lead others to Jesus yourself.

The "Romans Road"

Scripture	What It Says	Meaning
Romans 3:23	For all have sinned and fall short of the glory of God.	We're all sinners and can never be perfect like God. Sin isn't just big stuff like killing someone. It's anything we do that is wrong, according to God's standards.
Romans 6:23	For the wages of sin is death, but the gift of God is eternal life in Christ Jesus our Lord.	Because God is perfect and sinless, he can't allow any sinners into heaven. We deserve death as a punishment for our sins. But God gave us a special gift. He sent his son, Jesus, to earth.
Romans 5:8	But God demonstrates his own love for us in this. While we were still sinners, Christ died for us.	Jesus' whole purpose for coming to earth was to live a sinless life and to die for our sins. Because Jesus paid for our sins, we don't have to die and go to hell to pay for them. This is a gift. We don't have to do anything to get this gift—we only have to receive it.
Romans 10:9	That if you confess with your mouth, "Jesus is Lord," and believe in your heart that God raised him from the dead, you will be saved.	We receive this gift by admitting to God that we're sinners. We need to ask him to forgive us for our sins. Then if we turn away from our sins and ask Jesus to take over our lives, he will!

Rebecca St. James

Another thing that has helped me be a better witness is memorizing Scripture verses. Right now, I've got verses on cards on my fridge. Whenever I look at the fridge, I try to get the verses into my head. Sometimes it's helpful just to think, "If I had a chance to witness to (insert name here), what would I share?" People who don't know God want to know your experience with Him. They want to know, "What is reality to this person? How deep does this go?" If you share from your heart, that's what hits home with people.[11]

Forgiveness in the Gospel

ISAIAH 44:22 *I have swept away your offenses like a cloud, your sins like the morning mist. Return to me, for I have redeemed you.*

check this out

forgiveness
Psalm 130:3–4;
I Timothy 1:15–17

penance
punishing oneself to earn forgiveness

words to live by

When we point someone to Scriptures like those in the Romans Road, and they ask Jesus to save them from their sins, one of the things they'll want to know is if they're truly forgiven. What kind of forgiveness does God offer us in the Gospel?

Forgiveness is one of the best gifts in life. To know you're forgiven makes you feel free from guilt. Sometimes people live for years with guilt that burns into their minds and hearts and keeps them from experiencing any real joy in life.

Through believing the Gospel, God can change that. He offers forgiveness freely to anyone who will come to him, believe his Son died for their sins, and receive the gift. That's all he asks. We do nothing to earn his forgiveness—no **penance**, no reciting of Bible verses by altars, no praying on your knees in the cathedral. When we ask, God gives us forgiveness in Christ.

The verse quoted above gives us a picture of the greatness of God's love and forgiveness. In Isaiah 44:22 God says he has "swept away" our sins like the bright sun burns off a puddle left from a rainstorm. What happens? When the sun comes out, nothing is left. The puddle is gone. It's completely annihilated, out of existence. That's what God's forgiveness is like. He deals with our sins by forgiving us, and that means that as far as he's concerned, they no longer exist.

But there's more. Here's a chart of some other verses that talk about the reality of God's forgiveness:

Real Forgiveness

Scripture	Our Sins Are . . .	What It Means
Isaiah 38:17	put behind God's back.	Out of mind. God no longer thinks about them
Isaiah 43:25	out of God's remembrance.	Out of memory. God doesn't remember them anymore.
Psalm 103:12	put "as far as the east is from the west."	Out of sight. They're now so far gone that God can't even see them.
Micah 7:19	thrown into "the depths of the sea."	Out of reach. No one else can retrieve them and bring them back to God.
Isaiah 44:22	blotted out.	Out of existence. In God's eyes they don't even exist anymore.

These passages point out an important truth: God has placed our sins completely out of his thoughts, his sight, his memory, his (and anyone else's) reach, and literally out of existence. Think of the greatness of this truth. You can be forgiven for everything—past, present, and future—so that it's like you never committed that sin, at least in God's eyes! That's what we should always tell people when we share the Gospel: "You can be forgiven of everything you've ever done that was wrong!"

check this out

forgive
Matthew 6:9–13

two men
Luke 7:36–50

Getting Rid of the Junk in Your Life

> MATTHEW 6:14–15 ***For if you forgive men when they sin against you, your heavenly Father will also forgive you. But if you do not forgive men their sins, your Father will not forgive your sins.***

When we share the Gospel, we must make it clear that we can be forgiven of all our sins, mistakes, evil words and desires, everything. But you might wonder how that works out in your normal human relationships. Sure, God has forgiven you, but what about people who have hurt you? What about that grudge you've had for years? Do we offer others the same kind of forgiveness God has given us? Yes!

trespasses
sins

parables
stories with a specific point

In the passage above, Jesus says that we are to forgive the **trespasses** of others the same way God forgives our trespasses. But if we don't forgive others, he warns us, God will not forgive us.

Jesus told several **parables** to help people understand God's concerns about forgiveness. Two of these stories compare sin to money. In one, Jesus tells about two men who were forgiven and freed from their debts; one was forgiven for owing fifty dollars, the other was told he wouldn't have to pay back the five hundred dollars.

When he told this story, Jesus was talking to a leader of the Jews, a man who probably kept all the commandments from his early years and was very important. Meanwhile, a prostitute came into this man's house and, thankful that Jesus had forgiven her for her sins, put some very expensive perfume on his feet (in that culture, it was polite to wash someone's feet when they entered your house—remember, people traveled mostly by walking on dusty roads, and their feet got really dirty).

The Jewish leader was furious that Jesus would let a prostitute touch him. That was when Jesus told him the parable about the two people being forgiven for different debts. At the end, Jesus asked, "Which one will love the forgiver more?" The answer, of course, is the man who was forgiven five hundred dollars.

king
Matthew 18:23–35

The comparison is this: God has forgiven each of us for literally millions of dollars' worth of sins. When we understand how much God has forgiven us, we realize holding a sin against any of our friends or neighbors is ridiculous.

In the other parable, Jesus spoke of a man who owed a king more than five million dollars. The king was about to sell the man and his family into slavery, but the man begged, and finally the king forgave him for everything. This man was very happy until he went out on the road and met a fellow who owed him five dollars. This second man couldn't repay, and the first man had him thrown into prison. When the king heard of the incident, he called on the first man, telling him if he was forgiven five million dollars, surely he should have forgiven someone else a mere five dollars. Because this man wasn't willing to forgive the five-dollar debt, the king had him thrown into prison.

It's not just about money. These two parables show us that we should be willing to forgive anyone who has hurt us, or lied about us, or stolen from us, or done anything else. God has forgiven us millions of dollars' worth of sin, so we cannot rightfully refuse to forgive someone who has only done a few pennies of wrong against us!

How Others See It

Hannah Moore

A Christian will find it cheaper to pardon than to resent. Forgiveness saves the expense of anger, the cost of hatred, the waste of spirits.[12]

How did Jesus forgive others when they hurt him? The Bible contains a very specific case. When the Romans nailed him to the cross (remember, he was totally innocent of doing anything wrong!), the first thing he said was, "Father, forgive them, for they do not know what they are doing" (Luke 23:34).

On another occasion, a woman was brought to him who had been caught in bed with a man who wasn't her husband. The ones who brought her to Jesus said, "In the Law, Moses commanded us to stone such women. Now what do you say?" Jesus knew it was a trap. If he told them not to stone her, he would be violating the law of Moses (in the first few books of the Bible). If he said to stone her, he would be up against the Romans—only they could command that someone be executed. So what did Jesus do? He said, "If any one of you is without sin, let him be the first to throw a stone at her."

Then he started writing something in the sand—no one knows what. One by one everyone went away. When the woman looked up at Jesus, he said to her, "Woman, where are they? Has no one condemned you?" She answered, "No one, sir." He then said, "Then neither do I condemn you. . . . Go now and leave your life of sin." That's a brand of forgiveness we rarely see in the world, but that is what Jesus did with others when he had the chance. (See John 8:3–11.)

heart to heart

Are you holding a grudge against anyone? Who are you mad at? Can you think of people you know you should forgive? Forgive them first before the Lord. If this is tough, ask God to help you forgive them. Then forgive them to their face. It doesn't matter if they don't ask you to forgive them. Sometimes you have to make the first move.

Living a Life of Love

> EPHESIANS 5:1–2 ***Be imitators of God, therefore, as dearly loved children and live a life of love, just as Christ loved us and gave himself up for us as a fragrant offering and sacrifice to God.***

Another important element of living for Christ in this world is loving others. That's what God wants us to do the most while we're still down here on planet Earth. Paul once said in the Bible that only three things will continue after we get to heaven: faith, hope, and love. But, he added, "the greatest of these is love." "Love never fails," Paul also said in 1 Corinthians 13. If everyone lived with unconditional, perfect love in their hearts toward all people, we would not have to worry about any crime or sin, and then we'd know true joy and peace. Love is a simple thing, but how do we show it?

Perhaps another acronym will help. How do you L-O-V-E?

First, you have to listen. Let people know they have your undivided attention. They will tell you the secrets of their hearts and love you for caring about their lives.

Second, put others first. Be a servant. Take care of others. Your selflessness will stand out in today's "look out for number one" world, and you will never lack for friends.

Third, value people. Put a high premium on making people the most important priorities in your life. They and their needs count more than money, your career, a house, or a car—value people and they will feel important in your presence.

check this out

three
1 Corinthians 13
listen
James 1:19–20
others first
Galatians 5:13
value
Matthew 10:29–31

check this out

encourage
1 Thessalonians 5:11

Fourth, encourage. Wherever you go, praise people for what they're doing right. Appreciate them, and they will appreciate you.

When we love others by listening, putting them and their needs first in our lives, valuing them as people and encouraging them, we will find that such people will love us in return. When others feel loved, they're most likely to also want to hear about Jesus. So when we love everyone and anyone, God will open doors for us to share the Gospel with them and help them come to know God's love, which is the greatest love of all.

How Others See It

Karl Menninger

Love cures. It cures those who give it and it cures those who receive it.[13]

Mark Stuart

I've felt for a long time that the church needs to be better in tune with the basic everyday needs of people. And when I say "the church," I mean me, you, and everyone who claims to know Jesus. Churches have the tendency to spend a lot of time talking about sermons, doctrine, and theological issues, while there are real people hurting out there on the streets. Don't get me wrong, theology is important, but it shouldn't take so much of our time that we have no time left to help a family that needs food or a fourteen-year-old girl who's just discovered she's pregnant. If we never get around to dealing with these kind of problems, in my view, we are just playing at being the church.[14]

Steve Wiggins

People don't always need you when it's convenient for you. But when they need you, you need to be there for them. It's what Jesus would do.[15]

Final Thoughts

- Walking with God is something all Christians are expected to do. It involves, in its most basic form, the practice of four disciples: Bible study, prayer, fellowship in the church, and evangelism. As we incorporate these four practices into our lives, we will succeed as Christians.
- Walking with God is simplified in the term *walk*. Through it we see that a relationship with God is like a walk through mountains and valleys. The sights change. The weather changes. But God is always there, leading, helping, speaking, and listening.
- God's grace is essential to survival in this world. It is the means by which God gives us his gifts and power without cost. Through grace God gives us everything we need just for the asking.
- When we forgive others, we are showing our godliness. When we are forgiven, others are showing that God loves us and still cares for us even though we've made mistakes.
- To live a life of love is what the Bible is all about. How are we to treat others? How are we to look at God? Through the eyes and arms and hands of love. When we love, we are most like Christ, and that pleases God immensely.

Questions to Deepen Your Understanding

1. What are some of the things we can do to strengthen our relationship with God?
2. What are the steps we can take to truly understand the Bible?
3. What kinds of prayers should we bring to God?
4. How much does God forgive us?

read on

Some of Mark and Jeanette's favorite books about walking with Christ in daily experiences:

- *The Basics: Nailing Down What Gets You Up,* Mark Littleton, Christian Publications
- *Beefin' Up,* Mark Littleton, Multnomah
- *Can I Be a Christian Without Being Weird?* Kevin Johnson, Bethany
- *Dying of Embarrassment—& Living to Tell About It* (Devotionals for Teens), Lorraine Peterson, Bethany
- *Life, Love, Music, and Money* (Pretty Important Ideas on Living God's Way), Susie Shellenberger and Greg Johnson, Bethany
- *What's in the Bible for Women,* Georgia Curtis Ling, Bethany
- *A Young Woman's Walk With God: Growing More Like Jesus,* Elizabeth George, Harvest House

Chapter 8: Living in Your Family

Getting Along With Those You Live With

What's in This Chapter

- Parents: You Can't Leave 'Em, So Love 'Em
- Obeying Can Protect You—Honest!
- Tips on Obedience to Your Parents
- The Extended Family

Here We Go

Your dad is a tough old cookie. Sometimes he gets nasty.

Or your mom is stressed out all the time and just doesn't seem to have time for you.

Or you live in a one-parent home.

Or you're living through a parental divorce.

Do any of these situations speak to you? Of course, you could be in the perfect home. Your parents love you. Everyone gets along. The dog doesn't even have fleas. Still, you're going to want to know about many issues revolving around the home and living in it in a fulfilling, happy way.

If so, this chapter is for you. We'll look at a number of issues and will try to cover all the bases. And we'll try to offer some practical tips about getting along in the situation you might find yourself in.

Parents: You Can't Leave 'Em, So Love 'Em

EPHESIANS 6:1–4 ***Children, obey your parents in the Lord, for this is right. "Honor your father and mother"—which is the first commandment with a promise—"that it may go well with you and that you may enjoy long life on the earth." Fathers, do not exasperate your children; instead, bring them up in the training and instruction of the Lord.***

Strangely enough, the New Testament doesn't tell us too much about parents and children. This verse in Ephesians, along with a handful of others, gives us the primary lesson. Children are to obey their parents "in the Lord." That is, children should obey their parents because they—the children—are children of God ("in the Lord"), and this is what he requires.

Paul includes the fifth commandment and mentions that it's the first commandment with a promise. That is, when we honor and obey our parents, God blesses us with long life and good days. Obedience is that important to God.

check this out

parents
Proverbs 1:7–9; 2:1–9; 22:15

In the Old Testament, especially in the book of Proverbs, we can find many teachings about parents and children. Read through Proverbs and pick out some verses to memorize.

Why is obedience so important for children? Because children lack the wisdom of adults. Toddlers sometimes try to stick their fingers into electrical outlets. Preschoolers might run out into the street without looking. Elementary school children sometimes spend their money on cheap toys that they throw away the next day. Some middle schoolers would eat chocolate bars for breakfast and french fries for every meal if their parents let them. And some teens want to drive cars at high speeds. It takes wise parents to guide and direct their children into making wise choices.

Obeying Can Protect You—Honest!

for real

Ally, a seventeen-year-old, had this to say: "Recently, I did something I shouldn't have. My mom had told me not to be on the phone after ten o'clock at night. I didn't like the rule because sometimes a friend would call late in need of some encouragement, and I didn't want to say no. The night in particular, I got a call from my friend Chelsea, and I just thought, Well, I'll only talk for a little bit, *and then it turned into more than a little bit, and I lost track of the time. I guess I was laughing. I had just gotten off the phone when next thing I knew, my mom came up the stairs and stormed into my room. She asked me, 'Were you on the phone?'*

"'Yes, I was talking to Chelsea.'

"'You're not supposed to be on the phone after ten.'

"'I'm sorry.'

"'You're grounded for two weeks.'

"I really thought it was too much as I watched her leave with my regular phone and my cell phone. I felt good that I had been honest about it, though.

"The next day, my dad and mom talked to me about it, and they decided not to ground me for two weeks, but to restrict my phone-talking for two weeks. That felt better. It's also easier for me to obey now

that I have the restrictions. I can tell my friends that I can't talk after ten because 'of my parents,' rather than because I don't want to. In fact, it's even kind of a protection for me. I can always blame them for things I can't do when I might not really want to do them in the first place. (Okay, that's a joke.)

"But really, I do see the way being obedient to my parents' rules helps me. And when I really think about a rule I may not like, it usually makes sense.

"Anyway, I'm working on it. It's not always easy, but being a committed Christian also helps a lot because I know Jesus is helping me obey even when I may not want to. He gives me the power to obey with a smile."

How Others See It

Jaci Velasquez

I need a little more privacy. . . . But the thing is, I love living with my parents. And I love having my mom on the road with me. I'd be lost without her. So I feel kind of torn between needing them and wanting them to treat me like an adult.[1]

Obedience, the Tough Issue

PROVERBS 1:7–9 ***The fear of the Lord is the beginning of knowledge, but fools despise wisdom and discipline. Listen, my son, to your father's instruction and do not forsake your mother's teaching. They will be a garland to grace your head and a chain to adorn your neck.***

This passage speaks to the issue of obtaining wisdom. How do you get it? By listening to and obeying your parents. Why is obeying so important? Because it leads to wisdom, the basic skill for living well. When you obey, you learn to live well. Also, learning to obey our parents helps us learn to obey God more easily.

How do you become a teen who honors and obeys his or her parents even when you wish you could do otherwise? First, listen to them. Second, respect their ideas and opinions—they were young once. Third, accept that they are wiser than you are and probably know how to handle most situations. Fourth, do what they say even when you disagree. Chances are you won't regret it. Most parents want the best for their children and would never knowingly give bad advice or faulty instruction.

check this out

love
John 4:15

Why Obey in the First Place?

People obey authority figures for different reasons. Here are several Scriptures that explain some of those reasons:

Levels of Obedience

Response	Scripture	Meaning
Fear	Romans 13:3	You obey because you fear what the authorities will do if you disobey.
Tradition	Isaiah 29:13–14	You obey because it's what you learned growing up.
Reward	2 Corinthians 5:10	You obey to get a reward.
Wisdom	Proverbs 3:3–4	You obey because you know it's wise.
Respect	Proverbs 1:7	You obey because you respect the one asking for obedience.
Love	1 John 4:18	You obey because you love your parents.

Notice that this chart moves from the most negative reason to obey to the most positive reason. To obey simply because you fear your father is not a very good reason. Tradition also lacks integrity. Reward is getting better, but it's more like the dog that knows he'll get a bone if he lies down. Wisdom gets at the real issue—obedience is simply the smartest course of action. Considering the facts about your own experience and that of your parents, obedience makes sense. Respect is also a strong reason. When you obey even when you don't like what you have to do, you show respect for your parents' judgment and authority. Finally, the best reason to obey is love. When you obey because you love someone, you have reached the kind of obedience God truly values.

How Others See It

Rebecca St. James

One of the greatest things my parents have instigated, and I hope to do someday if I have a family, is they've encouraged a "no secrets" policy. That means everything is out in the open. There's nothing you can't talk about, which is wonderful.[2]

The Shepherd and the Lamb

A traveler sat with a shepherd in the Swiss Alps. The shepherd held a little lamb that had a broken leg.

"How did it happen?" the traveler asked sympathetically.

"I broke it," said the shepherd. He explained that this lamb was the most wayward of all his lambs and that it often went far away from the flock, eating the grass close to cliffs. Sometimes other little lambs followed this one and got lost or killed. So the shepherd had broken the lamb's leg to teach it to obey. "This one, when it is healed, will be the most obedient of all my lambs," the shepherd explained with tears in his eyes. "It will come immediately when I call. And it will never stray again."

For the Christian, God must sometimes break us to teach us to obey. Once we are broken, we will never forget the lesson, and our obedience will be strengthened. It's admittedly a tough way to learn, but it's one of God's greatest tools to teach us to follow him. Many Christians go through deep "brokenness" before they become very useful to God in serving him.

Tips on Obedience to Your Parents

- Remember that in most cases when a parent makes rules you may not like, it's because they're trying to protect you and keep you out of trouble—not make your life miserable.
- Most parents want their kids to be happy. So it's not normal for them to make rules just to make you unhappy. Remember, they do love you and care about you.
- Give your parents a break now and then. They're human. They'll make mistakes sometimes by going overboard with a punishment or rule. Learn to forgive.
- Most parents will listen to your objections to a rule or situation if you voice them. Once voiced, though, remember that you'll need to accept whatever decision they make.
- Obeying with a smile always helps things work out for the better. And sometimes, when your attitude is good, your parents will make changes in the rules because you've grown and are showing that you're mature enough to have some privileges.

You Can Pick Your Friends, but Not Your Siblings

1 John 2:9–11 *Anyone who claims to be in the light but hates his brother is still in the darkness. Whoever loves his brother lives in the light, and there is nothing in him to make him stumble. But whoever hates his brother is in the darkness and walks around in the darkness; he does not know where he is going, because the darkness has blinded him.*

If the New Testament only speaks a little about how children are to relate to parents, there's nothing specifically about how teens are supposed to relate to their brothers and sisters. The New Testament writers simply didn't address the issue.

However, if we look at the bigger biblical picture, there are plenty of lessons. Think about it—everything in the Bible about relationships certainly applies to a sibling relationship. How are you to treat your brothers and sisters? Love them. It's that simple. Love them by serving. Love them by giving. Love them by sacrificing. Love them by encouraging. All the ways we're to love each other as Christians applies to how we treat our brothers and sisters, even if they aren't believers.

How Others See It

Shelley Phillips

When I was in high school, my little sister was still in elementary school. Like a "typical" little sister, she could get on my nerves. And I could really tell her off. I was always making her cry.

During my senior year, my dad said to me, "Shelley, you're leaving for college soon, and what your sister will remember most about you is how you've treated her."

Dad's words hit me like a ton of bricks. I felt so bad. After that, I worked harder at being nice to my sister and at giving her a little more attention. One thing I'd like to say to people who have younger siblings is this: Start being nice *right now*. I'm glad I changed, but it would have made things easier on my sister, and on the whole family, if I'd tried a little harder to get along.[3]

Help! My Parents Are Going Through a Divorce

Malachi 2:16 *"I hate divorce," says the Lord God of Israel.*

How does God feel about divorce? He hates it, according to Malachi 2:16. Other texts—see Matthew 19:1–12, 1 Corinthians 7:10–16, and Matthew 5:31–32—make it clear that God does not want married people to get divorces. However, under certain conditions, like sexual immorality and desertion, God allows divorce, even among Christian parents.

But what about you when you face divorce? How can you survive this time when your parents probably fight and quarrel constantly, sometimes violently, and even may try to drag you into the situation to take sides?

More than half of all households today go through a divorce. More than three-quarters of second marriages end in divorce. It's an epidemic, but it's also something even Christian teens have to find a way to deal with.

When asked about their parents' divorce, this is how several different teens responded:

- "I hated it. I hated the fighting and both trying to get me on their side. Now I just feel like my life doesn't matter anymore."
- "It was actually kind of good to get away from all the quarreling and have some peace. Now my parents are both happier with their new situations, and that makes me happier."
- "I don't like having to go to one house and then the other on weekends and stuff. But I guess you can learn to live with just about anything."
- "I keep praying that my parents will get back together since neither of them have remarried. But I don't think God will answer that prayer."

Do any of these thoughts strike a chord with you? Obviously, every divorce is a little different. You'll have to decide how to handle the divorce in your home with the help of your friends, advisers, and extended family. But here are some thoughts on what to do:

For one, no matter what your parents may say, their divorce is not your fault. They're responsible for their actions. You couldn't have made this turn out better simply by having a better attitude or acting differently.

Second, you may just have to accept the situation as it is. Yes, pray about your parents. Yes, seek God for help. But remember, even God will not "make" someone do what he wants. Sometimes you just have to say, "Okay, God. This is it. I don't like it. But I accept it. Now what?"

think about it

Third, try to keep a good relationship with each parent. Work at being kind, understanding of their feelings, and listening. Don't try to defend the other parent to the one you may be talking to. Just be a listening ear.

What If One of My Parents Constantly Speaks Against the Other One?

There are some ways to handle this effectively. Listen, try to affirm the parent (not in agreement, but saying things like, "I can understand why you feel that way"), and resist the impulse to take sides, even if you think the other parent is wrong.

Another way to deal with it is to tell the complaining parent, "I really do not want to listen to this. If you need to complain, talk to a friend, but not me." If the parent won't abide by such a rule, tell them something like, "If you start complaining, I'm just going to walk out of the room." Watch that you don't say this in a smart-alecky way. You do have some power in this relationship, and it should be okay for you to voice your opinion, but take care to voice your feelings in a loving, respectful way.

The third way, but not the best, is simply to ignore the complaining. Nod your head as if you understand what's being said, listen, and leave it at that.

Remember one more thing. Jean Kerr, a humorist of your parents' generation, once said, "Being divorced is like being hit by a Mack truck. If you live through it, you start looking very carefully to the right and to the left." Your parents may both have been deeply wounded by their divorce. They once were in love and meant it to last. When it didn't, they probably came away terribly disillusioned, perhaps angry at themselves, the world, and God. Show your parents compassion. Things can be tough, especially for single moms. Finances might be very tight. So just give them a bit of a break. They're fighting a hard battle just surviving. Try not to make that battle worse.

Blended Families

Today, more than half of all families are blended. That is, there has been a divorce between your parents, and they have remarried. Sometimes they remarry someone who also has been divorced and has children. Many times, getting along is tough for these families because of rivalries, jealousies, favoritism, and other problems. While these things can be serious, nothing in the Bible speaks specifically to blended families. However, you do find many families in the Bible like Abraham's, Jacob's, King David's, and others where the father had several different wives who had children. These were not stepchildren, as in most of today's blended families, but half brothers and sisters. Still, they were a lot like the blended families of today.

Looking at the Bible, you immediately see the kinds of problems these families had. When Abraham took Hagar as a wife (at Sarah's suggestion because Sarah couldn't have children), it created rivalries and problems that continue today with the whole Arab/Israeli conflict.

In Jacob's family, there was so much jealousy toward Joseph (because Jacob favored him) that the other brothers tried to kill Joseph. He was later sold into slavery because his half brothers hated him so much.

King David's children committed rape, murder, and rebellion. Absalom so despised his father because of the family problems that he led a civil war against his father. In the end, he was killed, and David mourned for years because of his own failures with his children.

Clearly, there are many problems that any blended family can experience. Among them:

- Fighting and quarreling
- Jealousy
- Favoritism
- Abuse—sexual, emotional, and physical
- Deep and inconsolable anger
- Rejection
- Hatred
- Running away

Problems in the Blended Family

Here are some ideas on what to do and how to handle problems in blended families:

1. Talk to God about your situation. Get everything out in front of him, and ask him for his leadership and advice. He will answer.
2. Tell your parents what's going on. Try to show them real facts, not just feelings. Get everything out in the open.

3. Try to work out any problems with your stepbrothers and stepsisters. Again, talk, negotiation, and prayer together can help in many ways.
4. Refuse to give up on your family. If you need to go to school or other authorities, consider doing so. But don't just shut down and give up.

What If Nothing Changes?

Sometimes you will find yourself in a situation where nothing seems to change. The problems continue, your parents don't care, and you are miserable. What can you do?

First, keep building your relationship with God. He has promised that he will help you if you trust him. He will lead you and give you ideas that you can act on. Don't give up on him. Sometimes it will take a while before he can do what he plans to do. So hang in there, and believe he has your best interest at heart.

Second, examine yourself. Are you doing anything that is making the problems worse? Can you work at not saying things you know will be hurtful? Can you "turn the other cheek" to insults and some of the unkind things that get said? Can you see anything you can do that will improve things simply because you have a better attitude?

Third, seek the counsel of others—your friends in blended families, other Christians, pastors and leaders at your church. God has placed many resources around you. Use them to seek help and insight.

The Extended Family

> 1 Timothy 5:1–2 ***Do not rebuke an older man harshly, but exhort him as if he were your father. Treat younger men as brothers, older women as mothers, and younger women as sisters, with absolute purity.***

How is a Christian to treat members of the extended family? The same way he or she treats members of the Christian family: with love, honesty, kindness, and friendship. Uncles, aunts, grandparents, and cousins are all to be treated with care and respect. It's easy to forget such an attitude when so many families fight, argue, and end up with strained relationships. In a world where abuse and mistreatment abound, how are you to treat an uncle who ignores you or a cousin who puts you down every chance he gets? Again, the answer is love.

Did you know that most of Jesus' own family, except his mother, didn't believe that he was the Messiah when he was on earth? Not only didn't they believe in him, they thought he was crazy. Imagine having to live in that type of situation! But Jesus not only lived in that kind of situation, he showed love and respect.

check this out

family
John 7:1–5

crazy
Mark 3:20–21

Final Thoughts

- All young people are to grow up obeying their parents. Whatever makeup we find in our families—stepfathers, half brothers, whatever —we are to learn to obey those in authority over us. When we obey our parents, we please God.
- We are to treat the extended family—grandparents, uncles, aunts, cousins—the same way we are to treat everyone—by loving them as we love ourselves. It's a simple rule, but not easily followed. In fact, the only way to follow it is through the power of Christ.

Questions to Deepen Your Understanding

1. What is the primary thing we need to practice in our relationships to our parents?
2. How should we treat members of our extended family?

read on

Some of Mark and Jeanette's favorite books about getting along with those you live with:

- *Cars, Curfews, Parties, and Parents . . . (77 Pretty Important Ideas),* Susie Shellenberger and Greg Johnson, Bethany
- *Does Anybody Know What Planet My Parents Are From?* Kevin Johnson, Bethany
- *How to Live With Your Parents Without Losing Your Mind,* Ken Davis, Zondervan
- *Hugs for Teens,* Scott Krippayne, Howard
- *On the Homefront: A Family Survival Guide,* Katrina L. Cassel, Concordia
- *Preparing for Adolescence,* Dr. James Dobson, Tyndale

Chapter 9: Friendship, Dating, and the Big One—Marriage

Looking at Friendship, Dating, and Marriage

What's in This Chapter

- The Christian's Guide to Dating
- Successful Dating
- What If You Went Too Far?
- The Search for Mr. or Miss Right
- Finding Your Mate
- Getting Ready for the Big "M"

Here We Go

The starting place for good dating and marital relationships is building good friendships, first with teens of your gender, and then with teens of the opposite gender. As Proverbs 27:17 says, "As iron sharpens iron, so one man sharpens another." You will find that real friendships will sharpen and hone you in becoming a teen of real character. As you build such friendships, especially with other Christians, at times they will speak truth to you as if from God himself. In fact, that's one of the primary ways God speaks to us as his children: He uses the spiritual people in our lives to communicate his advice, guidance, and ideas to us. Sometimes he will even use people who have no real belief in him.

How Do You Begin Building Good Friendships With the Opposite Sex?

Just being with others in school is a big start. By learning to talk to girls and guys, you expand your abilities to converse and soon learn that the opposite sex isn't so crazy after all. The place to begin is in church and school. Getting into a mixed-gender Bible study group at church will allow you to see how others think and react to things you might say. A Bible study group is a great place to practice things like manners, tact, friendliness, and a million other things you'll need to get along in polite society.

Here are some ways you can work toward building good friendships:

1. Take the opportunity to sit down and talk with others at lunchtime, in classes, and other situations. You needn't be a con-

versational whiz here. Just ask a few questions. You'll be amazed at how being a listener will open you up to other teens and have them open up to you.

2. Spend time in small to large groups of both sexes. You can learn a lot simply by being there. You don't even have to say much most of the time. Just sit in and listen to what others say and what kinds of opinions they have.

3. Read books like the ones listed at the end of this chapter, listen to tapes, and go to conferences and retreats at your church where teens will attend. Spending a weekend with others is often a great way to get to know them on a deeper level.

The Christian's Guide to Dating

GENESIS 2:24 ***For this reason a man will leave his father and mother and be united to his wife, and they will become one flesh.***

2 CORINTHIANS 6:14–16 ***Do not be yoked together with unbelievers. For what do righteousness and wickedness have in common? Or what fellowship can light have with darkness? What harmony is there between Christ and Belial? What does a believer have in common with an unbeliever? What agreement is there beween the temple of God and idols?***

This famous verse is quoted much by youth pastors and leaders in the church to help guide Christians as they date, become engaged, and marry. It's an important principle and not one to take lightly, even though it's a tough one to follow. What does it mean for Christians who have reached the age to begin dating? Mainly, it means don't become linked emotionally, spiritually, or physically with teens who don't share your faith. Why is this?

Look at the different statements in the verse:

1. ***For what do righteousness and wickedness have in common?*** This is a tough one to look at because it suggests that you as a Christian are righteous—good, law-abiding, keeping God's rules—and unbelievers are wicked—evil, sinful, and rejecting of God. The problem is that many unbelievers are decent people and don't fit the description at all. Or do they? The truth is, you can't know the heart of others until you've gotten to know them intimately. And God's warning here is not to become intimate

with someone who doesn't believe in him. Why? Because deep down that person, no matter now nice on the surface, rejects God, his commandments, his plans, and his ways. By the time you find out how really bad someone might be to you, you could be hooked in ways that make it hard to let go later. God is saying, don't even get started in becoming close with an unbeliever.

2. ***What fellowship can light have with darkness?*** Pretty stark contrast, right? Light and darkness. But that's it. Christians are in the world of light. They see truth, God, and the world the way God see these things. Unbelievers are in the dark. They will not want to follow God's rules. So what kind of fellowship can you really have? Real fellowship occurs on the deep level of spirit-to-spirit. You'll never get to that level with unbelievers unless you're willing to compromise about a lot of things God may not want you to.

3. ***What harmony is there between Christ and Belial?*** Jesus on the one hand, the devil on the other. They're enemies. Satan wants to destroy Jesus and all he stands for, including those teens who follow him. Unbelievers, perhaps unwittingly, will try hard to destroy your beliefs in Jesus and your commitment to him. So, again, God says it's a mistake to get involved with them.

4. ***What does a believer have in common with an unbeliever?*** You go to church. You read the Bible. You memorize verses. You pray. You share your faith. Are such things important to you? They won't be to an unbeliever.

5. ***What agreement is there in the temple of God and idols?*** You can't have idols—idols like money, cars, rock music, drugs, drinking, and other things—in God's temple. But you may find that's what you'll be bringing there (in a spiritual sense) if you get deeply involved with unbelievers.

What About Dating to Share Your Faith?

Many Christian teens date unbelievers because they think they will be able to share their faith with these guys or girls and eventually lead them to Jesus. It happens occasionally that a Christian does actually lead a date to Jesus. But more often, unbelievers have more of an effect on believers than vice versa.

Perfect Charmer

Your mistakes can be a warning for others. Mike, age nineteen, tells this story: "I found a Christian girl I liked a lot, and after many discussions I talked her into dating me. I used all my charm and a lot of lies to move her in the direction I wanted her to go because I didn't believe as she did. Gradually she gave in until we began having sex. She felt guilty. I felt wonderful. To get her to do this, I used deception, outright lies, coaxing, and every other trick I could think of. Now I'm a Christian, and I see the evil of what I did. I'm starting to tell others about my tactics as an unbeliever to help Christians not make the mistake of dating teens like I was. I was the perfect charmer. And many unbelievers are. And it all leads to disaster."

Ultimately, it's your business whom you hang with and whom you date. But if you really want God's blessing on your life, you'd be wise to take his advice on the subject. He will show you the way if you let him, and you will find that his way is the best way. Try his way out. You may be surprised at how much fun you begin to have and how you stay off the dead-end streets.

Successful Dating

How do you go about having a fulfilling dating life? Some writers, like Joshua Harris, advocate dating only when you're really committed and have picked out someone you wish to court. For a lot of teens, though, this doesn't work, especially when you're young and not really ready or interested in marriage. What are some of the things you should consider as you prepare for the world of dating?

1. Make the decision to date only believers. You won't regret it, and it will win God's true blessings on your relationships.
2. Start slow. Don't let the first twinges of infatuation and the fun of a person you're seeing turn you into a puddle on the floor. Go easy. Get to know the person well before the first kiss. Spend time with the person in groups so you can see how he or she acts with others.
3. Set your limits. How far is too far for you? The Bible specifically says premarital sex is wrong (Hebrews 13:4; 1 Corinthians 6:9–10; and 1 Thessalonians 4:3–5). But what about kissing and

other things? You will have to have clear boundaries in these matters because some Christians will try to violate them. A good rule is "no touching below the neck."

4. Learn to converse and relate. It takes time to get to know someone of the opposite sex. Guys are very different from girls. So work at learning to talk things through. Read books. Go to youth group, and ask your leaders to teach on this subject.

What If You Went Too Far?

It happens. Perhaps it happened before you became a Christian. Maybe you were a Christian when you gave in to a date's demands and had sex on any level (not just intercourse—other forms of sex are just as bad). You can't go back to being a virgin again. What do you do if you've committed sexual sin?

First, admit it, and turn from it. Decide now that you won't date unbelievers, you won't give in to the demands of even a sinful believer, and you will set limits and boundaries. If someone you start dating puts pressure on you, decide not to continue in the relationship if that person won't change.

Second, remember that God's forgiveness erases everything. You can't get your virginity back, but you can become new and real inside your heart. Remember 2 Corinthians 5:17: "If anyone is in Christ, he is a new creation; the old has gone, the new has come!" When you become a Christian, you're a new person. God has wiped out your past. And even if you committed those wrongs while you were a Christian, it's the same thing: God forgives you, and those mistakes are gone.

Third, don't wallow in the past. Look forward to God's future blessings. God will bless you if you seek him. Don't think that he has turned against you or that he'll destroy your life now that you've messed it up.

The Search for Mr. or Miss Right

Marriage is one of the most sacred unions any person can enter into. Marriage is God's idea. He was the first matchmaker when he created Eve to be Adam's partner. It's his design that most people will eventually marry.

Nothing else will change a man's or a woman's life more than marriage. From the time we approach the teen years until we are actually married, most of us dream of the partner we will spend our lives with. We want someone who is kind, honest, gentle, truthful, and loving. But where do you find such a person?

Getting ready for marriage is something most of us, in some way or another, do from the time we're toddlers. We watch our parents—how they interact, what their relationship is like—and form opinions about what marriage is like and whether we want a similar relationship.

The stages of marriage in America used to be easy to chart: love, engagement, marriage, honeymoon, childbearing and raising, teen years, college years, empty nest, death of a spouse.

This pattern is not very common in America today. Divorce, unmarried parents, homosexual parents, and any number of other factors have changed the structure of marriage and the home in America. This 50/50 situation affects millions of teens and will influence how you and other teens approach marriage as you grow older.

How Others See It

Josh McDowell and Bob Hostetler

Everyone wants it. Without it, life would be, at best, incomplete—at worst, desperate. The yearning to give and receive love throbs in the heart of everyone, male and female.

People try in different ways to discover true love, real love, a love that is strong and deep, a love that lasts for all time. Yet the pursuit of love has caused more heartache and pain, more brokenness and bitterness, than all the diseases and all the wars in history.[1]

According to recent surveys by various research agencies, more than one-half of all American marriages suffer through a divorce. At least three-quarters of second marriages also fail.

Finding Your Mate

The dating process with a view to eventually getting married can be tough. I well remember those days of finding a girl I really liked only to discover she wasn't interested in me.

Dating can be fun and invigorating, though. You meet new people. You learn how to converse and relate to the opposite sex. You find out that everyone is different. No two girls or guys are alike. And that makes it both interesting and frustrating.

When I was in high school, my girlfriend and I quickly fell in love. We went to our junior and senior proms together. We spent much time intimately talking, having fun, and kissing. Gradually, though, I lost interest. At the end of our senior year, I broke up with her. And that summer I learned the truth about going through life without a sure date. I didn't find anyone who was as fun, conversational, and interested in me as my girlfriend had been. Before going to college, I quickly made up with her, I went off to college, and so did she. In those days there was no e-mail, no easy way to keep in touch, and the phone system was expensive. I wrote her letter after letter. She didn't reply. For a solid month, each day became more tense and panicked. She hadn't responded, and I feared she'd met and fallen for some young stud at college and had forgotten all about me. Each time I visited the post office I walked away with renewed terror that I hadn't gotten a letter from her. It became one of the most painful times in my life as I imagined all kinds of things that could have gone wrong.

Finally, though, she answered and apologized for the long delay. She soon came to visit me at my college for party weekend. It was a grand time, and I fell more deeply in love. When we parted at the gate for her plane ride home to the University of Rhode Island, we both wept. Later, though, she decided to break up with me permanently.

Over the next few years I searched for her in the eyes and hearts of every girl I dated. But I never found someone quite as good as her until I met my wife, Jeanette. That's a whole other story, but it illustrates how tenuous the dating process can be. I only tell you this because I want you to know: Dating and marrying eventually are worth the trouble. As Paul said, "Those who marry will face many troubles in this life, and I want to spare you this" (1 Corinthians 7:28).

The decision to marry is a perilous choice, and even the dating process can invite much trouble. You just never know what might happen, however in love you may feel with your mate. Enter it, as some say, "with eyes wide open." And stick with it "with one eye shut."

Getting Ready for the Big "M"

check this out

Jacob
Genesis 29:15–30

Solomon
Song of Solomon

GALATIANS 5:22–23, 25 *But the fruit of the Spirit is love, joy, peace, patience, kindness, goodness, faithfulness, gentleness and self-control. Against such things there is no law. . . . Since we live by the Spirit, let us keep in step with the Spirit.*

Scripture may not provide concrete answers about preparing yourself for marriage, but it offers plenty of advice on how to make yourself into who God wants you to be. God has revealed to us through his Word the characteristics that please him. If we strive to develop those characteristics, we will grow closer in our relationship to him. What better way to prepare for marriage than to be walking in God's path and strengthened by his presence? Instead of focusing on what kind of person you want to marry, perhaps you should focus on what kind of person you are becoming.

What steps should a teen take to ensure a happy marriage? Scripture does not provide a clear path. In fact, most marriages in Scripture were arranged marriages. Two fathers agreed that their children would marry each other, and the matter was settled. Sons and daughters had no choice whom they would marry. Love matches, the kind we treasure in America, were unheard of in Scripture except for a few, such as Jacob and Rachel and Solomon and the Shunnamite.

How Others See It

Heather Floyd

I would much rather be a content single person, to this day, than to be caught in a marriage where my husband doesn't really love me or in a dating relationship where I don't really like the guy I'm spending time with.

I feel like I'm really special to the Lord right now, because He's not finished with His time alone with me yet. He still has things that He wants to do through me as a single person that He can't do when I'm married. He doesn't want to share me yet.[2]

Everyone has an ideal picture in mind of the person he or she would like to marry. It is important to have standards and expectations. However, even those who find their "ideal" partner will eventually discover that everyone makes mistakes and no one is perfect. The trick to knowing if you've found the right person is truly understanding your relationship and knowing its strengths and weaknesses.

Josh McDowell and Bob Hostetler provide some good counsel in their book *Handbook on Counseling Youth*. They advise that a couple should ask a number of questions that will help them decide if their plans to unite are wise:

1. Are you both Christians? (2 Corinthians 6:14)
2. Have you sought God's will in a biblical manner?
3. Do you love each other with a biblical love? (1 Corinthians 13)
4. Do your parents approve? (Exodus 20:10)

These are the foundational questions. A number of others are also appropriate:

5. Do you help each other grow closer to God?
6. Can you talk?
7. Can you play together?
8. Can you work together?
9. Do you have mutual friends?
10. Are you proud of each other?
11. Are you intellectually on the same level?
12. Do you have common interests?
13. Do you share the same values?
14. Do you feel comfortable about how you make decisions together?
15. Do you help each other emotionally?
16. Do you have absolute trust in each other?
17. Are you more creative and energetic because of each other?
18. Can you accept and appreciate each other's family?
19. Do you have unresolved relationships in your past?
20. Is sex under control? Are you maintaining purity?
21. Have you spent enough time together?
22. Have you fought and forgiven?
23. Have you talked about each area of your future life?
24. Have you had counseling?[3]

Asking and answering these questions together with a counselor will help any young couple make a wise and intelligent decision. It's not all just about hormones; it's about a whole life. So make the most of it and pray that God leads you every step of the way. Are we implying that everyone has to get married to be happy? No way! Statistics tell us that most people will get married eventually. But don't rush it. If you put off getting married until you're in your late twenties or thirties, you can get college out of the way first (which is much easier for a single to do than a married person), and you may have the money and time to travel or do other stuff that people tend not to do after they get married. More people than ever are staying single longer. Sometimes that gives us time to get to know ourselves better—which can lead to a better marriage in the long run!

How Others See It

Dr. James Dobson

A Sunday school teacher gave me some advice when I was thirteen years of age that I never forgot. He said, "Don't marry the person you think you can live with. Marry the one you can't live without." There's great truth in this advice. Marriage can be difficult even when two people are passionately in love with one another.[4]

Terry Jones

Don't get married or date because it's the thing to do—because everyone you know is getting married or dating. Hearing so much about divorces has made me so glad that I have my husband, Chris, in my life. He's my perfect match. I can't imagine being with anybody else.

Marriage is such a wonderful thing that you really need to have it be with the right guy. If that means you're forty before you get married, then you wait for that guy and don't compromise yourself in any way.[5]

How Can You Meet the Right Person?

What steps can you as a teen take to find the right person to marry? Aside from the thoughts above, consider these steps:

1. When you first start dating, just proceed with the idea of getting to know others, learning to talk to them, trying new things together. Don't think you have to find the right guy or girl the first time you go out on a date. That's just not reality. You will probably date many people before meeting Mr. or Miss Right. So have some fun. Enjoy it. And keep yourself pure in the process.

2. Get used to going to places where you're likely to meet the right kind of person. Secular people may consider bars, dating services,

and the like. Some of these things, like dating services, might work in some cases. But where are you likely to meet the kinds of Christians you might wish to build a relationship with? Places like church, Christian singles groups, Christian dating services, and the like. These kinds of activities are just the kinds of venues where you might meet the right person.

3. Pray about it and keep God involved in every step of the process. That seems obvious, but many Christians fail to consider it as an important step. God wants your happiness as much as you do, and he's the heavenly Matchmaker. So keep him involved.

4. Start slow and build a relationship before taking more intimate steps. Of course because you are a Christian, premarital sex is ruled out. The intimacy of kissing and spending time alone can lead to compromises, so don't go too fast. You have plenty of time. Refuse the impulse to rush into things.

5. Consult with friends and others who can tell you things in real honesty. If parents or others who really care about you start to give you bad news about the person you're tight with, listen to them. They probably see things you don't. And they could help you avert a real disaster.

6. Get counseling from your pastor and others as you take the steps of engagement and marriage. They can advise and help you.

7. When you fall in love for real and think you've found the guy or girl you've looked for all your life, sit down with your prospective mate and talk about some of the rules you believe you should follow in marriage—rules like going to church, arguing fairly, and not engaging in any kind of abuse. Some experts say that things you agree upon before marriage will stick much more deeply than those that come out of the process after you are married.

8. Keep God in your home, let him lead, and face life together with gusto and hope. Hold nothing back in loving your mate perfectly.

A house is only a house until you make it a home. It's not easy. It takes work, but it can be done—with faith, love, honesty, and servanthood. Are you willing to make your house a home?

heart to heart

Celibacy—The Big Question

1 CORINTHIANS 7:8–9 ***Now to the unmarried and to the widows I say: It is good for them to stay unmarried, as I am. But if they cannot control themselves, they should marry, for it is better to marry than to burn with passion.***

Never marrying is a choice some Christians will make even from their teen years. Why? There are probably as many reasons as there are people. Some people don't want to marry because they truly want to serve God all out, and getting married would keep them from that. In fact, Paul suggests that some Christians should consider this a real option, according to 1 Corinthians 7:32–35. Paul was a celibate. So was Jesus. Who can discount what they accomplished in their lives?

Another reason some Christians don't marry is that marriage simply doesn't appeal to them, or they just never meet someone they wish to join with. There's nothing wrong with either of those attitudes. Such people should always consider that perhaps God has led them in that direction for a greater purpose, and they should seek to find what that purpose might be.

Still another reason some Christians don't marry is because of a problem like homosexuality. Having a homosexual orientation and not acting on it is one way many Christians deal with the problem. They simply accept their condition, refuse to act on their passions, and live a celibate life. It's a hard way to go, but it may be the only realistic path for people in that situation. Moreover, this is once again a clear marker toward ministry. Instead of bemoaning such a situation, teens who see this as their condition can turn it into a positive by ministering specifically to others in the same situation, or by throwing themselves into a ministry that benefits others.

Finally, there are those who long for marriage but simply never have the opportunity. I have a friend who just got married for the first time at the age of forty-five. Her husband was forty-four and also had never been married. It was an unusual situation, but she prayed about this for many years and finally found the right person, even though in the year before she met this man, she had accepted that she might never marry.

I also have another friend who is the same age and has never been married either. In fact, she has never really dated much because she was a little on the picky side, and she also refused to date anyone who wasn't a strong and committed Christian. Today she wonders if she has done the right thing. But she has a vibrant music ministry, takes care of her invalid parents, and has helped her sisters and nieces in financial ways because she has a well-paying job. Though she laments never getting married, she has experienced fulfillment in other ways that she says she could never regret.

Whether celibacy is something you should consider is a tough question that only you can answer as God leads you. Here are some things to consider:

1. Do you want to serve God all out in a way that you know you couldn't with a family to support?
2. Is your sexual passion level fairly low, and do you think you could live with not having a mate because of it?
3. Do you have an extended network of friends and family with whom you can share your deepest thoughts and secrets, like a husband would with a wife, or vice versa? In other words, being alone maritally does not mean you have to be alone spiritually or emotionally.
4. Do you sense God's specific leading on this issue? You will need his full support if you want to succeed in this. Seek him every step of the way.

The Gift "Wore Off"

Gabriel, a college student, tells this story: "I went into one of my teachers' offices to tell him I thought I had the gift of celibacy. He congratulated me and asked me what I planned to do. 'Serve God all out,' I told him. 'I really want to go for the absolute most I can do for him.'

"It was an exciting time for me, but that summer in a missionary program I met Marla. I fell fast and hard. I couldn't wait to tell my teacher what had happened. When I went to him, he asked, 'I thought you had the gift of celibacy. What happened?'

"I thought about it, and then with a grin, I had to say, 'I guess it just wore off.'"

for real

Final Thoughts

- Most young people will one day get married. God's plan and rules for marriage are clearly laid out in Scripture. As we follow them, we ensure that God's blessing will be upon our family and our marriage.
- As we grow up, we need to learn to build positive, healthy, God-honoring relationships. As we do that, we invite God's blessing to be upon every area of our lives.
- The dating process can be tough and frustrating, but it can also lead to one of the greatest joys in life: meeting and marrying the love of your life.
- Celibacy for Christians is a real option to consider, especially if you have a deep desire to serve God all out. Seek God about this, as it's not something to enter into lightly.

Questions to Deepen Your Understanding

1. As you consider marriage, what are some of the important things you need to do to prepare?
2. How do you know if you're ready for marriage?

read on

Some of Mark and Jeanette's favorite books about looking at friendship, dating, and marriage:

- *The Act of Marriage,* Dr. Tim LaHaye and Beverly LaHaye, Zondervan
- *Covenant Marriage: Building Communication and Intimacy,* Gary D. Chapman, Broadman & Holman
- *8 P.R.O.M.I.S.E.S.: Really Relevant Super Significant Promises for Teenagers Who Want to Fall in Love With Jesus Forever,* Dan Davidson and Dave Davidson, New Leaf
- *Saving Your Marriage Before It Starts,* Les and Leslie Parrott, Zondervan
- *Paul on Marriage and Celibacy: The Hellenistic Background of I Corinthians 7,* Will Deming, Eerdmans
- *Preparing for Marriage: A Guide for Christian Couples,* Donald J. Luther, Augsburg Fortress

Part Four

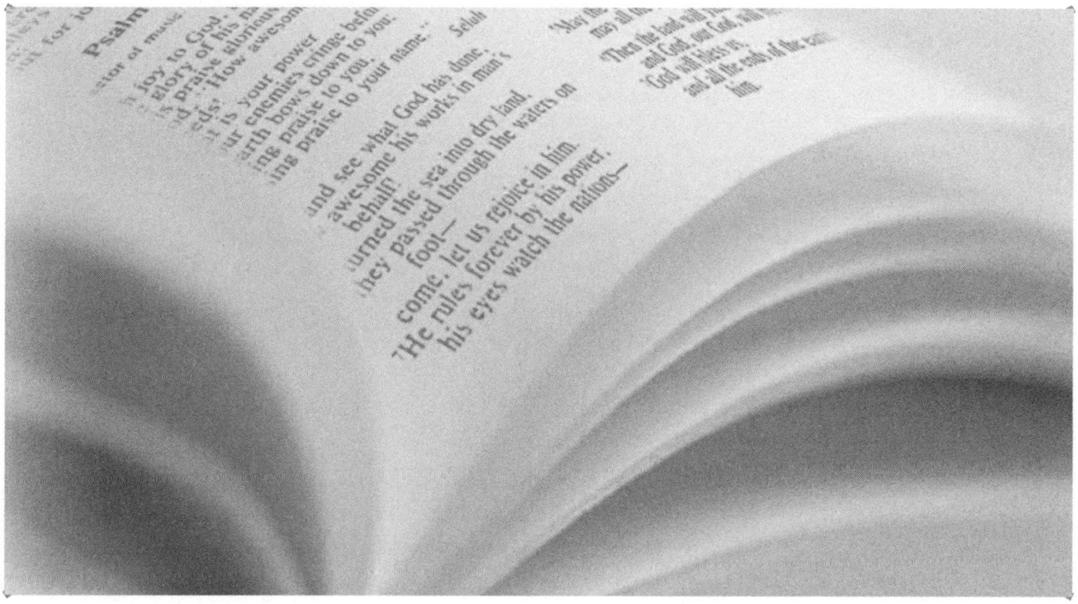

Stressed to the Max

Chapter 10: Life's Ingredients

Making Life Happy and Making It for God

What's in This Chapter

- School: "What's the Use?"
- Friendship, the Key to Long Life
- Finding the Job and Career You Always Wanted
- The Sweet Sound of Success
- Sports: Proceed at Your Own Risk

Here We Go

The different ingredients in a teen's life can make it pretty complex. It's hard to juggle all the different elements we'll talk about in this chapter. School is the first one. Oh, will it ever end? Yes, it will. Much sooner than you think. But while you're a teen, school is a huge part of your life. Making the most of it is essential to both your personal and spiritual success. We'll give you pointers for doing that in this chapter.

Friendship is another key element of living in our world. How do you build good, worthwhile, lasting friendships? What can you do to make your friendships fulfilling? Again, that's something we'll look at here.

Job, car, success—these are other aspects of life you'll be dealing with now or in the near future, if you aren't already. Amazingly, the Bible has principles that apply to each. As you study the corresponding Scriptures, you'll be amazed at how wisely God guides us in those areas.

Finally, we'll look at sports and entertainment, a couple of major parts of your world. You'll probably spend a lot of time in one or the other or both. How do you use them to contribute to your life, rather than control it? We'll be looking at what the Bible offers there too. You'll find that the Bible, though it was written thousands of years ago, speaks to us right where we are now. And you'll be happy to know that it offers wise and encouraging guidance, not just a lot of rules.

School: "What's the Use?"

> COLOSSIANS 3:22–25 ***Slaves, obey your earthly masters in everything; and do it, not only when their eye is on you and to win their favor, but with sincerity of heart and reverence for the Lord. Whatever you do, work at it with all your heart, as working for the Lord, not for men, since you***

know that you will receive an inheritance from the Lord as a reward. It is the Lord Christ you are serving. Anyone who does wrong will be repaid for his wrong, and there is no favoritism.

What does the Bible say to a teen in school? Though this passage from Colossians is addressed to slaves, it could apply to anyone who works on any level—whether it's in school, a trade, business, a profession, or any other form of work.

From this passage we learn several principles that apply to school. First, we are to obey. That means listening to and following the orders of our teachers. Sometimes that's difficult, especially when you don't particularly like the person who's giving the orders. But as they say in the military, "If you can't salute the person, salute the rank." Respect the position, if nothing else.

Most teachers honestly want to help their students. So when you obey them, you enable them to help you. Paul says you are to do this in "sincerity of heart" and out of "reverence for the Lord." Sincerity means not just on the outside, but from within. This means your heart is in what you're doing. Reverence implies respect and even fear. Remember, God has put the teachers over you. You answer to God for the way you respond to them, and they answer to God for the way they treat you!

The second thing about school is that we're to do our work there "heartily." That means with "enthusiasm," with a real desire to excel. Not many teens have that attitude. But when a teacher finds such a one, they'll do all they can to make his or her school experience positive.

The last thing is that you can be sure that God will reward you personally for your attitude, obedience, and enthusiasm in school. Think about that one. You may get rewarded in school with As and Bs and awards and athletic letters and so on. But in the end, you haven't been rewarded fully. God has something far greater for you in his kingdom, and he promises that you won't regret following him and doing his will in these matters.

You might wonder where the idea of school came from. School in the sense that we know it today was not common in biblical times. For one thing, girls never had schooling outside the home. In fact, many cultures didn't even consider girls as human, but as possessions, things you used for your own pleasure or needs. Girls were trained to do household and child-care chores, while boys were allowed to learn to read and study.

Christianity changed the concept of women being possessions. Women suddenly became the equals of men in God's eyes, and equally precious to him. What we know as **feminism** actually has its roots in Christianity, for it was the words of Jesus and the writings of Paul that set women free.

School, though, was a different idea. Normally, parents were responsible for their children's <u>education</u>—in fact, most of the schooling was done at home. Reading, writing, and math were the main exercises. In affluent homes, slaves were employed as tutors to teach the young men. In 75 BC, **Simon ben-Shetah** introduced mandatory elementary education for boys in the nation of Judah. Acts 19:9 (MSG) refers to the "school of Tyrannus," but we know no details about it.

check this out

education
Genesis 18:19;
Deuteronomy 6:7

feminism
a movement, often political, to further the cause of women

Simon ben-Shetah
ruler of Judah

How Others See It

Denise Jones

In high school, we faced problems and hassles like everyone else. But no matter what, we've tried to remain true to our commitment to Christ.[1]

Dr. James Dobson

One of the purposes of education is to prepare a young person for later life. To survive as an adult in this society, one needs to know how to work, how to get there on time, how to get along with others, how to stay with a task until it's completed, and, yes, how to submit to authority. In short, it takes a good measure of self-discipline and control to cope with the demands of modern living. Maybe one of the greatest gifts a loving teacher can contribute to an immature child, therefore, is to help her learn to sit when she feels like running, to raise her hand when she feels like talking, to be polite to her neighbor, to stand in line without smacking the kid in front, and to do English when she feels like doing soccer.[2]

Nicole C. Mullen

I wasn't cute [when I was in school]. Ladies from church would make clothes for me. Some girls on the school bus would make fun of me. "Homemade." That's what they would call me. But I remember thinking, "God still has a plan for me that these girls cannot touch."[3]

Friendship, the Key to Long Life

PROVERBS 17:17 *A friend loves at all times, and a brother is born for adversity.*

check this out

hang out
Proverbs 1:10–19; 4:10–19, 20–27

bad company
1 Corinthians 15:33

Good friends love at all times. They help each other get through tough times. They stick close. They don't give up on you or reject you when you make a mistake.

The Bible says a lot about friendship. Picking the right friends and growing in relation to them is extremely important in living a good life. Here are some of the great truths about friendship as found in the Bible:

- "A man of many companions may come to ruin, but there is a friend who sticks closer than a brother" (Proverbs 18:24). Some friends will love you so much that they will literally step in and help when your genetic brother turns away. That's a valuable person to have in your life. It's also the kind of person to look for as you build a friendship.

- "He who loves a pure heart and whose speech is gracious will have the king for his friend" (Proverbs 22:11). This verse shows how you can have an effect on others—even important people in the world, people whom you'd never guess you could influence. How? First, love a pure heart. That is, love a person who speaks the truth and acts honestly, who doesn't deceive or accuse. Second, speak graciously. Give words that build up and help people. When you have that outlook, guess what? People will trust you and love you—even kings or presidents!

- "If one falls down, his friend can help him up. But pity the man who falls and has no one to help him up!" (Ecclesiastes 4:10). Remember that all of us suffer moments of defeat or failure. All of us will get into trouble at times. It's then that you need a friend to lift you up when you can't lift yourself.

heart to heart

Proverbs is full of advice about what kinds of people to hang out with, and also who to avoid. It's up to you. You won't find helpful, supportive, loving friends in loser places. Friends make an important investment in our lives. They can make or break us, and you need to avoid bad company. Statistically, the reasons more teens get into trouble in life through drugs, drinking, violence, or other harmful activities is because they have friends who got them into it. When I was in high school, my best friend, Jon, talked me into trying marijuana, beer, and hard liquor, all in the same year. I began using these substances all through college, and it made my life sad and painful. Only becoming a Christian at the age of twenty-one saved me from a life that could have had a disastrous end.

Beware of whom you invite to be your friends. Make sure they have values similar to yours. If you don't, you can be sure that their values will soon rub off on you!

Loyal Friendship

We can show friendship in many ways. Sometimes it's a kind word that builds a relationship. Occasionally, it's an act of kindness that cements it or a special gift that makes a friendship firm and strong. One of the things that cemented my friendship with a guy in high school named Jeff Winter was Jeff's sense of humor and liveliness when hanging out with the guys. Jeff could always be counted on to help out, lend a hand, and just be there whenever someone was needed. We shared a lot of good times just hanging out in those days.

When I became a Christian, one of the first people I shared my faith with was Jeff. He tuned me out at first, but as Jeff tried to figure out what to do with his life, God spoke to him through another guy. Jeff thought back to our long talks and decided to make the commitment. Today, thirty years later, he is a pastor in a Presbyterian church, and we're still good friends. Why? Because Jeff remains a loyal friend even though he's over a thousand miles away. We've kept up with each other because we share memories, a love for Christ, and an enjoyment of each other.

How to Build Solid Christian Friendships

Finding committed Christians to build great friendships with can be difficult. Many Christians just aren't that concerned about knowing and serving Jesus. Others are there in name only.

My daughter Alisha has recently begun building some new relationships with Christian teens whom she wasn't really interested in until she became a highly committed Christian this past summer. What did she do?

First, she saw clearly how her friendships with unbelievers were dragging her down. She cites a Scripture she has memorized: "Do not love the world or anything in the world. If anyone loves the world, the love of the Father is not in him" (1 John 2:15). Alisha had a number of high school friends who got her involved in drugs, drinking, and the party scene. She was unhappy and unfulfilled and wondered what was wrong. When she started associating with Christian teens, her eyes were opened. "I really saw how being hooked up with unbelievers was messing me up," she says. "And I saw the real beauty and fun of Christian fellowship." So she began moving away from her old friends and building new relationships with these Christians.

Second, she specifically sought teens who she knew could build her up and help her in her new journey rather than those teens who were on the fringes as she had been. "It wasn't that I rejected anyone. It's just that I saw how I needed to be around people who were on fire and who really wanted to know and serve God. I discovered people who would really be like this, and now I'm building close friendships with them."

Third, she went to our church and the youth meetings with a whole new attitude. One night she came home and told me, "Dad, tonight I felt God's glory." The preacher that night had talked in a way that she said "was like God was speaking directly to me." She said, "It was awesome. I kept glancing at my friend Sarah sitting next to me, and she was as excited as I was. We were both so into it." Now Sarah and Alisha are not only close friends but accountability partners. They both want to serve God wholly and deeply.

Here are some ways to find friends like this:

- Go to church and build honest, open relationships with other teens.
- Open up about your real needs, hurts, fears, and hopes. Others will open up to you as you get honest with them.
- When you find someone who resonates with you, invite him or her to your house for a meal. Go to the mall together. Get to know your friend.
- Speak the truth to each other. Really lay it on the line. Don't hold back when you see that something is wrong.
- Be patient. If you're not connecting with anyone at the moment, talk to God about it. He will lead you if you call out to him.

Jesus and His Friends

Jesus developed close friendships with a number of people found in Scripture—Mary, Martha, and Lazarus, the disciples, especially James, John, and Peter. The amazing thing is that Jesus didn't seek out the famous, the powerful, the popular, or the cool people. He sought out friends he knew he could count on, and those people were the simple, everyday type of people you find in Scripture.

Look at the things Jesus did with those he chose to be with him:

- He looked at them in terms of potential instead of where they were at that moment (Mark 1:17).
- He specifically chose them and assured them he was their friend and not just their leader and master (John 15:15–16).
- He let them into the most intimate moments of his life (the Mount of Transfiguration, Garden of Gethsemane).
- He gave them nicknames and insights that were personal and encouraging (John 1:33–51 with Andrew, Peter, Philip, and Nathaniel).
- He spoke the truth to them, even when it hurt (Luke 22:31–34, about Peter's denials).

If Jesus were to stop by your youth group, whom do you think he'd hang with? I'd be willing to bet it would be the plain guys and girls who could be counted on to help, and not necessarily the good-lookers, the popularity seekers, and the playacting Christians. Who are you choosing for your crowd?

Finding the Job and Career You Always Wanted

> EPHESIANS 6:5–8 ***Slaves, obey your earthly masters with respect and fear, and with sincerity of heart, just as you would obey Christ. Obey them not only to win their favor when their eye is on you, but like slaves of Christ, doing the will of God from your heart. Serve wholeheartedly, as if you were serving the Lord, not men, because you know that the Lord will reward everyone for whatever good he does, whether he is slave or free.***

Do you have a dream? Is there a career you think about nearly every day, something you just want to do? Do you think God wants you to be fulfilled in your work? How can you take the steps to find the career that will give you that fulfillment and joy in life?

These are questions all teens ask themselves sooner or later. My son Gardner, who is only eight years old, has gone through a number of career ideas already in his young life. At the moment, he says he wants to be a geologist because he likes handling, identifying, and playing with rocks. However, he has at times also wanted to be a writer, a fireman, a soldier, and, for a long time, a superhero who saved people's lives. (He gave up on that one because he thought it "would be too hard without any superpowers.")

tentmaker
Acts 18:1–3

On the other hand, my daughter, Alisha, now seventeen and considering college, has fluctuated between counseling, writing, teaching, and, now, working in the criminal justice system. You'll probably find that you fluctuate among many different options as you move through high school and then college. Years ago, when I attended college, I had no idea what I wanted to do until I became a Christian. Before that, I was confused and scared. There just wasn't anything that really buzzed me. But after becoming a Christian and seeking God about it, I finally settled on the ministry. But even that changed over the years as I proved not to be a very good pastor. In time, though, God showed me he had gifted me in the area of writing, and that is what I began doing, to my great satisfaction and fulfillment.

We find in the just-quoted passage from Ephesians that Paul was addressing slaves. But the truths of the verses apply to anyone who has a regular job. Paul worked as a tentmaker to support himself in Corinth and other cities. He felt that all kinds of work were honorable in the eyes of God.

How should you treat your work in the eyes of God? This passage points out several important elements:

1. Obey your employers, and have respect for them as people.
2. Remember that you serve God first, not your employer, and that God will ultimately repay you. That means a paycheck isn't all you'll receive for the good job you did. God plans to reward you in heaven too.
3. Serve wholeheartedly. That is, put your heart into your work. If you don't like your work, ask God to help you do it the best you can anyway. In the end he will reward you.

Questions to Ask

The preceding are the fundamentals of work. Next comes the question of how to zero in on a career that you will find interesting and compelling. Here are some questions to ask as you pursue the career of your dreams:

1. What abilities or talents do you have? What gifts have others told you that you may possess and should exploit? In the parable of the talents, Jesus said, "To one he gave five talents of money, to

another two talents, and to another one talent, each according to his ability" (Matthew 25:15). While this refers to finances, the real issue is that Jesus says the differing amounts were given "according to his ability." That is, God gave each a gift on the basis of what God knew he was capable of doing. Isn't that the essence of your own abilities and talents? When I was in high school, I had a friend who was a wonderful artist. I remember marveling at his drawings and pictures. He even painted monster models so that they literally looked like miniatures of the real things. He had a great gift. And in time, he went on to become a graphic artist. Surely God gave him those abilities and wanted him to use them.

2. What grabs you? What would you really like to do that you might not now have the gifts for but that really intrigues you? Are you willing to get the training and put in the time to learn this skill? "Commit to the Lord whatever you do, and your plans will succeed" (Proverbs 16:3). I cringe when I go back and read some of my early productions from when I first started my work as a writer. But the desire was inside of me. The idea of writing something that ministered to others gripped me. I was willing to pay the price, and I learned over the years to craft my works with a level of excellence that didn't come with the initial package. In many careers it takes effort and learning to develop your skills. Rarely does one of God's gifts come fully formed.

3. If you're not sure what you might like to do, are you willing to try several different things? Remember, God will lead you: "In his heart a man plans his course, but the Lord determines his steps" (Proverbs 16:9). You may have great plans, but God will work out the path ahead of you and lead you in it if you seek him.

4. Last, are you seeking God about it? Have you asked him what he wants you to do? As Jesus said, "Seek and you will find" (Matthew 7:7). When I first became a Christian, I thought God wanted me to become a doctor. I had taken coursework in college toward that end, even though I didn't really want to be a doctor much—it just seemed like a good thing to do. I prayed about it for a while, and then one day God hit me with a call to the ministry. It jarred me at first, but as I saw him answer other prayers, I became more and more excited. Seeking God is one of the main steps toward finding the career of your dreams.

think about it

Should a Christian teen work? Certainly not at the expense of school or family or friendships. But if a teen is able to handle his course load and juggle a job, then why not? Scripture tells us only to work hard and to work to please the Lord in all we do. If we're doing that in our primary area of responsibility (i.e., school), then certainly other areas should be open to us.

Would You Lie to Keep Your Job?

Sometimes our jobs might tempt us to compromise. Maybe we'll be asked to dress in a certain way that doesn't honor Christ, or perhaps we'll be asked to lie or act unethically. What do we do?

Jerry is an example. He took a job in a manufacturing company in the customer service department. Each day he was faced with angry customers who sometimes cursed him out. He tried to do a good job, but often people weren't satisfied. One day he received a call from a manager who needed a part for a machine. Jerry checked into it and found he had the part available, and so he said that he could send the part overnight to the manager. After he got off the phone and began the process of filling the order, his boss walked into his little cubicle.

"Did you just get a call from so-and-so?" the boss demanded.

"Yeah. We have the part, and he's very happy," Jerry responded.

"The problem is that he also needs one of our people to go out there and install the part. I told him that couldn't happen today because we didn't have the part available. But the real reason is that I don't have any other people to go out there at the moment. You'll have to call him back and tell him you were wrong, we don't have the part."

"But we do," Jerry said, "and I already told him."

"Then you'll just have to lie about it," the boss said and stomped out.

Just nineteen, Jerry had never been in such a position. But he was a Christian. He knew he couldn't lie. So he prayed about it. God didn't seem to offer him an answer. He finally got up and walked slowly to his boss's office. "I don't know what to do," he explained. "I'm a Christian. I can't lie to this guy. We have the part, and I already told him. Can't we work out something else?"

His boss stared at him with anger. Then he said, "Fine. I'll handle it. But this could go in your file."

"That's okay. I guess I can deal with it."

As he walked away, a small voice inside his head whispered, "Like your boss is going to report you for refusing to lie!"

Jerry smiled and realized God had helped him work out a difficult situation.

When you find yourself in such a work situation, remember God. He can help in ways you might not think of or anticipate. It's always better to go his way than the wrong way, no matter how right that way may seem at the time.

Moreover, consider Jesus himself. He ministered to people, walked among people, and worked among people without ever compromising himself or the truth. We can also keep that goal in mind as we begin working for God in the real world.

It doesn't matter whose payroll you're on; you're working for yourself and for God. Remember Colossians 3:23–24: "Whatever you do, work at it with all your heart, as working for the Lord, not for men, since you know that you will receive an inheritance from the Lord as a reward. It is the Lord Christ you are serving." If your work has no dignity, then bring dignity to your work.

heart to heart

How Others See It

A. B. Zu Tavern

Work cannot always be agreeable: Since we shall have to learn it sooner or later, we might as well begin now to learn that we cannot always do just the things we like to do and work only when we feel like working. We shall also have to learn that we can't dodge paying attention to details.[4]

The Sweet Sound of Success

JOSHUA 1:7–9 *Be strong and very courageous. Be careful to obey all the law my servant Moses gave you; do not turn from it to the right or to the left, that you may be successful wherever you go. Do not let this Book of the Law depart from your mouth; meditate on it day and night, so that you may be careful to do everything written in it. Then you will be prosperous and successful. Have I not commanded you? Be strong and courageous. Do not be terrified; do not be discouraged, for the Lord your God will be with you wherever you go.*

check this out

long books
such as the book of Ecclesiastes

Success, even by biblical standards, is not something that comes easily to anyone. Strangely, the Bible speaks rarely of success. The passage above uses the word *success*, but you rarely find that word in the Bible. Success was in many ways a foreign concept to the biblical writers. What they sought was to please God. And pleasing God was success in their eyes. Human success didn't matter. All that mattered was doing God's will and living out the plan he had prepared.

words to live by

How do you gain real success in life? This passage from Joshua spells out a number of things God told Joshua to do just after he took over the leadership of Israel from Moses. God told him to first obey his laws in everything; second, to meditate on the Scriptures day and night; and third, to apply the Bible to the problems of life and to follow its teachings.

You might think success is a matter of vision, ambition, leadership, mental power, and a hundred other things. But God narrows it down to three basic principles:

1. Obey the Bible.
2. Meditate on the Bible.
3. Apply the Bible.

It's that simple!

How Others See It

Booker T. Washington

Success is to be measured not so much by the position that one has reached in life as by the obstacles that he has overcome while trying to succeed.[5]

think about it

Booker T. Washington's quote is right on. In the book of Revelation, in the letters to the seven churches in chapters 2 and 3, the idea of success is translated into the term *overcoming*. Overcoming disaster, problems, evil, inner temptation, and so on is what real biblical success is about.

If you want to speak about worldly success, the kind of success that involves lots of money, lots of power, lots of fame and popularity, lots of prestige, lots of stuff, then the Bible is the wrong place to look. Few people in the Bible had that kind of success, and when they did, it either went to their heads or became the subject of long books of the Bible about why it all means nothing. If you want worldly success, you'll probably have to love the world a lot, and the Bible has some hard things to say about that too. Mostly, the Bible promises things like persecution, hardship, trouble, and problems when it comes to what it'll be like living a Christian life here.

check this out

hard things
I John 2:15–16

abundant life
John 10:10

fruit of the spirit
Galatians 5:22–23

> **How Others See It**
>
> **Mike Jackson**
>
> Being able to share the Gospel with other people, and being a servant of the most-high God, that's the ultimate goal, the ultimate success in my life.[6]

If you want to talk about prospering and living abundantly in the midst of a tough world, then the Bible is for you. Jesus came to give us an abundant life, and that involves things like the fruit of the Spirit—love, joy, peace, etc. And who wouldn't exchange those realities for all the money on earth? So when you think of success in biblical terms, think of things like character, integrity, wholesomeness, decency, honor, and things like that. The Bible promises those in abundance to people who will follow Jesus without question.

To succeed in the world, you must assert yourself. To succeed in God's sight, you must deny yourself.

What Do Kids Need to Thrive?

Search Institute researchers feel they have found a miracle cure for teen ailments. They have identified forty specific "developmental assets" they feel are critical to success with teens.

Although many of these assets are missing in American teens' lives, researchers claim that students with at least twenty-six of the assets are fifteen times less likely to engage in risky behaviors. While teens need at least twenty-five of the thirty assets to do well, the average student only has sixteen. Researchers feel the key to developing more of the assets in teens' lives requires entire community involvement. If you'd like more information, check it out at *www.search-institute.org*.

Meanwhile, check your youth group kids and your own family against the following thirty prerequisites for success:

Checklist for Kids

1. I feel loved and supported in my family.
2. My parents are approachable when I want to talk about something serious.
3. I regularly have in-depth conversations with my parents.
4. Besides my parents, I have three or four other adults to approach for help.
5. I often have serious conversations with an adult who is not my parent.
6. My parents talk with me about school, sometimes help me with my schoolwork, and attend school events.
7. The atmosphere at my school is caring and encouraging.
8. My parents clearly express their standards for my behavior.
9. My parents set rules for me and enforce the consequences when I break the rules.
10. When I go out, my parents check on where I am going, who I will be with, and how long I'll be gone.
11. I can only spend a limited number of nights out of the house for recreation.
12. My friends are a good influence. They do well at school and avoid risky behaviors such as alcohol and drug use.
13. I'm in the band, orchestra, or choir, or take musical instrument lessons. I practice one or more hours each week.
14. I'm in sports or other school organizational activities at least one hour each week.
15. I'm involved in nonschool sports or other organizations at least an hour per week.
16. I attend a religious program or service at least once a month.
17. I do the best I can at school.
18. I hope to continue my education beyond high school.
19. My grades are above average.

20. I do six or more hours of homework each week.

21. I'm interested in helping others and trying to improve their lives.

22. I'm concerned about global issues such as world hunger.

23. I care about other people's feelings.

24. Because of my values, I won't have sex during my teen years.

25. I can stand up for my beliefs.

26. I'm good at making decisions.

27. I make friends easily.

28. I'm good at planning ahead.

29. I feel good about myself

30. I expect to have a happy future.

When James Garfield, twentieth president of the United States, was principal of Hiram College in Ohio, a father asked him if his son's course of study might be simplified so he could get through more quickly. Garfield replied, "Certainly. But it depends upon what you want to make of your boy. When God wants to make an oak tree, he takes a hundred years. When he wants to make a squash, he requires only two months."

Finding God's Will

As a Christian teen, I was very concerned about finding God's will for my life and having a successful life. After high school, I went to a Bible school, still uncertain about what I wanted to do with my future. I'd been writing devotional articles for a national magazine since I was fifteen years old, and I wished I could be a writer. But I was afraid I wasn't smart enough for that. And surely God wouldn't let me do that because I'd enjoy it too much, I thought.

Then one night I heard comedian Mark Lowry speak to a youth rally. He said, "Young people, God wants to make your dreams come true." Mark went on to tell us that God didn't give us dreams to frustrate us, but to use them to accomplish his glory. Mark talked about how we often think God is going to make us do something we don't want to do with our lives—like going to be missionaries in Africa ("I hate safari hats and khaki pants!" Mark revealed). But God is not a cosmic killjoy. He designed us to be able to do what we like to do with our lives. I began to think about that.

A few months later, at another teen rally, I heard now-TV-personality John Ankerberg speak. John asked, "How do you know if your dreams are your dreams for your life or God's dreams for your life?"

He explained that when we're pursuing selfish dreams, we want to get the attention, the glory, the benefit. But when we pursue God's dreams for our lives, God gets the glory. For instance, if a football player wants to be a football star so he can get attention, applause, and all the girls and money, it's probably just his dream for his life. But if a guy wants to be a great football player so he can glorify God through it, then it just may be God's plan for his life.

That night, I committed my dreams to God. I realized that the seeds of the wishes in my heart may have been planted there by him for a purpose.

Today, I make my living as a freelance writer. Every year it only gets better. I have worked on a number of significant books in the last few years, and I find my career to be even more fulfilling than ever. It's hard sometimes. I face many deadlines, and I have three young children and a husband. I try to balance everything, but there are moments when I want to scream, "What are you doing, God?" But he always comes through. It's then I bow and say, "Thanks, God."

The truth is, don't be afraid to dream. Explore your abilities, your interests, your goals, and your desires. Dream of what can happen in your life. Commit those dreams to God and don't be surprised if he makes them come true.

Sports: Proceed at Your Own Risk

1 CORINTHIANS 9:24–27 ***Do you not know that in a race all the runners run, but only one gets the prize? Run in such a way as to get the prize. Everyone who competes in the games goes into strict training. They do it to get a crown that will not last; but we do it to get a crown that will last forever. Therefore I do not run like a man running aimlessly; I do not fight like a man beating the air. No, I beat my body and make it my slave so that after I have preached to others, I myself will not be disqualified for the prize.***

Going for the Gold

What makes teens, especially guys, click? Probably more than any other aspect of our world, it's sports. Teens are into sports more than ever, and Hollywood moguls know that if they want a movie to generate a large box office, it must appeal to teens. Sports movies are usually big attractions in the teen market. Think of movies like *Friday Night Lights, Rudy, Remember the Titans,* and *The Waterboy*. Each of these received a lot of attention from the teen market.

Sports is not a foreign issue in the Bible. The sports analogy in the preceding quote from 1 Corinthians was a favorite device of Paul's. He often used athletic illustrations to make his point. But he also pointed out that bodily discipline—working out, athletics, and so on—isn't as profitable for the soul as holiness is.

athletic illustrations
2 Timothy 2:5;
Hebrews 12:1;
1 Timothy 4:8

But how do you take advantage of the values of the sports world? Paul tells us that we should:

- Run a good race. Give it your all. Make sure what you're doing is at maximum potential.
- Train well. Prepare yourself. Don't expect to win the race unless you've put yourself in winning condition.
- Don't run aimlessly. Set goals and do your best to reach them. Keep your goals in front of you.
- Don't get disqualified. Keep the rules.

Paul is speaking of running the spiritual race. But certainly in running a spiritual race, you must figure out how worldly sports and entertainment fit in. When you run well, train hard, keep your mind on your goals, and resist making fatal mistakes under the guidance of the Spirit, you will see how sports and entertainment can fit into your schedule and your life. Anything less is a cop-out.

How Should a Christian Look at Sports?

Are you obsessed with your sport? Getting in shape? Winning medals? Being the best?

Here's a good verse to consider as you analyze this issue: "For physical training is of some value, but godliness has value for all things, holding promise for both the present life and the life to come" (1 Timothy 4:8).

Did Paul mean you should not devote yourself to your game? Is he saying we should never engage in sports? Probably not. In fact, he uses a powerful illustration in 2 Timothy 2:5 to encourage his young friend Timothy to play his ministry game righteously: "If anyone competes as an athlete, he does not receive the victor's crown unless he competes according to the rules." It's certainly a good rule for playing a sport, and also for serving God.

But what's the bottom line for a Christian? Can he or she be as devoted to a sport as to the church, the youth group, Bible reading, or serving God?

Certainly God wants us to excel at what we do. Many athletes today in baseball, football, and basketball offer tremendous testimony to the world of how they look at what they do. For instance, Mike Sweeney, star hitter and first baseman for the Kansas City Royals, has found a platform speaking to Christians about his faith and how it has impacted his game. At a difficult crossroads of his baseball career, he faced a tough decision. But he came at it from a spiritual standpoint:

"I was on my knees when I saw the vivid picture of my life—it was so detailed. It was a picture of a tandem bicycle. And I was on the front seat of the bike, trying to steer where I was going. And it struck me, 'That's why I feel all this pressure, because I'm trying to steer.' I cried my eyes out that evening. It was a time of brokenness, a time when I said, 'God, I cannot do this on my own. I realize I've been trying to do this baseball thing [myself] for years.'

"When I had given my life to Christ, I thought I gave him everything. But it was apparent that night that I was trying to do baseball all on my own. That night, my prayer was, 'Lord, I don't know where I'm going to go. I don't know what spring training has in store for me, but it's time for me to get on the backseat.' My commitment was that, come Easter Sunday, I was going to get on my knees and praise him no matter what. I told God, 'I realize that with you on the front seat of the tandem bicycle, you're going to steer me wherever you want to steer me, and I'm going to get on the backseat and pedal my heart out. I'm not going to get sidetracked looking to my left and to my right; I'm going to keep my eyes focused straight ahead on you.'"

That's the kind of attitude every Christian teen should have, both on the field of play and off. If you let God lead, if you give him first place in your life, he will enable you to use your talents and gifts in ways that will change you and your world. He may tell you, "I want you to play baseball well. I want you to go all the way." Or he may say, "The sport is nice, and you're good at it. But I have other plans."

No one can tell you God doesn't want you to play a sport. You've just got to keep it in perspective.

How Do I Know When Sports Have Gotten Out of Control for Me?

Paul told the Corinthians, "'Everything is permissible for me'—but not everything is beneficial. 'Everything is permissible for me'—but I will not be mastered by anything" (1 Corinthians 6:12). What did Paul mean? In God's world, you as a Christian have the right and privilege to make any choice you want in any matter, so long as it doesn't violate God's clear commands and it's also beneficial. Ask, does your sports involvement benefit you spiritually, drawing you closer to God? Does it help you grow in love for your family and your friends? Are you using it for God's glory? If so, then it's beneficial. But what if your involvement in a sport makes you offensive and disagreeable when you lose? What if it causes you to take risks and do things you know God wouldn't want you to do? If that's the case, then it's no longer beneficial, and you may need to step back and take a hard look at how your involvement in sports is affecting your life.

Paul says he "will not be mastered by anything." That means sports can get you "out of control" sometimes. It can dominate your thoughts and actions. It can become so obsessive that you forget about God, church, friends, and others. If that's what is happening to you, then it has mastered you. The only master you should want in your life is Jesus himself. Don't let something like sports become your whole life.

The Rock Climb

I'm not a crazy sports guy. I don't watch sports much on television. In high school, I played tennis on the varsity. I also wrestled and participated in gymnastics. But I was never really great at any of it. I have found one sport, though, that scares me to death.

Ever go rock climbing? Now there's a sport that is tough! Scaling a cliff, even if there are plenty of handholds and footholds, scares the wits out of me.

Fortunately, I have always gone rock climbing with people who know how to do it. They tie us in on something called a belaying line (how I love the technical terms—makes me feel like a real Everest-killer), and then as we climb, some very alert (I mean extremely alert) person at the top reins in the line so that if you slip and fall, you only fall a few feet.

That's the way it's supposed to work with us novices anyway. Of course, one guy ended up as a pancake on the pavement, but let's not talk about him right now.

The last time I went rock climbing was a few years ago, but I still get shivers just picturing the scene in my head. Somehow, scaling a cliff with nothing to hold on to but those little nooks and crannies in the rock seems a bit bonkers, out-of-your-mind, and crazy, don't you think? But then every youth group has to do it sooner or later—maybe it'll impress the girls.

On one climb, I remember coming up against a jutting of rock where I had to hang out over dead air a moment to get around it. I was up there, hanging on to a little lip of rock about a quarter of an inch wide, and people below me yelled:

"You can do it!"

"Hang in there, it's only a little farther!"

"Just think, if you die right here, we have the rocks to cover your body with!" (He was the local youth group comedian.)

"Don't worry, we won't let you get hurt."

Right, as long as the belaying guy is still paying attention, I should be okay, I thought. Oh, did I say guy? You pictured someone about two hundred pounds, a linebacker on the football team, right? No, my guy was a shrimpy little girl of fourteen who weighed less than eighty pounds. They wanted her to try belaying because she needed to learn to be tough!

I huffed with exhaustion as I tried to reach the next handhold, my legs dangling in space. I didn't want to fall. After all, I was one of the leaders in the youth group. We had been taught this was how you built real fellowship. Man, and I thought all you needed was cookies and fruit punch.

Desperately, I lunged to get a fingerhold only inches out of reach.

And that was it! I fell—a few feet—then dangled from the belaying line like a rag doll. The seventy-eight-pound belaying wonder had come through!

"Take a rest and try it again," a leader told me.

"Yeah," I said, "in about ten years."

---

redeem the time
Ephesians 5:15–17

But I did try it again that day, and I want you to know that I beat that mountain. "Brothers, I do not consider myself yet to have taken hold of it. But one thing I do: Forgetting what is behind and straining toward what is ahead, I press on toward the goal to win the prize for which God has called me heavenward in Christ Jesus" (Philippians 3:13–14).

Sticking with the Christian life is a lot like rock climbing. You suffer falls, mistakes, and slipups. But you keep trying. At other moments you're Spider-Man climbing up the edge of a building.

Walking with Christ and being a Christian calls for a simple game plan: Hang in there until you get to the top. You struggle for a handhold—maybe it's memorizing some new Scripture, or having a quiet time a few times a week. You dig in your fingers and pull up. Soon you're going for another handhold—getting victory over that temper, or keeping pure in your relationship with a girl or guy. As you climb up the rock face, sometimes you fall. But the belaying line holds you. You don't get hurt. You just start in again where you are and get back into the climb.

What does Paul say he does here in Philippians? Press on. Keep taking those steps. Keep finding those handholds. The Christian life is a climb up a cliff. So don't give up. Even when you fall, pull up again and keep on going. One day you will face Jesus and he will say, "Well done, good and faithful servant."

How Others See It

Bryan Diemer

God has given me a talent to run, which is wonderful. But more importantly he's given me a platform to spread his word. Being involved in sports gives me many great opportunities to witness.[7]

Scripture is not against sports at all; rather, it tells us to learn to redeem the time and make the most of the time we have for the kingdom of God. In Matthew 6:33, Jesus spelled out our top priority. It's not having fun. It's not being number one. But this is what he says: "But seek first [God's] kingdom and his righteousness, and all these things will be given to you as well."

What You Can Do

Just imagine what would happen in sports events if every Christian involved made Christ's teachings and guidance his priority. You might establish these principles:

- Respect your game, yourself, and those you're matched against.
- Commit yourself to doing your best first; second, be loyal to the team; and last, pay attention to the number of points your team is scoring.
- Make it a priority simply to enjoy the contest, whoever wins.
- Love those you're playing with and against, as well as the fans, coaches, and God.

With such guidelines in place, if Christians practiced them, it would be nothing less than a revolution!

However you come at the sports option, remember that you will answer to Christ for your use of time and life and resources while on earth. God does not begrudge us a little fun. But when it becomes an obsession, when you will do anything to win, even cheat, when you eat and sleep and think and breathe the pastime that beguiles you, then you have lost control. That's a dangerous spot to be in. But keep it in balance, enjoy it, and let God always have first place to say, "Stop!" if necessary, and you will always succeed.

Just Entertain Me!

> EPHESIANS 5:3–4 ***But among you there must not be even a hint of sexual immorality, or of any kind of impurity, or of greed, because these are improper for God's holy people. Nor should there be obscenity, foolish talk or coarse joking, which are out of place, but rather thanksgiving.***

The entertainment world of today is one of the biggest markets for teen dollars and sense. The movie industry caters specifically to the teen market, because they're the ones who go to the most movies. Often, teens will attend a movie they like over and over, running up the take. Producers love it, and every month several movies come out that are specifically targeted to you as a teen.

Then there's the Internet and the many other resources that have come to the forefront in the last decade. With the Internet, we find teens on Web sites like MySpace.com where they talk to teens all over the world. Many temptations have come with this: pornography, gambling, and online games and videos. There are many dangers for the average teen. Let's look at some of them and do some evaluation.

First, go back and reread those verses from Ephesians. Paul specifically cites a number of habits, attitudes, and actions to avoid. What are they?

- ***Immorality***. That's any kind of sexual involvement, either spiritual or physical, that is out of bounds for Christians. Pornography is certainly immoral from a Christian standpoint. So is phone sex and any other kind of sex, except sexual relations in the confines of marriage. The world may say it's okay and to "come on down—we're having fun," but from God's point of view, it's a satanic trap.

- ***Impurity***. Again, this is anything that incites disgusting, sexual, hateful, or racist thoughts. Going to a political Web site where your friends rail against minorities or talk about intimacies you know you should keep to yourself can destroy your relationship with Jesus.

- ***Greed***. Anything that makes you want more, more, more is greed, whether it's money, possessions, food, or whatever. Watch out there; Satan is tempting.

- ***Obscene speech***. Should you watch movies with a lot of filthy talk in them? It's up to you. But it's probably not healthy and can lead you to use that kind of talk in your normal life.

- ***Foolish talk***. That pertains to gossip and inane discussions. Sure, some fun is okay. Cracking a joke here and there, playing a role for effect, we all do that at times. But when you're spending hours on the phone talking about nothing, maybe you need to have a heart-to-heart talk with God about it.

- ***Coarse joking***. Dirty, sexual, racist, and vulgar jokes and the like are things that should not find a way to our tongues. Take care when watching sitcoms or dramas on television and especially cable that you don't emulate their offensive and belittling humor.

You have a lot of freedom to explore the Internet and other activities to your heart's content. There are many good things and great sites on it that are worth visiting over and over. But when you expose your mind to the garbage you find in many of those places, you're giving the devil an opportunity to distract you from what really matters. A good truth is found in 2 Corinthians 10:5: "We demolish arguments and every pretension that sets itself up against the knowledge of God, and we take captive every thought to make it obedient to Christ." Every thought? How is that possible? It is when you work at it. God wants you to have a clean mind, free from the gutter-level material filling the airwaves today. If you let your mind be filled with sewage, your heart will soon be little more than a septic tank of gunk that takes away your joy, peace, and love for others.

How Can You Choose Edifying Entertainment?

heart to heart

How can a young Christian like you find entertainment that is not only worth your money and time, but will draw you nearer to Jesus and make you fall more in love with him every day? It's not easy, and you're going to have to say no to most of what's out there. But here are several resources to use and actions to take:

- Ask your Christian friends about resources that they have found helpful and search them out.
- Read reviews of movies before you see them. There are many good reviews at *christianitytoday.com*, *pluggedinonline.com*, and *christian answers.com*.
- Refuse to watch programs on network or cable television that you know are not edifying because of the coarse joking, sexual innuendo, and so on. Sure, they may be funny. But not everything that's funny is healthy.
- Read good books and don't spend a lot of time in gossipy phone calling. Spend time in the Bible every day too.
- Don't give sexually oriented material a second of your time. Just say no.

What If I'm Addicted?

It's easy to get involved with Web sites and materials that will soon have you going back day after day, hour after hour. Whether it's playing games online, watching pornography, playing Dungeons and Dragons, or pursuing one of many other enticements out there, some Christian teens will become seriously caught and influenced by those resources. What if this is happening to you or a friend?

1. Get help from a parent, a friend, a counselor, a pastor. Many churches have recovery groups that will give you support and insight into how to overcome your addiction.
2. Believe God wants you out of this addiction and that he can help you on the inside. Jesus said, "Apart from me you can do nothing" (John 15:5) and "The Spirit in you is far stronger than anything in the world" (1 John 4:4 MSG). God can give you the power to overcome this problem from the inside out, where you really need the help.
3. If you fall, get up, decide not to fall again, and go on. And if you fall again, remember this truth from Psalm 37:23–24: "If the Lord delights in a man's way, he makes his steps firm; though he stumble, he will not fall, for the Lord upholds him with his hand." God is with you, right now, holding your hand to prevent you from "falling headlong," as another translation says it. Trust him, and he will empower you.
4. Keep fighting, keep with the plan, don't give up. James said, "Resist the devil, and he will flee from you. Come near to God and he will come near to you" (James 4:7–8). God holds all the cards. The devil is just a paper tiger. Don't let him bamboozle you into thinking he can run your life no matter what you do.

Final Thoughts

- Friendship is an important facet of growing up. And selecting the right kinds of friends is crucial. God shows us the way, especially in the book of Proverbs, about how to select friends who will last and who will be loyal to the end.
- Whatever kind of work we do, Scripture tells us to do it "heartily," as if we were working directly for the Lord. Why? Because we are. And one day, he promises to give us our real wages for doing a great job.
- Everyone longs for success, but spiritual success is different from worldly success, which involves wealth, prestige, power, and popularity. God's kind of success means that we have pleased him and him alone.
- Sports and entertainment are an important part of life, but we must beware of making them too big a part of our lives. They have their place, but keep them in it and all will be well.

Questions to Deepen Your Understanding

1. What are some of the most important things to remember about building friendships?
2. How should we go about selecting our friends?
3. What are your thoughts about sports? Where do you stand with them?
4. What does the Bible say about sports and physical fitness?

read on

Some of Mark and Jeanette's favorite books about making life happy and making it for God:

- *Could Someone Wake Me Up Before I Drool on the Desk?* Kevin Johnson, Bethany
- *Fillin' Up,* Mark Littleton, Multnomah
- *God's Little Instruction Book for Teens,* Honor Books Staff, Honor Books
- *Guys and a Whole Lot More: Advice for Teen Girls on Almost Everything!* Susie Shellenberger, Revell
- *The Real Deal: A Spiritual Guide for Black Teen Girls,* Billy Montgomery, Cook, Judson
- *Right From Wrong,* Josh McDowell and Bob Hostetler, Word
- *Slam Dunk,* Dave Brannon, Moody Press
- *Sports Heroes Series,* Mark Littleton, Zondervan

Chapter 11: Tougher Issues

Asking Tough Questions and Dealing With Tough Issues

What's in This Chapter

- Loving Your Enemies
- Time: Get Control or Be Controlled!
- In the Heart
- Worth the Pain

Here We Go

Tough issues, tough answers. That's what this chapter is about. Many issues in life do not have easy answers. Sometimes the Bible offers simple answers to hard questions. Sometimes it offers rather hard answers to simple questions. That's why we have the Bible. It helps us come to grips with tough issues in a tough-minded, spirit-footed way. Take this chapter with a grain of salt—the salt of God's Word. Let it sink into your spiritual palate and discover that some of these answers make sense.

Loving Your Enemies

> MATTHEW 5:43–48 ***You have heard that it was said, "Love your neighbor and hate your enemy." But I tell you: Love your enemies and pray for those who persecute you, that you may be sons of your Father in heaven. He causes his sun to rise on the evil and the good, and sends rain on the righteous and the unrighteous. If you love those who love you, what reward will you get? Are not even the tax collectors doing that? And if you greet only your brothers, what are you doing more than others? Do not even pagans do that? Be perfect, therefore, as your heavenly Father is perfect.***

The most personal place of our lives is our self, our personality, our in-the-world being. This is where we operate, where we draw lines and step over lines and live along lines. God wants us to be thinking people. He doesn't want us to simply accept what he says and not understand the reasoning behind it. God wants us to have minds full of faith and wisdom. That calls for a double-pronged attack at problems. It takes both faith—acceptance of what God says no matter what—and wisdom—skill for making it work in real life. When you combine those two abilities, you have a strong working, driving wheel for your life.

This passage shows Jesus' view of hatred and enemies. His words radically altered the thinking of people the world over because no one had ever heard of loving your enemies before. Jews based their idea of revenge on three similar passages in the Old Testament, the first being, "If men who are fighting hit a pregnant woman and she gives birth prematurely but there is no serious injury, the offender must be fined whatever the woman's husband demands and the court allows. But if there is serious injury, you are to take life for life, eye for eye, tooth for tooth, hand for hand, foot for foot, burn for burn, wound for wound, bruise for bruise" (Exodus 21:22–25).

check this out

revenge
Exodus 21:22–25;
Leviticus 24:19–20;
Deuteronomy 19:21;
Romans 12:17–2

The original intent of this passage was simply justice in criminal cases. It was not a command to take revenge.

heart to heart

Jesus corrected the idea of revenge in Matthew 5 by telling his listeners to love their enemies. This was a wholly new idea. What did it call for? To love them like the Golden Rule says: "Do unto others as you would have them do unto you" (see Matthew 7:12; Luke 6:31). Pray for them as you would pray for yourself or your own family. In another passage, Paul says we are to let God have revenge and not take it ourselves. Hatred turns your insides out. When you allow yourself to hate, you harm yourself far more than the one you hate, unless your hatred moves you to evil action. In which case, the judgment of God will tell on you. And yet how easy it is to harbor hostility toward others. The guy who stole your girlfriend. The girl who made the cheerleading squad when you didn't. The fellow who made first string ahead of you. The rival in the orchestra who has first chair.

Hatred is a cancer that can eat you up. You've got to let it go. But how?

How Others See It

Henry Wadsworth Longfellow

If we could read the secret history of our enemies, we should find in each man's life sorrow and suffering enough to disarm all hostility.[1]

Harry Emerson Fosdick

Hating people is like burning down your own home to get rid of a rat.[2]

George William Russell

If we allow ourselves to hate, that is to insure our spiritual defeat and our likeness to what we hate.[3]

One way to overcome hatred for someone in your life is to get to know the person on a deeper level. Pray for them—not that God will punish them, but that God will bless them. You cannot pray for someone like that for long and continue to hate them. Jesus is adamant. You cannot hate your enemies, for even God doesn't hate his enemies, but he blesses them the same way he blesses the righteous. If God, who has more reason to hate people who use his name in vain and commit all kinds of evil acts, loves them, how much more should we?

Blowing Hatred Out of Your Heart

> **Galatians 6:9–10** ***Let us not become weary in doing good, for at the proper time we will reap a harvest if we do not give up. Therefore, as we have opportunity, let us do good to all people, especially to those who belong to the family of believers.***

A good way to overcome hatred is to do good. Paul wrote these words to the Galatians when some of them were corrupted by old Jewish influences, especially in the area of the Jewish law. Some were possibly applying the idea of revenge to even other Christians. Paul told them to do something radical: Do not become weary in doing good. It's so easy to lose heart when someone fights you, puts you down, even spreads rumors about you. But if you do good to them, Paul assures us that God will let you "reap a harvest," meaning God's blessing will come to you in a special way. Every time you have an opportunity, Paul says, take that time to do good. To whom? To all—enemies included—and especially to other Christians.

How do you get rid of hatred according to Jesus and the Scriptures?

1. Pray for the one who has hurt you, as Jesus said.
2. Forgive them. Even if they will not listen to you or think they've done something wrong, you can still forgive them, before God and the world.
3. Do good to them in return. This is the thought of Paul in Romans 12:17–21 and the passage above. When we do good, we deflect the hostility of hatred and turn it toward healing. It may leave a scar, but so did the nails in Jesus' palms and the spear in his side. The scars remain. They are badges of God's love and care.

blesses them
I Peter 3:8–22; 4:12–19

How Others See It

Ann Landers

Hate is like acid. It can damage the vessel in which it is stored as well as destroy the object on which it is poured.[4]

A Prayer on a Sunken Ship

Emmett Dedmon, a World War II veteran, had always wanted to visit the Pearl Harbor Memorial. He had been stationed on the battleship Arizona *when the Japanese bombed Pearl Harbor. He had escaped but lost many friends on that ship. As he and his family arrived to see the memorial in Honolulu, he was aghast to see two tour buses of Japanese visitors arrive to see the memorial at the same time. Bitter waves of anger welled up inside him as he watched the Japanese walking up the ramp and standing around the large hollow in the floor that looked over the ship containing the bodies of over a thousand men. As Emmett looked at the foreigners, he thought,* This was supposed to be my day. This was my country these men died for. And it was because of their country that these men died!

But as he stared at the Japanese, suddenly all of them fell to their knees and clasped their hands in prayer. What they prayed Emmett would never know. Perhaps the same thing he and his family prayed as they stood in the same room. Moments later they boarded a launch for the trip back to shore. Everyone was silent. But Emmett writes, "The sun seemed to shine more brightly than ever on a morning I shall always remember."[5]

What About Racism?

Racism is a serious problem in our world. Many groups—Hispanics, whites, African Americans, Asians, Middle Easterners—harbor consistent and deep hatred for one another. Sometimes this dates back to centuries ago when wrongs were done by one group or another. Racism is often based on how you were raised, what your parents thought and said, and what you were taught by friends and others around you. Many cities today are plagued by crimes committed by gangs created to fight against other races in their community. What does the Bible say about racism?

First, Paul told us that in God's eyes, there is no difference between one person and another. He wrote to the Galatians, "There is neither Jew nor

Greek, slave nor free, male nor female, for you are all one in Christ Jesus" (Galatians 3:28). Paul wrote to people who were extremely racist in their outlook. Jews hated Gentiles. Greeks despised Romans. Arabs disliked Jews. But Paul was saying that in God's kingdom, there are no differences. All are equal in the eyes of God—equal citizens, equally loved, equal in the gifts of salvation. There is no particular way for one group and a different way for the other. In God's world, all people are the same in terms of value.

Second, bigotry and hatred for an enemy were specifically condemned by Jesus. He said in the Sermon on the Mount, "You have heard that it was said, 'Love your neighbor and hate your enemy.' But I tell you: Love your enemies and pray for those who persecute you, that you may be sons of your Father in heaven" (Matthew 5:43–45). Clearly, Christians cannot hate or disrespect a person because of the color of his skin, or even because of a person's being a traditional enemy. You are not only to pray for such people, but you are also to love them.

Third, be a peacemaker. Jesus said in Matthew 5:9: "Blessed are the peacemakers, for they will be called sons of God." Peacemaking is a difficult task in today's fractured world. It takes tact, compassion, integrity, and, above all, perseverance. In some cases, no matter how hard you try, people will not make peace with one another, as you can see in the Arab-Israeli conflict even today. But sometimes, when you work at it, you can help a few or more people come together, talk, and work out their differences. This is something Martin Luther King Jr. worked toward in the 1960s to establish peace between blacks and whites. We have seen it in many smaller situations in efforts that presidents and diplomats have made with the Arabs and the Israelis, with the Protestants and the Catholics in Northern Ireland, and in many other places in the world. Truly, such people are sons of God. Why? Because what was the mission of the Son of God himself? To make peace between mankind and God. He accomplished that by dying on the cross. You as a peacemaker will not have to go that far, but it will be costly. Some people will hate and reject you because of such efforts. Just remember that God is on your side and will guide you through whatever tangle you find yourself facing.

Fourth, the primary truth of Scripture, "Love your neighbor as yourself," certainly applies to everyone in your community and the world around you. Hatred and prejudice were rife in Jesus' world. One of the reasons some people hated him so much was because he preached this message of love and acceptance. You will probably find some people despising you for such a stand, but do not fear. God is with you and will empower you.

What About Cliques?

It is perfectly normal for you to hang out with your friends. It's also natural to gravitate to those who have similar interests and beliefs. However, sometimes cliques become a means to manipulate and control others, reject outsiders, and make life miserable for anyone who can't break into the clique. How should a Christian look at this tough issue?

The Bible does not refer to anything about cliques, but it does tell us repeatedly to reach out to others, embrace strangers and outsiders, and to be kind and loving with everyone we cross paths with. Once again, love is the Christian principle. Love everyone, be a peacemaker, show compassion and kindness, and don't give up. As Proverbs 11:30 says, "The fruit of the righteous is a tree of life, and he who wins souls is wise." While winning souls might refer to converting people religiously, it can also refer to winning over adversaries to a new point of view and willingness to get along.

Decision in a Bus Terminal

God sometimes speaks to us in the strangest places and circumstances. One such experience happened to me (Mark) in a bus station after a convicting conversation in a car where my friends had a stash of drugs.

I sat alone in the bus terminal, fuming. I had gotten a ride from college to home, but on the way I discovered the car had drugs in it. I knew I had to get out. So I did. The people in the car let me out in the middle of nowhere, and after retrieving my bags, I turned around, then stuck out my thumb. Guess who was in the next car on the road: a policeman. I knew then this was going to be a very bad day.

The officer stopped and told me to hop in. "I'm going to give you a ticket for hitchhiking and take you to the bus station. Hitchhiking is illegal. Don't you know that?"

I knew I couldn't lie. I had recently become a Christian. "Uh, I think I knew that."

"Why did you get out of that car between towns anyway? Was there a problem?" I didn't want to get my friends in trouble either. I said, "Difference of opinion about some things. It didn't work out."

"Yeah, we cops know about them."

Hmm. What was I supposed to say about that?

The officer just cruised along, and we talked about the dangers of hitchhiking, then sports. I told him I had recently become a Christian and explained how it had changed my life. He listened with interest but said little. When we reached the bus station, he suddenly said, "I decided not to give you the ticket. But get a bus, okay?"

I nodded. "I will. Thanks."

I walked inside and found out I'd have to wait two hours until the bus to Philadelphia arrived. It would cost twelve dollars. I didn't have much money, and my earlier ride was only five dollars. I felt cheated. Why did God have to let these things happen? I was feeling real hatred at that moment—for the guys whose car I had been in, for the policeman, and even a bit toward God. The world was full of jerks! I waited impatiently, feeling angrier and angrier. As I sat there fighting the Spirit in my heart, three students walked in with Bibles in their hands. They began passing out tracts. I figured they were Mormons, Christians, or atheists with a sadistic streak. Anyway, I decided I didn't need to hear something like, "Don't you know God has a wonderful plan for your life?" Yeah, and I've just seen it happen!

But the Spirit had other ideas. "Go to them," he seemed to be saying. "Just tell them you're a Christian."

No way. I was mad.

The Spirit finally won. I got up, and as if I were turning myself in after a crime spree, I said, "Yeah, I'm one too."

With excitement they questioned me about how I became a Christian and what I was doing. They were students at a local Bible college. In fact, one of them said his parents were driving to a town near Philadelphia the next day. Would I like to stay the night, get a good meal, have some fellowship, and meet a lot of Christians?

I was amazed, but I bit and had a great weekend. (It only cost me three dollars to get home in the end!)

That experience taught me a valuable lesson: Trust the Lord in difficult times, even when I'd rather sit and fume and hate. Anyone can trust him when things are going great—that's easy. But when you're in the middle of a terrible, horrible, very bad, no good day and you can say, "Lord, I trust you anyway!" that's when you're really cruising as a Christian.

check this out

deal with lying
Proverbs 6:20–24

What circumstances have invaded your life lately that have made you angry, even stirred up hatred inside you? Take a look at them and think about trust. What God wants you to do at this moment is trust him anyway. Even if it looks bad. Even if it continues to look bad. That's just our mind talking. Our heart tells us, "God can never make anything good come out of this." He'll amaze you if you let him.

Those Sweet Little Lies

> EPHESIANS 4:25–27 ***Therefore each of you must put off falsehood and speak truthfully to his neighbor, for we are all members of one body. "In your anger do not sin": Do not let the sun go down while you are still angry, and do not give the devil a foothold.***

Paul wrote these words in Ephesians to Greeks who were probably well versed in the art of lying. It was as much a part of their culture as ours. Scripture speaks to the problem of lying with one basic principle: "Put off falsehood and speak truthfully." When? In every situation. Paul was not speaking about social conventions (like telling your girlfriend she looks beautiful even if she isn't Cindy Crawford) or simple situations where the blunt truth might hurt ("Hey, where did you get that haircut—at the zoo?"). He meant that we should speak truth in situations where truth was required—answering honestly to questions that involve who did what (Mom: "Who forgot to clean out the dishwasher tonight?")—and owning up to the truth when you've done something wrong (Dad: "All right, who put the dent in the fender?").

How is your truth-telling meter doing today? Any white lies? Any black lies? Any big, little, or in-between lies? It's not easy to avoid, but once you stop lying, you begin to enjoy something many people have never experienced: a clear conscience.

An epidemic of lying is happening in our world. "Everyone lies," some say, and it's almost true. Recent studies show that more Americans feel comfortable with lying than ever. In fact, 45 percent of born-again teens believe lying is sometimes necessary, compared to 71 percent of non-born-again teens.[6]

How do you deal with lying in your life? How do you overcome the impulse to lie when you're in a tight spot, or when you want to come off as important, or when you simply want to get out of a situation? The passage above is helpful. Simply remember that we are "members" of one another. Christians are like a body. What body, if the thumb was hit by a hammer, would lie to itself and say, "The hammer didn't really hurt"? We belong to each other. That's why lying is so horrible to God. He hates lying because it destroys the body of Christ. This is to say nothing of the fact that God's first major statement against lying comes in the Ten Commandments.

Ten Commandments
Exodus 20:16

> **How Others See It**
>
> **Abraham Lincoln**
>
> No man has a good enough memory to be a successful liar.[7]

The problem with lying, as Abraham Lincoln points out, is that when you lie, you have to remember whom you spoke to, what you told them, when, and where. The next time you see them, you have to remember the whole scenario, and if they tell someone else, you may have to lie again to cover your tracks. Mark Twain said, "One of the striking differences between a cat and a lie is a cat only has nine lives."

Why do people lie? Sometimes people lie to protect someone else's feelings. Others lie to make themselves look better. Sometimes teens lie, like to their parents, to stay out of trouble. But actually, when you tell the truth, getting along with the world is much easier.

"Lying hurts people," an eighteen-year-old said. "When people find out, they are disappointed you didn't think you were a close enough friend or family member to tell them the truth."

Did Jesus ever lie? He was sinless, which we know from numerous passages, so he could never have told a lie. In fact, one of the things about Jesus that troubled his enemies was that he told them the truth—about himself, about them, about God, and about the world. Certainly, Jesus did not go around bluntly clubbing people with the truth—"You're an ugly toad compared to so and so." "I know everything about you and I'm going to start listing all your sins right now!" No, Jesus was gentle, kind, loving, but he also spoke sober truth. It's when we combine the personable qualities of love and goodness with truth and integrity that we have a real impact on the world, just like Jesus did.

Drowning in a Sea of Lies

EXODUS 20:16 *You shall not give false testimony against your neighbor.*

This is number nine of the Ten Commandments, given on Mount Sinai to Moses. The Ten Commandments lay out ten of the primary rules people can use to get along. Following them would ensure the nation lived in harmony. God gave the Ten Commandments as the primary statements of how to help people get along and live in peace. They're simple, succinct, and direct. Anyone who memorizes them and keeps them will go a long way toward living a Christian life.

The ninth commandment said we are not to "give false testimony." This was a legal expression for use in court. When you appeared to give testimony about someone's actions or person, you were never to lie or perjure yourself. But how often do we see people willing to lie not only on the street but also in the courtroom, where the penalties are much greater? This commandment, though, was not just meant for court situations; it was meant for any normal situation where you are "telling a story" or speaking the truth about someone. If people followed this commandment, we would not have:

- Lies about people spread around viciously
- The spreading of false rumors
- Exaggeration and gossip
- Politicians and government people deceiving the public
- Any kind of public or private lying

Imagine such a world. How do you stop lying? Scripture is clear on the basic process:

1. Admit to God your problem. (1 John 1:9)
2. Ask him for help and wisdom in overcoming it. (James 1:5–6)
3. Determine to tell the truth always. (Ephesians 4:25–26)
4. When you have lied, go back and make it right as soon as possible. (Proverbs 28:13)

How Others See It

Charles R. Swindoll

When we feel we must lie to someone who trusts us and whom we love, we are trapped in what psychologists call a "double-bind."

Whatever we do, we lose. That is what an unfaithful husband, for example,

> faces when he returns home to a wife he genuinely loves. He wants to restore his sense of closeness with her, but he knows he cannot tell her what he has done. So he lies. Lying becomes a habit.
>
> The lies are often unconscious and unspoken and therefore not marked by pain. This is the ultimate act of self-deception. Instead of resolving conflict, it perpetuates it; the deluded person lives a lie. He is sick and does not feel the fever.[8]

stealing
Exodus 20:15;
Proverbs 6:30; 30:9

Five-Finger Discount: Stealing

EPHESIANS 4:28 ***He who has been stealing must steal no longer, but must work, doing something useful with his own hands, that he may have something to share with those in need.***

Paul told the Ephesians to stop stealing, which assumes he knew they were doing so. The Ten Commandments expressly condemn stealing. Many other passages speak to the issue, especially in Proverbs. Stealing is simply to take what doesn't belong to you. Taking pens from school is stealing in God's eyes as much as robbing a bank. Pilfering from the Youth Fund is stealing as much as using a computer to hack into a company's accounts and transfer funds to your account. The Bible is clear that even when a man is poor and out of work and his family is starving, there is no reason to steal.

The worst kind of stealing, though, is the kind that is directly against God. Stealing his worship. Stealing his place in the world. Stealing his place in your heart. Such stealing is evil because it steals from the One who is so willing to give. It shows doubt of his power to provide even in hard circumstances. God is obligated to his people to provide, and truly there are few reports in the world where Christians are starving or going hungry. Yes, many heathen and pagan peoples are suffering, but there is a truth in Scripture that God keeps. It's found in Psalm 37:25: "I was young and now I am old, yet I have never seen the righteous forsaken or their children begging bread." Those who reject Christ are on their own, and often their own religions prevent their people from helping them (such as in Hinduism, where the law of karma says you are only getting in this life what you sowed in the last). But as a faith, Christians have always led the way in bringing justice, freedom, and help to those in need.

The sad truth is that more and more teens and adults are willing to lie, cheat, or steal to get what they want. According to a report by the Josephson Institute of Ethics:

- Thirty-seven percent of high schoolers say they stole from a store in the past twelve months.
- Sixty-five percent have cheated on an exam, an increase of 4 percent.
- Seventeen percent of college students say they stole.
- Twenty-four percent say they'd lie to get or keep a job.[9]

God Said It, We Believe It, That Settles It!

Exodus 20:15 *You shall not steal.*

Like lying, stealing was also prohibited by the Ten Commandments. God forbade stealing from anyone, not just people in Israel but those outside as well. Over and over God warned the Israelites not to resort to wrong means for right ends.

Why did God consider stealing such a serious offense? For one thing, stealing hurts the person you stole from, whether you took a small thing or a large thing. The commandment was not only to prevent problems, but to prevent pain. Another reason not to steal is because it leads to all kinds of other corruption. When you steal, you have to lie about how you got what you stole. You may also use what you stole for other crimes. And you may involve others in your stealing. Today, one of the biggest problems in the United States is teens in gangs who rob stores at gunpoint and commit other crimes. Stealing is just the beginning of many other kinds of sin.

What would Jesus advise us to do if we have stolen something? Jesus spoke directly to the issue in several places. One is an interesting example about paying taxes. Many people don't like paying taxes. For a teen, income taxes and sales taxes can take a big bite out of his or her income. Jesus talks on one occasion to Peter about taxes, asking if princes have to pay the king taxes. No, Jesus says, for that reason we don't have to pay taxes to God because we're his children. On the other hand, Jesus reminds Peter that others may not understand this principle, so he says, "But so that we may not offend them, go to the lake and throw out your line. Take the first fish you catch; open its mouth and you will find a four-drachma coin. Take it and give it to them for my tax and yours" (Matthew 17:27). Jesus provided a way for Peter to pay the tax so he wouldn't offend or get into trouble with the authorities.

This principle is found all through Scripture: When you have a problem, go to God and he will help you solve it with integrity and love. It's when we try to solve such problems on our own that we get into trouble.

What should you do if you have stolen something? Take it back, or if it's gone, repay the person you stole from. Confess to them your crime and don't hesitate to make it right. The theft will be on your conscience until you do. If your conscience doesn't warn you, then you are probably stealing a lot and **hardening** your conscience, which is dangerous to do.

How do you stop stealing if it's a problem for you? First, stay away from people who tempt you to steal. They will only destroy your life. Second, go to God and ask for his power to keep you from stealing again. Third, make a decision not to steal but to earn money so that, as Ephesians 4:28 says, you will have something to give to those who have need. That's the best course and the God-pleasing one.

check this out

take it back
Exodus 22:1;
Isaiah 63:17

conscience
Hebrews 4:7

God has planned
Ephesians 2:10

hardening
refusing to listen to the Holy Spirit

Time: Get Control or Be Controlled!

> EPHESIANS 5:15–17 ***Be very careful, then, how you live—not as unwise but as wise, making the most of every opportunity, because the days are evil. Therefore do not be foolish, but understand what the Lord's will is.***

Paul warns us to be careful how we use our time. His first comment is to be "careful, then, how you live—not as unwise but as wise." Using your time wisely involves the core of your life. We all have the same amount of time, but we don't all use it the same way. Paul wants us to be wise—skilled in our use of time. How do you use time wisely? Paul says by "making the most of every opportunity." The Bible teaches that God has planned to put "opportunities" in your days. These will be events, situations, a chance to encourage a friend, help others, show love, or give you a chance to witness to your belief in Christ. God has planned for those opportunities to come your way! But how can you be ready for them if you're wasting time playing computer games, watching TV, or listening to music? None of those things are wrong, but when they start to control you, then they're bad.

Notice that Paul says "the days are evil." What he meant is that it's very easy to waste it in foolish pursuits, even evil ones, for the devil is always ready to give idle hands something to play with. How you manage your time will determine how your life will turn out. If you use it wisely, you will find at the end of your life that you have done some remarkable things. Time is the great equalizer. Everyone has the same amount each

think about it

day. But many let it slide through their hands like sand, and they end up disappointed, disjointed, and dismayed.

By age eighty, an average man has done the following:

Slept	26 years
Worked	21 years
Been entertained	8 years
Eaten	6 years
Been angry	6 years
Waited on tardy people	5 years
Been in transit	5 years
Conversed	4 years
Been educated	3 years
Studied and read	2 years
Shaved	228 days
Scolded children	26 days
Tied his shoes	18 days
Blew his nose	18 days
Laughed	46 hours
Attended church and prayed	5 months

How Others See It

Benjamin Franklin

Dost thou love life? Then do not squander time, for it is the stuff life is made of.[10]

Paul J. Meyer

Experience proves that most time is wasted, not in hours, but in minutes. A bucket with a small hole in the bottom gets just as empty as a bucket that is deliberately kicked over.[11]

Jesus was one of the wisest users of time in history. Think about this: He had approximately three years to implant in the world a team of people who would ultimately start a faith that had to last forever!

time for everything
Ecclesiastes 3:1–8

Three years is nothing! Think how fast first through third grades went, or even your high school career! But that's all Jesus had. Those three years were packed with all sorts of activities—healing, preaching, counseling, guiding, and discipling. And yet Jesus did it.

How? He prayed, we know, for long periods before he ever embarked on a great mission. He sought out his Father for advice and direction in all circumstances. And he stuck to the plan. Many times, he refused to go along with what others wanted him to do because he had his own plan for the day.

Similarly, you must make time for the things that matter, or your day will fritter away to nothing. If you have to speak to a class or assembly or club, you must prepare during the week. A javelin thrower must throw a javelin ten thousand times to get one chance to appear in the Olympics. That takes time. There is a time for everything, if you'll just make the time to do something.

Jesus Had the Time of His Life

> MARK 1:35 ***Very early in the morning, while it was still dark, Jesus got up, left the house and went off to a solitary place, where he prayed.***

According to this passage, Jesus rose a long time before daylight so he could pray. He found an isolated place where he could think and talk with God, clearly showing how important he felt this time was. Perhaps part of this time was spent asking God to help him plan his day. He might have prayed:

- "Who do I need to work with closely today?"
- "Help me prepare for the people I will meet."
- "Give me wisdom for what to say to the Pharisees when they criticize."
- "Keep me on target."

Martin Luther, the great religious Reformer of the 1500s, said, "I have so many things to do today that I shall have to spend the first three hours in prayer."[12] Three hours? In prayer? When you have a lot of things to do, it seems only intelligent to pray less rather than more. But that's where

planning
Psalm 90:12

days are evil
Ephesians 6:13

you're wrong. We may not spend three hours a day in prayer, but when we spend time with God, he makes the rest of our day go further.

> **How Others See It**
>
> Jonathan Edwards
>
> Resolution: To live with all my might while I do live and never to lose one moment of time.[13]

Develop Your Personal Planner

> ECCLESIASTES 11:1–2 ***Cast your bread upon the waters, for after many days you will find it again. Give portions to seven, yes to eight, for you do not know what disaster may come upon the land.***

This passage shows a person who plans his day ahead, in fact his whole year. He sows his bread on the waters. This a figurative expression for giving your wealth and food to others who have need. They will help you in due time. Divide your portion into seven or eight parts. That is, don't take everything, but give a little to everybody and in the end you will find each has enough. Planning like this helps one to live wisely.

This is a wise way to plan your use of time. Often, by giving time now to someone in need, you save time later. If you plan the football game and prepare well, you won't spend as much time worrying and fretting on the field and afterward. If you take time to make encouraging comments to others now, they'll encourage you when you need it later. The expression "What goes around comes around" is an echo of this verse. When you use your time to do good, chances are that others will do good to you. If you use your time to do nothing but play computer games, your computer unfortunately will give back nothing. Too much time in that activity is a waste. Consider how to use your time serving and helping others, and in the end, you will find much of it will come back to you in refreshing waves of goodness and love.

What does the Bible tell us about making the most of our time? Three thoughts. One, use wisdom in planning your day. Think it through. Be wise. Be discerning. Prioritize. Do the things that matter first, and if you don't get to the things that don't matter, it doesn't matter!

Two, learn to redeem the time. To redeem means to "buy back" or to "purchase" time from the thing that holds it hostage. What holds time hostage? Evil. "The days are evil," said Paul. Evil will easily fill up your day, so you've got to redeem the time—you will have to make an effort to make sure it doesn't go to waste. The devil will throw anything he can into your path to keep you from the important things. What are the important things? Building the kingdom of God. Serving others. Giving and sacrificing your life for the needs of others. Meditating and praying. Worshiping. Accomplishing important works. You're the one who calls the shots. So call them wisely.

check this out

do God's will
I Thessalonians 4:3

Third, do God's will. Doing God's will for your life is paramount. Most of the time you will have choices between doing things that waste time and doing things that value time. Make the right choices and you will be doing God's will and pleasing God in the process.

In the Crowd

> 1 TIMOTHY 2:9–10 ***I also want women to dress modestly, with decency and propriety, not with braided hair or gold or pearls or expensive clothes, but with good deeds, appropriate for women who profess to worship God.***

Paul wrote these words to Timothy, who was leading the church at Ephesus. Evidently, the appearance of some of the women was distracting people from worship. Modest appearance was especially important in Paul's day because extravagant appearance was associated with sexual promiscuity (see Illustration #11).

Illustration #11
Women's Hairstyles in Paul's Day—If you had lived in the Greek or Roman world in the first century, you would have seen women with hairstyles like these.

Today, we too need to make sure our lives are focused on God. One of the things that can blur a God-centered focus is peer pressure. So-called "friends" can convince us to do things we wouldn't do on our own. Fashions, what's "in," and who counts are all parts of being in the crowd. We must guard ourselves from making mistakes we have to live with forever.

If you worry a lot about what your friends will think if you don't wear the right clothes, maybe you should change your friends. Some teens, unable to afford the designer duds, shoplift them and are caught. They have to pay fines and even spend time in jail. Clothes aren't worth that.

Just Don't Sweat It, Okay?

> MATTHEW 6:25–30 *Therefore I tell you, do not worry about your life, what you will eat or drink; or about your body, what you will wear. Is not life more important than food, and the body more important than clothes? Look at the birds of the air; they do not sow or reap or store away in barns, and yet your heavenly Father feeds them. Are you not much more valuable than they? Who of you by worrying can add a single hour to his life? And why do you worry about clothes? See how the lilies of the field grow. They do not labor or spin. Yet I tell you that not even Solomon in all his splendor was dressed like one of these. If that is how God clothes the grass of the field, which is here today and tomorrow is thrown into the fire, will he not much more clothe you, O you of little faith?*

In this text, Jesus points out the folly of worrying about clothing. In Jesus' day, the Jews were as concerned about the right clothes as anyone today. Never has a human being lived who wasn't interested in how he looked. Even in the Garden of Eden, when Adam and Eve sinned, the first thing they wanted to do was to clothe themselves. Eve was probably a little fashion conscious when she chose fig leaves over bark!

As Jesus spoke, he knew his listeners wanted to look their best. As a result, people wasted many hours preening themselves so they'd look "cool." Jesus points out, though, that worrying about such things—whether you're "in" because of your clothing, whether you'll be able to get "the right dress or tux" for the prom, whether you'll have Abercrombie & Fitch or have to settle for Kmart—is in many ways a complete waste of energy and mind power. Jesus pointed to a basic reality everyone in his audience knew about: lilies. "Look at them," he said. "If God dresses them like that, even better than anything King Solomon, the richest man in history, could wear, then you can be sure God is capable of doing the same for you."

In the end, Jesus assures us, God promises to provide us with what we need, so why worry? The Bible is strong on this point. Don't spend time fretting and worrying about whether you're keeping up with your friends. God will reward those who are faithful in the true matters of life.

Can It Be Wrong If I Want It?

> JAMES 4:1–6 ***What causes fights and quarrels among you? Don't they come from your desires that battle within you? You want something but don't get it. You kill and covet, but you cannot have what you want. You quarrel and fight. You do not have, because you do not ask God. When you ask, you do not receive, because you ask with wrong motives, that you may spend what you get on your pleasures. You adulterous people, don't you know that friendship with the world is hatred toward God? Anyone who chooses to be a friend of the world becomes an enemy of God. Or do you think Scripture says without reason that the spirit he caused to live in us envies intensely? But he gives us more grace. That is why Scripture says: "God opposes the proud but gives grace to the humble."***

If you've been praying to afford designer jeans or whatever, or if you've pestered God about that new shirt your mom said no about, and God didn't give it to you, you need to consider something else. It's not that God doesn't answer prayer. It's what James says. If you ask God for the wrong things, he will not answer. It's better to be in his will wearing rags than out of it wearing Hilfigers!

James spells out several reasons families have trouble—quarrels and hatred and fights—because we want the wrong things. How many times have you fought your mom or dad about some new haircut or style of clothing you wanted? It can be a real battle in some homes. But James says such attitudes are wrong. You're not getting what you want because you don't go to God in the first place. If you discussed it with him, maybe he'd lead you to find what he will give you.

Another reason you don't get what you want is because you ask with "wrong motives." When we ask God for things he refuses to give, the problem isn't the fact of prayer, it's the act of prayer: You want something just for yourself. It's selfish. And it's useless. Yes, God knows what we need and will provide that.

check this out

follow his example
I Corinthians 11:1; 4:16;
Philippians 3:17;
I Thessalonians 1:6

Look at your life and determine what you really want: Is it the right clothing, or the right attitude, the right outlook, the right relationship with God? Which is the most important? As you answer these questions, all the other elements will fall into place. Don't think it's the clothes that make you. What makes you you is how you appear in the eyes of God, who looks on the heart.

Peering at Pressure

ROMANS 12:1–3 *So here's what I want you to do, God helping you: Take your everyday, ordinary life—your sleeping, eating, going-to-work, and walking-around life—and place it before God as an offering. Embracing what God does for you is the best thing you can do for him. Don't become so well-adjusted to your culture that you fit into it without even thinking. Instead, fix your attention on God. You'll be changed from the inside out. Readily recognize what he wants from you, and quickly respond to it. Unlike the culture around you, always dragging you down to its level of immaturity, God brings the best out of you, develops well-formed maturity in you.*

I'm speaking to you out of deep gratitude for all that God has given me, and especially as I have responsibilities in relation to you. Living then, as every one of you does, in pure grace, it's important that you not misinterpret yourselves as people who are bringing this goodness to God. No, God brings it all to you. The only accurate way to understand ourselves is by what God is and by what he does for us, not by what we are and what we do for him. (MSG)

Peer pressure is an amazing thing. Through its influence, you can become a joyful, committed Christian who wants to be like others who are like Christ. Or peer pressure can lead you to do illegal deeds that could land you in prison. Some peer pressure is good. The other kind is clearly bad. This passage from Romans, especially verse 2, points out the problem. We are not to be "so well-advised to [our] culture that [we] fit into it without even thinking," but we are to be "changed from the inside out." We are to let the Spirit of God influence us so that we become more like Christ. In fact, Paul frequently told his listeners to follow his example and "imitate" him, as well as other people in other churches, clearly a form of peer pressure.

What is the pattern of this world? It's to do the things people in the world tell you to do: wear the right clothing; go to the right stores; get in with the right kids; do the things the kids want you to do. When we get sucked into the attitude of being willing to do anything to please those around us ahead of God or our families, we're in grave danger. The wrong teen can lead you down a path that will end in disaster.

Josh McDowell and Bob Hostetler write frequently to teens like you. They report that many teens in churches get involved in immoral and sometimes illegal behavior. A survey of 3,795 teens in evangelical churches throughout the U.S. and Canada revealed that:

- Two out of every three teens in evangelical churches (65 percent) lied to a parent, teacher, or other adult.
- Six in ten (59 percent) lied to their friends.
- One in three (36 percent) cheated on an exam.
- Nearly one in four (23 percent) smoked a cigarette or used another tobacco product.
- One in five (20 percent) tried to physically hurt someone.
- One in nine (12 percent) had gotten drunk.
- Nearly one in ten (8 percent) had used illegal, nonprescription drugs.

They conclude that "much of this sort of behavior is influenced by peer pressure."[14]

Do you feel the same pressures from your friends? Hanging out with the wrong people can lead to wrong behavior as the Bible frequently says, for example in 1 Corinthians 15:33: "Bad company corrupts good character." Think hard about whom you allow to persuade and influence you. Growing up, I was close friends with a number of teens who were into drinking and drugs. The single mother of one of my friends went on a trip every summer to England. We turned his house into "party zone number one." Everything from gambling and sex to drunkenness and illicit drugs went on there. At the time, I never thought about it as being wrong. Later, when I became a solid Christian, I saw how being around those guys led me down a bad road.

think about it

How Others See It

Sharon Scott

From our media, children learn more at earlier ages, and of course imitate what they see. The media also reinforces peer pressure. If you want to have a good personality and be popular, you have to wear a certain brand of jeans or use a particular toothpaste.[15]

How Do You Know What to Do?

What tests can you use to determine what behavior is right or wrong? Here are some thoughts:

- Learn and know the Ten Commandments. They're found in Exodus 20:1–17. They're a good guide for living in general and knowing right and wrong.
- There are a number of other Bible verses you should know and be familiar with: Galatians 5:17–21 is a list of all kinds of sins to avoid; so is Romans 1:18–32; 2 Timothy 3:1–7; and 1 Corinthians 6:9–10. If you have questions about whether something is right or wrong, these are good lists to consult.

Beyond this, though, what are some good principles for issues not mentioned in the Bible? Consider asking these questions:

- Does what I want to do glorify God (i.e., make him look good and worthy of respect)? 1 Corinthians 10:31: "So whether you eat or drink or whatever you do, do it all for the glory of God."
- Will it show love to others? Romans 13:10: "Love does no harm to its neighbor. Therefore love is the fulfillment of the law."
- Does it confuse me or make me feel guilty to do this? Does it give me peace? 1 Corinthians 14:33: "God is not a God of disorder but of peace."
- Will it benefit me or master me? Will it build others and me up, or will it tear down relationships and my own heart? 1 Corinthians 6:12: "I will not be mastered by anything."
- Will it wound another person or hurt him spiritually? 1 Corinthians 8:12: "When you sin against your brothers in this way and wound their weak conscience, you sin against Christ."
- Does what I am doing honor God? 1 Corinthians 6:20: "Therefore honor God with your body."

Ultimately, if in asking these kinds of questions you're still not sure what to do, ask God for wisdom. James said, "If any one of you lacks wisdom, he should ask God, who gives generously to all without finding fault, and it will be given to him" (James 1:5).

Sex and Teens

GENESIS 2:18–25 *The Lord God said, "It is not good for the man to be alone. I will make a helper suitable for him." Now the Lord God had formed out of the ground all the beasts of the field and all the birds of the air. He brought them to the man to see what he would name them; and whatever the man called each living creature, that was its name. So the man gave names to all the livestock, the birds of the air and all the beasts of the field. But for Adam no suitable helper was found. So the Lord God caused the man to fall into a deep sleep; and while he was sleeping, he took one of the man's ribs and closed up the place with flesh. Then the Lord God made a woman from the rib he had taken out of the man, and he brought her to the man. The man said, "This is now bone of my bones and flesh of my flesh; she shall be called 'woman,' for she was taken out of man." For this reason a man will leave his father and mother and be united to his wife, and they will become one flesh. The man and his wife were both naked, and they felt no shame.*

Sex is one of life's most powerful impulses. Perhaps that is why God reserved it for marriage. Only within the confines of marriage can such an experience be protected, guarded, and enjoyed. When people violate God's plan in any way, they run the risk of dire consequences. In the case of sex, when one engages in premarital sex, one runs the risk of disease, personal life change, and possible legal consequences that few of us would ever want to face. What is God's plan for sex?

In the above Scripture we see that God's plan for sex involves three elements:

1. Leaving your birth family
2. Remaining faithful to your spouse
3. Becoming one with him or her

When you follow these three elements, you're more likely to find success. A person who leaves his or her birth family, is faithful to his wife (does not have intimacy with any other person), and becomes one with her (sexually, emotionally, and spiritually) finds that God will bless that kind of marriage. But when couples live with parents, when there are illicit outside sexual relationships, or when couples do not keep themselves pure within their relationship, disaster can result.

check this out

commands
Hebrews 13:4

What's wrong with premarital sex?

- *A good sexual relationship takes time, commitment, and effort.* This rarely happens without the commitment of marriage.
- *Sex is a learned behavior.* You don't learn sex simply by reading books or looking at pictures. Within marriage, sex can be enjoyed as you learn together. But one-night stands lead to disillusionment. Sex was made to be shared in an atmosphere of trust, and trust is not created unless there is commitment, legal and public. It's just too easy to walk away otherwise.
- *Premarital sex is not God's way.* He counsels us to "keep the marriage bed pure" and warns that he will personally judge those who violate his commands.

How Others See It

Jaci Velasquez

I have personally committed myself to remain sexually pure until I'm married. It's not always easy to keep this commitment, but I believe God has someone very special for me. And I am willing to wait.[16]

Speaking Up

for real

Halfway through her junior year, Lynn decided she wanted to go back to the public high school after spending a couple of years in a Christian school. She felt she wasn't growing like she wanted in the Christian school and wanted a challenge. She also wanted to reach out to those who didn't believe.

The public high school was a bit of a shock. Girls talked about sex constantly. Lynn remained quiet in most of the discussions, though she did listen, wondering whether most of it was even true.

In April, she was sitting in her drama class when one of the girls who had left school early the day before sat down. Lynn casually asked, "How come you left school yesterday?"

The girl laughed. "Oh, my boyfriend and I went to his house. We did it five times. We even took a shower together." Everyone was soon talking about their own exploits, when suddenly Katy, a girl Lynn was not friends with, remarked, "I must be the last American virgin."

It made Lynn laugh, and before she thought about it, she said, "So am I!"

The other girls just chuckled, but suddenly there was a bond between Lynn and Katy that hadn't been there before. They became friends, and Lynn began inviting Katy to her youth group meetings at her church.

Before long, Katy was coming regularly. In time, Katy became a Christian. Lynn puts it all back to that one moment of honesty in a girls' gossip session. What if she had been ashamed of her virginity? What if she hadn't spoken up? When more young people own up to their convictions about sex, it will have an impact on the world. One at a time.

check this out

passages
I Corinthians 6:9–10;
I Timothy 3:1–7;
Matthew 15:19;
I Thessalonians 4:3–5

A Little Biblical Advice About Sex

HEBREWS 13:4 ***Marriage should be honored by all, and the marriage bed kept pure, for God will judge the adulterer and all the sexually immoral.***

words to live by

What does the Bible advise concerning premarital sex? Simply put, avoid it. Wait until marriage. That is the only way the Bible looks at it. Anything else is foolish and fraught with danger. People are to honor marriage as God's plan for sexual relations. When we honor the institution of marriage as God's plan for families and for sex, God promises he will honor us when it comes time for us to get married and raise a family. Other passages single out "fornication"—having sex with other partners before marriage—as a sin. Fornication has many bad effects, including the harm it does to your spirit and your relationship with God.

How do you resist the impulse of premarital sex? It's not easy, especially if you're in love with someone you think is the greatest person you've ever met. And that's the danger. When you let your feelings and hormones take over, pregnancy can result, or you can get a sexually transmitted disease.

How Others See It

A. C. Green

Keeping my body pure from immorality is another part of my overall conditioning. It affects every part of life, not just the physical. When I became a Christian, I made a vow like Samson's, but my strength wasn't in anything external; it was in my word. I resolved not to be with a woman until I married. My convictions were obvious when I joined the Lakers but not proven, so a few players taunted, teased, tempted, and tried me to see if I'd hold up to my standards. . . . I always have a choice to make. If I'm tempted by some woman or even a TV commercial, I don't have to look. I don't have to treat women like a piece of meat in a shop even if that's how they treat themselves. . . . We all have the power of choice. But once used, our choice has power over us. We have to live with the consequences.[17]

How Others See It

Austin O'Brien

I'm definitely a strong supporter of sexual purity. Sex is something you should share only with your spouse—not only because God says so, but sex inside a lifetime of marriage is on a whole deeper level than simply the act of sex itself.[18]

It's Tough to Remain a Virgin

"It's not that I don't want Jesus to return," Nicole said forlornly, "I just don't want him to return before I get married!"

I (Jeanettte) grinned. I understood exactly what Nicole meant because I'd voiced those same words myself years earlier—and actually, not that many years earlier. My friend Mary Ann had a more colorful way of saying it: "I don't want to die a virgin!"

Sex is such a widely pushed action in our world. We're made to believe there's something wrong with us if we're not hopping in or out of bed. I didn't get married until I was thirty-five, and I remained a virgin until then. So I know it's tough to be a virgin. But as those who have lost their virginity before marriage can attest, sex outside of marriage isn't all the fun it's portrayed.

My first summer job was as a waitress. I returned to moonlighting as a waitress a few years later when my day job wasn't bringing in enough money. Sometimes my boyfriend would come into the restaurant, and the other waitresses would good-naturedly tease me. They were always talking about sex. I usually stayed pretty quiet. One night they started asking me pointed questions about my sexual experiences with my boyfriend. I finally told them, "We're both virgins. We don't do sex outside of marriage."

That shut the other girls up fast! They were shocked. But a few minutes later, Marta looked at me with her big brown eyes wistful. "So you're really a virgin?" she quietly asked. When I replied yes, she said, "That must really be kind of nice."

Since then I've talked to a lot of Martas. And I've learned from them that sex outside of marriage isn't the end-all it's portrayed to be. Too many times the guy (or girl) moves on to someone else. And that love you thought would last forever ends. All you have left is the bitter memory that you gave an intimate part of yourself to someone who, in the end, didn't care enough to stick around.

It's tough to remain a virgin in our society. But a lot of your peers are doing so. Sex is not a passion that can't be controlled. You just have to be wise and careful—like not letting yourself get into situations in which you'll be tempted; like putting on the brakes before you want to when it comes to displaying affection; like not even allowing yourself to imagine "what if?"; like making yourself accountable to someone like your parents—letting them know what's going on in your heart and mind and dating life. Controlling the desires (after all, they're normal, God-given longings) is not easy. But it's possible. And it's a lot easier than living with the pain that comes with sex outside of marriage. I know. I made it—and so can you.

In the Heart

Genesis 1:1 *In the beginning God created the heavens and the earth.*

Finally, we come to the most secret place of all, our hearts. What does God want us to keep there? What truths, ideas, realities, emotions is he concerned that we develop inside our hearts? In this section, we'll look at a couple of subjects that concern the heart.

The Bible and Science

Many people believe we have the heads-on confrontation of science with faith in the first verse of the Bible. The Bible says God created the heavens, the earth, the seas, the animals, the birds, the fish, and all other creatures. Ultimately, God finished his creation with a crowning touch: the making of humankind through Adam and Eve. The Bible says nothing about evolution, a long process of creation, or anything like that.

The theory of evolution, on the other hand, presents the idea that creation occurred over a long period of time, with various animals and plants occurring through a process of natural selection, in which the stronger defeated the weaker and the stronger survived. Several things need to be considered.

The argument between the Bible and evolution is probably not as dire as some think. It's true that they oppose each other in the sense that they begin with different starting points. Some people say, "This could only have come from God; therefore, I'll find evidence that fits the Bible." Others may say, "I will search on absolutely scientific grounds. There's no room for religion or the supernatural here."

Today, many scientists are turning away from the old ideas of evolution as they were proposed by Darwin. The fossil record, which Darwin thought would show many of the former species that ultimately led to today's animals and plants, hasn't helped. No real transitional forms have been found in the fossil strata. And in fact, most admit that at one point, the Cambrian Explosion, many life-forms appeared out of nowhere. They just came suddenly, with no previous record of existence in earlier strata. That's a big problem for classic evolutionists.

Another problem is the so-called mechanisms of evolution—mutation and natural selection. Since the vast majority of mutations are destructive, no one has been able to show that they could have been the means of producing new life-forms. Moreover, a number of scientists today argue that almost everything in the human body is irreducibly complex. That is, for something like the eye to function, more than one hundred different parts have to operate correctly at the same time, or the eye couldn't exist. This is true of numerous biological functions, which simply could not have come together by some vague process of mutations and natural selection.

Even though evolutionists argue that their theory is built on more scientific grounds than any theory of intelligent design, the fact is that no one has ever observed the creation of a new life-form through that process. There is simply an assumption that evolution is so.

Some scientists support the intelligent design theory, which claims that the complexity of life requires a designer, just as a Rolex watch requires a technically knowledgeable designer. The number of scientists who support intelligent design is increasing.

How Others See It

Oswald Chambers

If the Bible agreed with modern science, it would soon be out of date because, in the very nature of things, modern science is bound to change.[19]

Why Believe the Bible?

ROMANS 1:18–23 *The wrath of God is being revealed from heaven against all the godlessness and wickedness of men who suppress the truth by their wickedness, since what may be known about God is plain to them, because God has made it plain to them. For since the creation of the world God's invisible qualities—his eternal power and divine nature—have been clearly seen, being understood from what has been made, so that men are without excuse. For although they knew God, they neither glorified him as God nor gave thanks to him, but their thinking became futile and their foolish hearts were darkened. Although they claimed to be wise, they became fools and exchanged the glory of the immortal God for images made to look like mortal man and birds and animals and reptiles.*

learn
2 Corinthians 1:3–11

Why does the Christian choose to believe that God is his Creator and the creation is God's gift? It isn't because he has more facts than the scientist. He doesn't. It isn't because he's smarter than the scientist. Sometimes he is; sometimes he isn't. It isn't because he's worked through all the material, given everything an open, objective glance, and then opted for faith. That's impossible; there's too much material, and no one is that objective. Then what is the reason?

This passage from Romans points out that two things are evident about God from creation to all people: (1) God is powerful, and (2) God has a divine nature, a personality. He is a person possessing personal attributes like mind, emotions, and a will. God has made this clear to each person so that "they are without excuse." That is, people can't say, "Well, God never told me about himself, so how can I believe in him?" Just looking around at the world tells a person that much. But it's not enough to have complete faith in God. It's just enough to convince a person that God exists. So why, then, do Christians take the step from believing God exists to believing he created the world?

The answer is found in Scripture: "By faith we understand that the universe was formed at God's command, so that what is seen was not made out of what was visible" (Hebrews 11:3). The reason Christians believe God is the Creator and we are his creation is that we have this little thing called faith, which Paul said is a gift from God (Ephesians 2:8–9).

We should learn from science, to be sure. In fact, one of the great truths coming out of modern science is how perfectly balanced our universe is. It's like a magnificent and perfect timepiece. If one gear were out of place, it wouldn't work. Dr. Hugh Ross, an astrophysicist, has shown repeatedly that there is a majestic design in our universe that calls for an incredibly intelligent Creator. If the universe were expanding at 1 percent less or more than it is, for example, it would either collapse (if less) or blow to pieces (if more). If the earth were tilted on its axis just a degree or so less or more, life couldn't exist. This marvelous design speaks of a wondrous designer, the Christian God. Belief in God is not only sensible, but it's also intelligent and reasonable.

done bad things
Galatians 6:7–8;
I Peter 2:18–25

> **How Others See It**
>
> Albert Einstein
>
> Science without religion is lame; religion without science is blind.[20]

When Things Go Wrong and You Get Hurt

> JAMES 1:2–8 ***Consider it pure joy, my brothers, whenever you face trials of many kinds, because you know that the testing of your faith develops perseverance. Perseverance must finish its work so that you may be mature and complete, not lacking anything. If any of you lacks wisdom, he should ask God, who gives generously to all without finding fault, and it will be given to him. But when he asks, he must believe and not doubt, because he who doubts is like a wave of the sea, blown and tossed by the wind. That man should not think he will receive anything from the Lord; he is a double-minded man, unstable in all he does.***

Going through a period of suffering is one of life's hardest experiences. Going through it without God would certainly make much suffering unbearable. But with God in your heart, suffering can be a way for God to give you grace and growth.

Suffering has many causes and many reasons, and often to ask God why it happens gets you nowhere. In this passage, we see some strong guidelines for dealing with the problem of suffering and evil. First, James tells us to ask God for wisdom when we suffer. Why? To tell us why we're suffering? Perhaps. But more likely to tell us what to do now that we're in the middle of it.

Sometimes suffering happens because we have done bad things. Sin always leads to suffering. However, that is not the universal cause. Often God simply does not reveal why we're suffering. You may ask, "Why does my best friend have leukemia?" or, "Why was Chad killed by that drunk driver?" or, "Why couldn't I make the team?"

Often, a specific answer isn't possible. What God will tell you, though, is what to do in the midst of your trouble: how to love and help your friend go through her time of pain with leukemia, how to minister to Chad's family, or what to do instead of playing on the team. God's wisdom usually helps us understand what to do in the midst of a situation rather than the whys behind it.

> ### How Others See It
>
> **Eugenia Price**
>
> The Bible clearly states, "As ye sow, so shall ye reap." There is no promise anywhere that any human beings will be exempt from the consequences of sin, past or present. He can be empowered not to sin in the same way again, but God does not make pets of his followers. If we break ourselves over his moral laws, we must be willing to submit to the consequences. And we can do this if we know that we do have access to his life every minute of our lives.[21]

check this out

perfecting
Hebrews 12:3–11

How to Survive When Your Life Caves In

HEBREWS 12:5b–6 ***My son, do not make light of the Lord's discipline, and do not lose heart when he rebukes you, because the Lord disciplines those he loves, and he punishes everyone he accepts as a son.***

The Hebrews passage reveals that suffering sometimes happens because God is perfecting us, making us like Jesus. God lets us go through troubles because he loves us. This is called discipline, and it's a common truth in Scripture. We are disciplined by God for our good, to make us into the kind of people he wants us to be. That means going through hard times, bitter experiences, suffering, persecution, and troubles. We didn't cause these hard times by our sin. We didn't ask for them. But our Father in heaven knows what to do because he is wise, loving, and perfect.

This is not a very happy reason for pain to some. "You mean God did this to me to make me a better person? I'd rather be the same as I was before!" To be sure, there are many people who feel that way. But God is more interested in making us holy than in making us happy. Why? Because only through becoming holy will we actually become happy. Remember that holiness isn't being pious or religious, it's being like God—loving, kind, good, patient, at peace, full of friendship, and joyful. That's real holiness.

heart to heart

Few of us enjoy having our character molded by God, which means that he is making changes in attitudes, outlooks, behaviors, and so on. It is a never-ending process until we arrive in heaven, perfect and fully mature. But that doesn't mean we have to just knuckle under and grin and bear it.

What Help Can I Get From the Bible When I'm in Pain?

Here are several thoughts and verses that can give you strength as you go through your own trial of suffering and hurt:

- Your suffering is going to result in something good: maturity and completeness. God will take that suffering in your life and use it to shape and mold you into the person he truly wants you to be. (See James 1:2–5.)
- Suffering will produce perseverance in your life, the ability to hang in there and grow in character, hope, and love. (See Romans 5:1–4.)
- God promises to "work" everything that happens in your life, including pain and suffering, "for the good of those who love him." (See Romans 8:28.) There are good things up ahead that God has planned. Keep the faith and refuse to give up, and one day you will see clearly how he made your life turn out to be good and joyous.
- Paul argued that our "sufferings are not worth comparing with the glory that will be revealed in us" (Romans 8:18). In other words, no matter how bad it gets for you in this life, the next life will be so incredible that when you get there, you won't see any comparison. It will all be just a part of the process of getting you to the ultimate place and time: heaven itself.
- God's plans are not to destroy you or maim you but to "prosper you and not to harm you, . . . to give you hope and a future" (Jeremiah 29:11). Trust that he knows what he's doing, and that he will ultimately get you there.

How Others See It

C. S. Lewis

God whispers to us in our pleasures. He speaks to us in our conscience, but he shouts to us in our pain.[22]

John Michael Talbot

I can look back at my darkest periods and realize that these were the times when the Lord was holding me closest. But I couldn't see his face because my face was in his breast—crying.[23]

Worth the Pain

Have you ever had braces? If you have, you know the pain they can cause. And if you haven't, you've probably heard a friend complain about them. What is it about braces that causes so much pain? Usually the most pain comes when the braces are tightened. The orthodontist tightens the braces to get the teeth to move to a new position. Even a tiny fraction of movement can cause pain. Then, as the teeth move just a tiny bit to the new position, the orthodontist comes in and tightens the braces again, moving the teeth just a fraction more.

The process of tightening and moving goes on for at least a couple of years. But when it's done, the person is usually glad he or she has gone through the process. For one thing, the teeth look better and straighter. But even better, the teeth are now better tools. The teeth will better serve their owner for a lifetime of chewing and talking.

No pain is fun. Suffering is a drag while we're going through it. But the end result is often worth the pain.

Thomas Carlyle, an English writer, said, "All thought worth thinking is conceived in the furnace of suffering."[24] Ultimately, how we respond to suffering goes in two directions: one, up; the other, down. We may go down to bitterness and rejection of God. Or we may go up to God's will and live in joy. You may never know the reasons for your or your loved one's suffering. But you can be sure of this: God will go with you through it, being there to comfort, guide, help, and encourage all the way.

go with you
Isaiah 43:1–3

How Others See It

Michele Akers

The famous French painter Renoir said, "The pain passes, but the beauty remains." He should know; the brilliant Impressionist artist continued to work even though he suffered severe arthritis. Eventually, he had to have his paintbrushes tied to his fingers. Renoir reminds me that even though it can hurt to follow our life's calling, the beauty and joy of the finished product far outweigh the pain of the moment.

Just as fire purifies metal, so adversity can purify our faith and reveal our true character. Our reaction to trials shows how strong we are, how we really think, and what we really believe. Pain can eliminate the dregs in our lives to reveal the true and lasting things. Pain grabs our full and immediate attention. It also brings us to the end of ourselves. When this happens, either we become closed and bitter or we become more open to God's promises and better.

I've learned that the second way brings all the benefits: I suddenly seek God with everything I have, realizing He is my only source of salvation and strength. If we let it, pain can allow us to see God more clearly and enable us to depend on Him. God will never shield us from life's adversities, because pain can produce the beauty of true character and a deeper, more powerful faith.[25]

Final Thoughts

- Hatred is a terrible sin when it relates to people and God. We may hate what others do, but we are not to hate them personally.
- Lying is a serious sin that displeases God, yet it is very much a part of the American lifestyle. Avoid lying at all costs, but if you do lie, make it right quickly, lest you be caught in terrible traps.
- Stealing is another of those sins Scripture warns us about. Do not steal, ever, even if in a bind of some sort. Trust God, and he will meet your needs. He will never put you in a situation where you must steal to survive.
- Managing your time comes under one heading in the Bible: Redeem it. Make the most of it. Use it for the glory of God, and when you arrive at his heavenly kingdom, you will have much to be thankful for.
- Peer pressure and other pressures—to wear the right clothes, to go with the right crowd—are things we all have to face. But face up to them with God's Word and guidance in your heart, and you will not fall in with the wrong bunch.
- Science and suffering pose great problems for all people, but the Bible offers strong answers that help us to not only learn but also grow closer to God in the process.

Questions to Deepen Your Understanding

1. Why is lying such a serious sin?
2. What is the main truth we should know about time management?
3. How do the Bible and science conflict?
4. What would you tell someone about God that might help them during a time of suffering?

read on

Some of Mark and Jeanette's favorite books about asking tough questions and dealing with tough issues:

- *Bad Connection (The Secret Life of Samantha McGregor),* Melody Carlson, Multnomah
- *Don't Check Your Brains at the Door,* Josh McDowell and Bob Hostetler, Word
- *Geek-Proof Your Faith: How to Handle 12 Tough Issues Without Looking Stupid,* Greg Johnson and Michael Ross, Zondervan
- *Honoring the Body: Meditations on a Christian Practice,* Stephanie Paulsell, John Wiley and Sons
- *The Politically Incorrect Guide to Darwinism and Intelligent Design,* Jonathan Wells, Regnery
- *The Power of Integrity: Building a Life Without Compromise,* John F. MacArthur, Crossway

Chapter 12: Let's Get Serious

Tackling the Really Hard Stuff

What's in This Chapter

- Abortion: Killing Off the Next Generation
- Homosexuality: Wrong, Right, or Something Else?
- Drugs: Right, Wrong, or Just Okay?
- Drunkenness: You Can Have Fun Without a Beer
- Smoking: You Can Be Cool Without a Cigarette in Your Mouth
- Suicide: The Final Statement
- The Occult Firestorm
- Abuse: The Quiet Crime
- You and Your Money
- Roundup of Other Issues
- Enjoying the Beat of Life
- Partying: If It's Fun, Is It Still All Right With God?

Here We Go

Some problems are far more serious than a mere disagreement with your parents or peer pressure. They range from getting pregnant and ending the pregnancy by abortion to pursuing the party lifestyle. Wherever you are as a follower of Christ, you're sure to encounter most of these problems. You will find them difficult, painful, and heartrending if you're involved in them personally. But God does not want you to be without hope. In his Word he has provided strong, sympathetic answers that will guide you on your way to making the decisions that will make your life.

Abortion: Killing Off the Next Generation

> **Psalm 139:13–16** ***For you created my inmost being; you knit me together in my mother's womb. I praise you because I am fearfully and wonderfully made; your works are wonderful, I know that full well. My frame was not hidden from you when I was made in the secret place. When I was woven together in the depths of the earth, your eyes saw my unformed body. All the days ordained for me were written in your book before one of them came to be.***

Abortion is a primary issue of our time. Approximately 1.5 million abortions are performed in the U.S. yearly. That's three abortions every minute. The total number of American war deaths before the wars in Iraq and Afghanistan was 1,205,291. The total number of abortions in the U.S. since 1973 is over 25 million.

check this out

biblical perspective
Hosea 9:11;
Jeremiah 1:5;
Romans 9:11

It's easy to see how abortion is a social problem, but what makes it a spiritual issue? The Bible tells us not to kill—you've probably known the Ten Commandments since you were a child, so that's nothing new to you. Abortion is simply killing a child. The Scripture in Psalm 139 tells us that God has known us since before we were born, while we were still in our mother's womb. What is the biblical perspective on abortion? From the passages in Psalm 139 and in Galatians 1:15, we learn that God fashions and shapes the fetus in the womb. When exactly this starts, we do not know. Presumably it begins at conception because the embryo at that point has all the DNA necessary to build a human being. This indicates that God works as early as conception to begin shaping a human being.

People who perform abortions usually don't refer to the unborn child as a baby. They call him or her "tissue" or a "fetus." But the reality is that this is a baby. Just because he's inside his mother's womb rather than outside doesn't make him any less human. He's growing and developing, and he's very definitely a child. If you ever have questions about that, just look at pictures or a video of unborn children at even the early stages.

When we stop to acknowledge and realize the baby's humanity, the issue seems a lot simpler. Sure, sometimes it's inconvenient to have a child. But inconvenience isn't justification for killing a baby.

How Others See It

Charles R. Swindoll

How would you like to be that baby inside the womb of a woman who isn't sure she wants you to live any longer?[1]

John Willke

I have a right to free speech, but not to shout "fire" in a theater. A person's right to anything stops when it injures or kills another living human. Should any civilized nation give to one citizen the absolute right to kill another to solve that first person's personal problem?[2]

---

for real

A Small, Sad Voice

Jean Staker Garton, author of Who Broke the Baby? *decided to become a pro-life activist after one incident with her young son. She recalls, "All our children were in bed; the late television news was over, and I was putting the finishing touches to a presentation for medical students scheduled to be given the next day. As I reviewed some slides that might be used, there appeared on the screen a picture of an abortion victim, aged two and one-half months' gestation; her body had been dismembered by a curette, the long handled knife used in a D and C (dilation and curettage) abortion procedure. Suddenly I heard, rather than saw, another person near me. At the sound of a sharp intake of breath, I turned to find that my youngest son, then a sleepy, rumpled three-year-old, had unexpectedly and silently entered the room. His small voice was filled with great sadness as he asked, 'Who broke the baby?' How could this small, innocent child see what so many adults cannot see?"*[3]

What are the options for a teen who becomes pregnant? Often, the best option is to bring the baby to term and let the child be adopted. Authors Josh McDowell and Bob Hostetler reveal that of more than 1.5 million abortions performed yearly in the U.S., over a half-million are teens aborting their children. If these babies were brought to birth, much of the adoption problem in the U.S. would be mitigated. Married folks who cannot conceive would have the opportunity to raise a healthy child in a loving home where they could grow up to be responsible Americans and Christians.

The physical effects of abortion are staggering, according to the Institute of Medicine, National Academy of Sciences. In teens and older women who have had abortions, the following is true of any subsequent pregnancies:

- 85 percent miscarriage rate
- 47 percent higher labor complications
- 83 percent higher delivery complications
- 67 percent more apt to have premature babies.
- Miscarried their "wanted babies" twice as often[4]

Would you consider abortion in the following situations?

1. There's a preacher and his wife who are poor. They already have fourteen kids. Now she finds out she's pregnant with the fifteenth. They are living in tremendous poverty. Considering their poverty and the excessive world population, would you consider recommending she get an abortion?

2. The father is sick. The mother has TB. They have four children. The first is blind. The second is deaf. The third is deaf. And the fourth has TB. She finds she's pregnant again. Given the extreme situation, would you consider recommending abortion?

3. A man raped a thirteen-year-old girl, and she got pregnant. If you were her parents, would you consider recommending abortion?

4. A teenage girl is pregnant. She's not married. Her fiancé is not the father of the baby, and he's very upset. Would you consider recommending abortion?

In the first case, if you choose abortion, you have just killed John Wesley, one of the great evangelists in the nineteenth century. In the second case, you have killed Beethoven. In the third case, you have killed Ethel Waters, the great gospel singer. If you said yes to the fourth case, you have just declared the murder of Jesus Christ.

What If You're a Pregnant Teen and Thinking About Abortion?

What if abortion right now seems like the only way out? What path can you take that might be best for you and your baby? Here are some thoughts:

- Don't just listen to the pro-choice crowd. Get the facts from the other side. Contact your local chapter of the Right-to-Life, Majella Society, or another pro-life organization, and give them a chance to make their case. This could be the most important decision you've ever made.
- If you have any question whether you are carrying a baby or just some tissue, seek wisdom from the Bible. Read the passages listed above and ask God to lead you. He will guide you and give you wisdom if you ask him. (See James 1:5–6.)
- Think about the consequences of having an abortion. You may even want to talk to a Christian who had an abortion and ask her how an abortion changed her life.
- Bringing a baby to term is not as difficult as you might think. What is difficult is raising that child without a father and with you still in your teens. You can bring a child into the world, give her up for adoption, and even keep in touch with the adoptive parents. You

don't have to forget about the child as if she never existed. Many adoptive parents would be happy to let you have an influence on your baby's life.

- Pray, alone and with others, about your pregnancy. Seek God. What is he saying to you? Listen to your heart. God will speak with you. He will lead you and encourage you to do the right thing.
- Resolve not to let this happen again. Choose to wait until you're married to ever have sex again. A first mistake doesn't have to lead to another if you take the right steps to prevent it.

Homosexuality: Wrong, Right, or Something Else?

ROMANS 1:26–27 ***Because of this, God gave them over to shameful lusts. Even their women exchanged natural relations for unnatural ones. In the same way the men also abandoned natural relations with women and were inflamed with lust for one another. Men committed indecent acts with other men, and received in themselves the due penalty for their perversion.***

Homosexuality has long been debated in the world and in the church as an alternative lifestyle. Is it really an alternative? Many teens regard the gay lifestyle as just another dish in a huge buffet of choices: "You're bi? You're straight? You're gay? It's all the same to me." One teen says, "If it makes me happy, why shouldn't I do it?" And another, "It's just a little fun. What's wrong with that?"

What does the Bible say about homosexuality?

The passage from Romans uses the word *unnatural*. The writers of the Bible considered homosexuality abnormal and "against nature." In Leviticus 18:22, the Hebrews were commanded to detest men who "lie with a man as one lies with a woman." The verse concludes, "That is detestable." First Corinthians 6:9–10 lists several wrong sexual behaviors, including "male prostitutes" and "homosexual offenders." First Timothy 1:10 singles out "adulterers and perverts," along with "slave traders, murderers, and those who kill their fathers or mothers." Scripture cannot be used to support homosexuality.

Is Homosexuality the Worst Sin of All?

LEVITICUS 18:22 ***Do not lie with a man as one lies with a woman; that is detestable.***

In some places, preachers speaking on the subject of homosexuality often make it sound like it's the worst of the worst of sins. But they don't really have much scriptural support for that idea. The truth is that when you look at the passages cited above, you see that homosexuality is listed with other kinds of sin, from gossip and adultery to rebellion and disobedience. Obviously, Paul never singled out homosexuals as horrid sinners. They were simply caught in a lifestyle that was sinful, just as telling dirty jokes was sinful. He never assigned a level of badness to it.

Jesus himself told his listeners that "looking on a woman lustfully" was the same thing as actually committing adultery. He did not mean a lustful gaze was as bad as adultery, but he meant that it was a kind of adultery that was still sinful. So in many ways, mental and emotional lusts, desires, and hopes are sins in similar manner to the acts. Of course, thinking about murdering someone is not the same as actually killing a person, but the thought itself is still a sin in God's eyes.

While homosexual thoughts, feelings, and deeds are not a worse sin than others, they're still a sin.

Is homosexuality genetic, or are some people born with a bent or a natural inclination to become homosexuals? Like all sins, sometimes there is something in a person that can be passed on to children. God told Moses that he "visits the iniquity of the fathers onto the children for four generations" (see Exodus 20:5). That means God causes sinful people to pass onto their children the same tendencies, through example, training, or possibly genetics. Researchers have found that alcoholic parents can pass along a tendency to become alcoholic to the children. I have personally known people who refused ever to take a drink because of their parents' problems, for fear that it would lead them down the genetically same road.

Similarly, researchers have reached different conclusions about homosexuality. Some studies seem to indicate that there may be a genetic aspect to homosexuality; other studies have shown no connection. In some studies, twins are both heterosexual or both homosexual; yet in still other studies, one twin is heterosexual and the other is homosexual.

What, then, is the answer? So far, it's wise to consider the research inconclusive. But even if there is a genetic connection for homosexuality, the problem remains that the Bible calls it sin. Having an alcoholic gene or a fat gene, for instance, does not excuse drunkenness or gluttony.

Some researchers believe that homosexuality is a learned behavior that can be overcome if the person with the affliction has the support, willpower, and spiritual strength to face it and overcome it. If, as the Bible shows, homosexuality is a sin like any other sin, it can still be confessed and left behind. It does not have to control the person with the sin. Also, since it may be a learned response to personal tastes and tendencies, it can be unlearned. But it's not easy.

What Are the Alternatives?

Perhaps you agree that homosexuality is sinful. But what do you do if you know you have this inclination and it's very powerful? Here are a couple of thoughts:

1. If you have the desire, strength, and willpower, you may be able to live as a heterosexual. There are organizations for Christians (Exodus International is one) that help you stop homosexual behavior and turn from it. One of the leaders of that group told me they have had tremendous success through such strategies as Christian conversion, repentance, faith, and genuine Christian love. One of the primary elements needed for help is a support group. Many churches offer recovery groups that meet on their property. Getting involved in such a group is essential for success for those who take this option.

2. In many cases a homosexual will say that his or her sexuality prevents him from ever being heterosexual, that he simply isn't attracted to the opposite sex. But because of the scriptural ban on homosexual relations, he can lead a celibate lifestyle. Biblically, that's a wise and helpful alternative. Jesus said in Matthew 19:11–12, referring to people who choose celibacy for various reasons: "Not everyone can accept this word, but only those to whom it has been given. For some are eunuchs [people who remain unmarried or do not engage in sexual activity] because they were born that way; others were made that way by men; and others have renounced marriage because of the kingdom of heaven." What does Jesus mean? Some Christian homosexuals can simply give up all sexual relations because God has given them that special power. And there are some who will renounce homosexuality to serve God more completely. These are worthy reasons to turn from the gay lifestyle and find a way to reach fulfillment through other means.

How Can Christians Make a Real Stand About Homosexuality in the World Today?

In a world that supports homosexuality, how can we be strong in our moral stand? And how can we help homosexuals? Here are some tips for dealing with homosexuality:

1. ***Right and wrong.*** Be absolutely clear in your own mind that homosexual behavior is wrong. Know what the Bible says on the subject.
2. ***Power.*** Sex may be the strongest force in your life. You will not be able to resist its pull from willpower alone. A person gains new strength when he becomes a Christian.
3. ***Love.*** Love does not equal sex. It is particularly cruel to homosexuals to suggest that it does. Jesus' own example shows that it's possible to love while abstaining from sexual relationships.
4. ***Fantasies.*** Be careful with unchecked fantasies. Brood on anything long enough, and it will take over your life.
5. ***Friendship and support.*** The Bible bans homosexual behavior, but it does not forbid same-sex friendships. Friendship and support, especially from more mature Christians, are essential.
6. ***Forgiveness.*** If you've practiced homosexuality, learn to forgive those who are hostile. Many people have a negative reaction from Christians, for example, then reject Christianity itself. To see things objectively demands forgiveness. Bitterness only clouds the issue.

Drugs: Right, Wrong, or Just Okay?

GALATIANS 5:19–21 *The acts of the sinful nature are obvious: sexual immorality, impurity and debauchery; idolatry and witchcraft; hatred, discord, jealousy, fits of rage, selfish ambition, dissensions, factions and envy; drunkenness, orgies, and the like. I warn you, as I did before, that those who live like this will not inherit the kingdom of God.*

The Bible doesn't say anything about drugs other than alcohol. However, in this one passage, an interesting word is used for "witchcraft." It's the Greek word *pharmakeia,* from which we get the word *pharmaceutical,* or *drug.* In the Bible, it appears that drugs were available and used under certain conditions, but always under the heading of witchcraft. Drugs were considered a form of witchcraft.

Today, illicit drugs are available to almost anyone who seeks them. But some drugs, especially cocaine and its derivatives, are extremely dangerous. Emergency rooms are full of people with drug overdoses of all sorts.

But that might not be your experience. Perhaps you've tried marijuana or some of the other less powerful drugs, and you think it's just a form of recreation. No harm done. You just had a little fun. Perhaps the primary verse on this issue actually talks about drinking, but the application applies. Ephesians 5:18 says, "Do not get drunk on wine, which leads to debauchery. Instead, be filled with the Spirit."

The point of this verse is that a Christian should be controlled by the Holy Spirit, not a substance taken into his body. When teens are controlled by drugs, they may feel compelled to do things, commit crimes, and attempt risky behaviors because of the influence of the drug. There is also the impact on the body from drugs. Smoking marijuana can cause lung cancer. Other drugs can induce a heart attack or other trauma. Overdoses are common and occur easily.

Should you use drugs? The Bible does not give any specific directive about them. But from passages like Ephesians 5:18, we can be sure God does not approve of such actions. There is nothing in the Bible that would justify the use of drugs for recreational or fun use.

What Should You Do If You're Involved With Drugs?

The answers for drug use are the same as for other wrong behaviors. Do they build you up? Do they benefit you and others? Does your use of drugs glorify and honor God? Are you putting yourself in danger? Honestly answering such questions will go most of the way in helping you deal with these issues.

Here are some other steps to take:

1. ***Get help.*** Many churches and Christian counseling services will offer you real support and guidance in taking steps to turn away from drugs.

2. ***Stop hanging out with other teens who use drugs.*** They will influence you in ways you won't be able to fight.
3. ***Build new friendships with committed believers*** who walk closely with Jesus and don't use drugs.
4. ***Commit your life to Jesus*** and take steps to learn to relate to him and walk with him.

Taking such steps will give you the support and power you need to overcome this dangerous problem.

Taking a Stand

Brad Daugherty, a sixteen-year-old Christian student, has faced the problem of living his faith in a secular world. "It's real hard to get the balance between a Christian worldview and a secular worldview you find in high school," he says. "With organizations like FCA, you find a niche with Christian people, so that helps a lot. But in classes like biology that teach evolution, you face a real difference. It's amazing to me how people don't acknowledge things were created rather than that they just happened."

What are some of the pressures he must deal with? "Sexual pressures, the way guys talk," he says. "It's hard to take that without letting it soak. No matter how much you try to tune it out, it's going to stick. Locker-room talk, what they've done with their girlfriends, what so-and-so did to someone else. I don't feel like I'm left out, but I know there are people who aren't nearly as strong in their faith. I've known people for years and years, and you wouldn't think they'd do anything. But then you find out they went to a party and got drunk and had sex with someone they were going out with for only a week, and these are people who claim to be Christians. The pressure is to drink, use drugs, smoke, use bad language, talk about others in a nasty way."

Brad believes he often has to take a stand. "A lot of Christians who get out in the secular world just sink into their shell and don't try to stand up for what they believe in. When somebody's around me and using foul language, I'll say, 'You don't need to be saying that.' Or, 'At least around me, don't talk like that.' If someone invites me to a party or asks me to do something I know is wrong, I just say, 'I don't do that kind of thing.' A lot of times, it's not even bad stuff. But I'd have to skip church to do this thing. I try to put God first. I have to ask, 'If I do all these other things, even good things, will it take me away from God?'"

Brad tries to influence his friends for good. Frequently, people ask him what he believes, and he's always amazed at the responses he gets. He has led some of his friends to Jesus in the process of simply trying to influence them for good.

check this out

dangers of drunkenness
Ephesians 5:18–22

Drunkenness: You Can Have Fun Without a Beer

PROVERBS 23:29–35 ***Who has woe? Who has sorrow? Who has strife? Who has complaints? Who has needless bruises? Who has bloodshot eyes? Those who linger over wine, who go to sample bowls of mixed wine. Do not gaze at wine when it is red, when it sparkles in the cup, when it goes down smoothly! In the end it bites like a snake and poisons like a viper. Your eyes will see strange sights and your mind imagine confusing things. You will be like one sleeping on the high seas, lying on top of the rigging. "They hit me," you will say, "but I'm not hurt! They beat me, but I don't feel it! When will I wake up so I can find another drink?"***

words to live by

This passage points out the dangers of drunkenness. What are they? Woe. Sorrow. Strife. Complaints. Bruises. Bloodshot eyes. It "bites like a snake and poisons like a viper." You'll have hallucinations. You'll be confused. You'll feel like you're going to and fro at the top of the mast on a ship. You'll get into fights, but you won't feel the pain. Until later. Alcohol is an altogether bad trip. There is virtually nothing good about it, even though the Bible in no way condemns drinking wine as your normal beverage. But why? Because in biblical times, water could easily be polluted. It was difficult to find pure, good water all the time. So to rid themselves of the fear of disease and sickness, they drank wine, which when fermented passes on no germs.

There's no reason to drink wine or beer or any other alcohol today. But what should you do if you've been involved in drinking and want to get out of it?

1. ***Seek help.*** Your church, your Christian friends, parents, counselors, and the like can all be resources you can tap. James, a Christian who got involved in his church's recovery program says, "I don't know how I could have done it without support. But the people who were around me gave me the strength I needed to say no to drinking."

2. ***If necessary, flee the situation.*** Paul told Timothy, "Flee the evil desires of youth, and pursue righteousness, faith, love and peace, along with those who call on the Lord out of a pure heart" (2 Timothy 2:22). Samuel said, "My parents told me that if I ever got into a situation where I was uncomfortable or where people were putting a lot of pressure on me, I should call them and they'd come and get me immediately. I did that at a party, and they came and I was really relieved. I kind of didn't believe them at first, but when they came through, I knew they loved me even more than I thought."

3. ***Don't put down your friends who drink,*** but when asked about it, explain to them your position. Again, Paul told Timothy, "The Lord's servant must not quarrel; instead, he must be kind to everyone, able to teach, not resentful. Those who oppose him he must gently instruct, in the hope that God will grant them repentance leading them to a knowledge of the truth" (2 Timothy 2:24–25). Loreen, a senior, said, "A lot of times, people ask me why I'm not drinking or using drugs. I'm always afraid they'll put me down. But when I explain and use the Bible and all that, it's amazing. Some people just stand there totally astonished. Several have said to me, 'I wish I could believe those things.' And I've helped some find Jesus that way."

Here are some facts about alcohol or drug addiction:

1. ***Addiction is deadly.*** Regardless of the type of drug used, it can kill.
2. ***Addiction is progressive.*** Untreated, the problem always becomes worse, not better.
3. ***Addiction is more powerful than the individual.*** Willpower is no match for it.
4. ***Once an addict, always an addict.*** Whether the individual is using drugs or not, the effect of subsequent use grows in intensity.
5. ***Addiction is nondiscriminating.*** The problem hurts anyone in its path, especially close family members, and has no respect for social or economic status.

With these facts in mind, it's wise not to have anything to do with alcohol.

Smoking: You Can Be Cool Without a Cigarette in Your Mouth

1 CORINTHIANS 6:19–20 ***Do you not know that your body is a temple of the Holy Spirit, who is in you, whom you have received from God? You are not your own; you were bought at a price. Therefore honor God with your body.***

We have no Scriptures expressly forbidding or advocating its use, but we do have many Scriptures that indicate we are not to treat our body as anything but the temple of the Holy Spirit. We need to be careful what we put into it.

What are the dangers of smoking? Smoking does no good but does lots of bad. Consider this list:

1. One cigarette causes a rise of ten to fifteen points in your blood pressure and causes the heart to work 10 percent harder.
2. Cigarette smoke contains at least nineteen poisons, among them carbon monoxide, nicotine, furfural, and acrolein.
3. Carbon monoxide prevents red blood cells from uniting with oxygen.
4. Nicotine constricts blood vessels, raises blood pressure, gives a pep feeling followed by depression until another cigarette is smoked, and puts a yellow stain on teeth and fingers.
5. Furfural causes tremors and twitching, short-windedness.
6. Acrolein causes a violent action on nerve centers, producing degeneration of brain cells, very rapid in boys. Degeneration is permanent.
7. In girls and women, smoking causes loss of their schoolgirl complexion, making them look prematurely old. Their face becomes ashen, and their skin drawn and haggard.
8. Smoking causes heart disease.
9. Smoking causes lung cancer, lip cancer, tongue cancer, throat cancer, and even bladder cancer.
10. Smoking gives bad breath.
11. Smoking is highly unattractive to most people.
12. Smoking may cause lapses in memory and mental ability.

How Others See It

James I

A custom loathesome to the eye, hateful to the nose, harmful to the brain, dangerous to the lungs, and in the black stinking fume thereof, nearest resembling the horrible Stygian smoke of the pit that is bottomless.[5]

From the National Center For Chronic Disease Prevention and Health Promotion:

- More than 6,000 people under the age of 18 try their first cigarette each day. More than 3,000 people under the age of 18 become daily smokers.
- The number of adolescents who become daily smokers before the age of 18 increased by 73 percent from 1988 (708,000) to 1996 (1.226 million), rising from nearly 2,000 to more than 3,000 people under the age of 18 who become daily smokers. If the rate of smoking initiation among young people had held constant since 1988, then 1.492 million fewer people under the age of 18 would have become daily smokers by 1996.
- In the 1960s and 1970s, the rate of first-daily smoking was highest for people ages 18–25. Since the late 1980s, however, the rate of first-daily smoking was similar for adolescents aged 12–17 and young adults ages 18–25.
- Among people ages 12–17, the incidence of first use of cigarettes per 1,000 potential new users has been rising continuously during the 1990s and has been steadily higher than for people ages 18–25 since the early 1970s.
- At least 4.5 million adolescents (aged 12–17) in the United States smoke cigarettes.
- Young people vastly underestimate the addictiveness of nicotine. Of daily smokers who think that they will not smoke in five years, nearly 75 percent are still smoking five to six years later.
- Seventy percent of adolescent smokers wish they had never started smoking in the first place.

Help for Smokers

1. There's power in Jesus. If you want to overcome this problem, Jesus will supply the power to do it. It won't be easy, but it can be done.
2. If you can't quit cold turkey, consider trying something like the patch or other resources on the market that help people quit. There's a tremendous movement in the U.S. today to get people to quit smoking. Many resources have been discovered and invented.
3. Get into a support group. Many churches offer groups, much like AA or AlAnon, that help smokers quit. Walking your mile with others helps tremendously.
4. Trust God. He will get you through this if you're committed and willing.

check this out

power
Ephesians 5:18–22

can't quit
1 Timothy 5:23

support
James 5:13–16

trust God
Proverbs 3:5–6

Moses
Numbers 11:10–15

Jonah
Jonah 4:1–3

Suicide: The Final Statement

1 SAMUEL 31:3–6 ***The fighting grew fierce around Saul, and when the archers overtook him, they wounded him critically. Saul said to his armor-bearer, "Draw your sword and run me through, or these uncircumcised fellows will come and run me through and abuse me." But his armor-bearer was terrified and would not do it; so Saul took his own sword and fell on it. When the armor-bearer saw that Saul was dead, he too fell on his sword and died with him. So Saul and his three sons and his armor-bearer and all his men died together that same day.***

There are four suicides in Scripture: three in the Old Testament and one in the New (Judas Iscariot, the disciple who betrayed Jesus and then took his own life in regret).

Teens attempt suicide for many different reasons: depression, rejection by peers, a major mistake, low self-esteem, addictions, horrid family lives, abuse, homosexuality, pregnancy, and a lack of hope for the future.

Depression is a primary cause of the desire for suicide. Moses at one point asked God to kill him because he was depressed. The same thing happened with Jonah after he brought a great revival to the enemy city of Nineveh.

think about it

Researchers have found that depression is a common reason for teen suicide. The reason for the depression can be manifold, but the dark feelings,

check this out

all things are possible
Matthew 19:26

the sense of despair, and the idea that nothing will ever be right again can lead teens to attempt suicide.

About 5 percent of all teens suffer from significant depression, including adjustment disorder with a depressed mood, dysthymia, major depression, or, occasionally, bipolar disorder (manic-depression). Because these diseases can have significant genetic components, those who suffer from a family history of depression may enter into depression during their teen years.

Other symptoms of depression may appear as headaches, stomachaches, persistent boredom, and changes in eating or sleeping patterns. If depression seems a possibility, getting a diagnosis is the first step. The same symptoms can indicate other problems, like sleep disorders, substance abuse, or early stages of schizophrenia.

Although antidepressant drug treatments work well for adults, they seem less successful for depressed teens. Active and focused talk therapy is more effective. Sometimes, an examination of the home environment can bring changes and improvement.

Severe depression is often chronic. As many as 70 percent of school-age children and teens treated for major depression will see the symptoms reoccur within a five-year span. Most depressed kids, however, respond to various combinations of psychotherapy, family therapy, drug treatment, and environmental improvements. The earlier the disease is diagnosed and treated in teens, the faster and more complete recovery they'll experience.

If You're Considering Suicide

What should you do if you're experiencing an impulse to commit suicide? The first thing to do is get help. Talk to a parent or a counselor. Express what's inside you. If you're depressed, try to talk out the reasons why. There are a multitude of reasons for depression, and depression is often a biochemical imbalance. That means you're not thinking clearly. With medication therapy, those feelings can clear up in a matter of days.

think about it

A second line of defense is to realize that God forbids suicide. It's murder, the ultimate murder, self-murder. When you realize that God does not want this and can help you get beyond it, you can realize there's hope. Human strength cannot win, but with God, all things are possible.

A third course is to check yourself into a hospital. There you will get the rest and time you need to recover and find your balance again, and you would be under the care of a psychiatrist.

Last, Moses, Elijah, and Jonah all overcame their impulses to die. It's possible to work your way out of this pit through God's help and love. From 1975 to 1977, I (Mark) personally suffered from severe clinical depression. I fought the desire to kill myself nearly every day. At one point I was hospitalized for a month because I told my doctor that I was afraid I was really going to kill myself. After more than two years of pain, struggle, and terrible emotions, I came out of it and have never faced such devastating feelings again. While your depression may go on and on with no end in sight, God promises, "Blessed is the man who perseveres under trial, because when he has stood the test, he will receive the crown of life that God has promised to those who love him" (James 1:12). I found this verse utterly true in my own trial by fire. After coming out of the depression, I experienced a continuing joy and hope in life that I could only consider the "crown of life" that James refers to.

check this out

Elijah
I Kings 19:4

How Others See It

Karl Menninger

Hope is the major weapon against the suicide impulse.[6]

---

everyday insights

While Mark has had his own experiences with suicide, I (Jeanette) also faced this choice some years ago. I remember telling myself, "If I killed myself, no one would know for hours." Actually, it wasn't the first time I'd thought that. For a few years in my life, it seemed as if I constantly faced the temptation to end it all.

Then, on that specific day, I remember realizing that's just what suicide is: a temptation. For some reason, Satan was tempting me to end my life. If Satan wants me out of the way that much, God must have some pretty neat plans for my life, I thought. It stood to reason that if Satan was so fervently out to destroy me, maybe God was going to use me in some effective way.

After that time, when the temptations hit, I recognized them as temptations and resisted them, just as I resisted other temptations.

If you've ever been plagued with thoughts of suicide, don't feel that you're alone. Remember, God must really have some great plans for your life if Satan wants you to end it so badly. And treat suicide like any other temptation—don't give in!

check this out

infect
Luke 17:2;
Deuteronomy 12:31;
Ephesians 6:10–18;
1 Peter 5:7

The Occult Firestorm

DEUTERONOMY 18:10–12 ***Let no one be found among you who sacrifices his son or daughter in the fire, who practices divination or sorcery, interprets omens, engages in witchcraft, or casts spells, or who is a medium or spiritist or who consults the dead. Anyone who does these things is detestable to the Lord, and because of these detestable practices the Lord your God will drive out those nations before you.***

It happens slowly, carefully, almost without your knowing. It may start with astrology and reading about your sign in the horoscopes. It can move on to playing with Ouija boards, then séances. Soon, there's involvement with fortune-tellers, channelers, Wicca, New Age crystals, and possibly even satanists who practice abuse, rape, animal and child sacrifice, and all kinds of evil ceremonies, actions, and beliefs. It can snare you and trap you and ultimately kill you if you get involved.

That's probably why this Scripture is so stern. In fact, some verses, like Leviticus 20:27, command that people practicing the occult should be put to death. God knows what demons can do to young people. And demons love to infect teens with their evil. This passage lists several kinds of occultic practices that existed even in the days of Moses (1440 BC):

1. ***Divination***—trying to foretell the future using things like cards, dice, bones, and animal entrails.
2. ***Sorcery***—the use of special drugs in making people do your desires.
3. ***Interpreting omens***—giving the meaning of an event like an eclipse, a sudden storm, or other phenomena.
4. ***Witchcraft***—using spells and dolls and other ritual objects to influence people or events.
5. ***Medium or spiritist***—a person who talks to and gains advice from demons.
6. ***Consulters of the dead***—trying to call up people who have died as in a séance or other means.

God says to not only stay away, but to run away, as fast as you can, and never look back when approached by people who practice these rites.

Oppression occurs when a demonic presence oppresses a person at all times during the day. This person has opened himself up to demonic forces but has not gone all the way into possession. King Saul was oppressed by a demon, but not possessed. Possession is when a demon takes up residence in your body and actually controls what you do and say. You are held in a spiritual prison in which the demon has entire power over you. The many cases of demon possession in the New Testament are evidence that this is true and can happen to people who are open to demonic presences.

check this out

King Saul
I Samuel 16:14

demon possession
Matthew 8:28–34; 9:32–34

destroy you
I Peter 5:8–9

How Others See It

Josh McDowell and Bob Hostetler

Technically, ritual abuse is not necessarily derived from satanic practices. Yet the goal of ritual abuse appears to reflect the basic foundation of satanic worship and belief. The victim is indoctrinated into a system where good is bad and bad is good. There may also be forced submission to worshiping a designated god. In addition, belief in supernatural powers such as demons and monsters are used to control and terrorize.[7]

What Do I Do Now?

What should you do if you have become involved with the occult?

1. ***Stop it, get out of it, get away from it, make a complete break with it.*** Even if it seems fun now, the ultimate goal of all demonic influence is destruction through suicide or other means. They want to destroy you.

2. ***Destroy all vestiges of the occult in your life.*** Any books, potions, artifacts, jewelry, and whatever else is connected to the occult, get rid of it. Don't give it to another occultic member; you'll just destroy him in the process. Burn the artifacts or books. Make them utterly useless, and then bury the ashes and rid yourself of them entirely. In Ephesus during the visit of Paul, the new believers burned all the scrolls and artifacts connected to the occult at one point, and the text says, "In this way the word of the Lord spread widely and grew in power" (see Acts 19:18–20). You may be surprised to see how God works in your life and in others when you make an honest rejection of all things occultic.

3. ***Decide now to make a break with all people who have influence on you in this area.*** Do not associate with them. Decide once and for

all that you will lead a life for Jesus and accept him and no other as Savior and Lord. Follow him and leave behind all who would deter you from that purpose. If you believe you are oppressed or possessed by a demon, the first thing to do is realize that it has control over you. You're still in there, but you need to force yourself to get to someone who can help in casting out the demon, either a minister who knows something about exorcism, or some other person who can lead you to such people.

Demonism

There are many instances in the Gospels in which Jesus cast out demons. The demons frequently tried to irritate Jesus by announcing things like, "We know you are the Son of God." On other occasions, the demons asked to be sent into other beings, in one case a herd of pigs. Jesus did not tolerate demonic activity in his presence, and he dealt with it immediately. He commanded demons to "come out" or to "go into the abyss." He warned people to have faith in God and proclaimed that anything done in Jesus' name had God's mark of approval.

Abuse: The Quiet Crime

MATTHEW 5:21–26 ***You have heard that it was said to the people long ago, "Do not murder, and anyone who murders will be subject to judgment." But I tell you that anyone who is angry with his brother will be subject to judgment. Again, anyone who says to his brother, "Raca," is answerable to the Sanhedrin. But anyone who says, "You fool!" will be in danger of the fire of hell.***

Therefore, if you are offering your gift at the altar and there remember that your brother has something against you, leave your gift there in front of the altar. First go and be reconciled to your brother; then come and offer your gift.

Settle matters quickly with your adversary who is taking you to court. Do it while you are still with him on the way, or he may hand you over to the judge, and the judge may hand you over to the officer, and you may be thrown into prison. I tell you the truth, you will not get out until you have paid the last penny.

Abuse—physical, mental, sexual, and otherwise—is becoming more common in our society. Child abusers are hard to stop or catch since they hold the children they abuse in bondage. The child comes to believe that he deserves the abuse, or even that this is normal behavior. Thus, these children do not resist because they know nothing different. Children who were abused often grow up to be abusers themselves.

check this out

Abel
Genesis 4

Tamar
2 Samuel 13:1–19

confronted
Matthew 18:15–17

church discipline
Galatians 6:1

This passage in Matthew points out the seriousness of the crime of abuse. While Jesus does not refer specifically to abuse here, he does speak to the issue of anger, murder, and offensive put-down type of language ("raca" and "you fool"), which are all at the root of abuse. When you spiritually murder a person through emotional abuse or actual sexual or physical abuse, Jesus says you're in danger of judgment. Firing hateful words and put-downs at people puts one close to hellfire. These were not lightly spoken words. Jesus was serious. In God's eyes, how we treat others is a huge issue, and people who engage in hurting others will pay dearly for their crimes.

There are several examples of abuse in Scripture, one of the most horrible being the murder of Abel by Cain. We don't know at what ages this atrocity happened, but it is quite possible both young men were in their teens. The rape of Tamar by Amnon is another example of family abuse. An older brother rapes a younger sister. It qualifies as a double sin, for Tamar could have been as young as thirteen at the time. Unfortunately, God does not promise to keep anyone from abusive situations. What he does promise is that he will be with us through it (Matthew 10:16–32; Isaiah 43:1–2) and give us the wisdom to deal with it (James 1:5–6).

What If You Are Suffering Abuse?

Abuse should not happen in Christian homes, but it does. What should you do?

1. ***Abuse in the home should be confronted.*** Report to your pastor or youth pastor what's going on. Listen to their counsel. If your parents are Christians, or if the abuser is a Christian, church discipline (see Matthew 18:15–17) can be brought to bear upon him or her. That may bring relief. Often an abuser will threaten you, "If you tell on me, I'll really hurt you next time." Or, "If you go to anyone about this, they'll just laugh at you and call you a liar." Some even say, "This is the way it is with all relatives. It's the normal thing, so don't think anyone will even say anything about it." Don't believe these lies. Go to a friend or someone you trust and tell them everything. If necessary, you may have to involve the police. But don't let this person hoodwink you into believing what they're doing to you is normal or can't be stopped.

2. ***Show your abuser what the Bible says about his or her behavior.*** You may want to do this with a youth pastor or trusted friend present. If necessary, you may have to go to government authorities to get final and complete action against the person. The truth is, you don't have to just take it. Abuse in whatever form should be confronted, confessed, and terminated.

3. ***Find a support group at your church or in the community to help you in the recovery process.*** The abuser inflicted you with great wounds. It will take some time to regain your sense of self and find real hope and joy in life. Remember that others around you will be sympathetic, listen to your story, offer advice—both personal and biblical—and stand with you through any dark night.

4. ***When the time is right, work at forgiving the person who abused you.*** Let the bitterness and anger go. As Paul said in Ephesians 4:31–32, "Get rid of all bitterness, rage and anger, brawling and slander, along with every form of malice. Be kind and compassionate to one another, forgiving each other, just as in Christ God forgave you." Forgiveness is a process. Saying it once or twice may not rid your mind of the feelings of pain and hurt. But every time you recall or feel those memories coming into your mind, stop and pray: "Jesus, take these thoughts away. Let me be free of the anger and bitterness and forgive again." This process may take a long time. But gradually, as you refuse to dwell on the negative and hurtful feelings, God will replace them with wholesome, kindly thoughts that do not drag you down.

You and Your Money

How Others See It

George MacDonald

A beast does not know that he is a beast, and the nearer a man gets to being a beast, the less he knows it.[8]

1 TIMOTHY 6:9–10 ***People who want to get rich fall into temptation and a trap and into many foolish and harmful desires that plunge men into***

ruin and destruction. For the love of money is a root of all kinds of evil. Some people, eager for money, have wandered from the faith and pierced themselves with many griefs.

It's been said that Jesus said more about money than any other subject. That is probably true when you consider that many of his parables are about money or wealth and the use of it, as well as other teachings. The Bible has a lot to say about money. But what are its primary teachings? How should you as a Christian regard money and its lure and wiles?

The primary verses on the subject are found in Paul's first letter to Timothy. Please note that it's the "*love* of money" and not money itself that is called the "root of evil." Our world is filled with people who wish for more money. John D. Rockefeller, at one time the richest man on earth, was once asked what he really wanted in life. He said, "One more dollar." That's the attitude many have. "If only I made more money, I could have what I really want." Or "If I just had a better paying job, I could really soar." Or "If I just had a hundred bucks, I'd be happy."

All those people are probably wrong. If they received a million dollars today, they'd probably lament tomorrow that it wasn't two million.

What does the Bible teach about money that relates directly to you as a Christian? John Wesley, the great evangelist of the eighteenth century, was once said to have quipped, "Earn as much as you can. Save as much as you can. Give as much as you can. And then you can spend as much as you want." Let's take those ideas one at a time.

- ***Earn as much as you can.*** Proverbs 10:4 says, "Lazy hands make a man poor, but diligent hands bring wealth." Diligence is the key. Work hard. Persevere at it. Learn your business, and you will excel. Some people have greater gifts than others, and their earning power reflects that. But for you, probably it comes down to how much you can earn at a part-time job. What is this saying? Without becoming obsessive or greedy, simply earn all you can during your average week. If it's minimum wage, make the most of it. If you have a business mowing lawns or something like that, negotiate to get the best prices. Go for the maximum without resorting to cheating, stealing, lying, or other practices.
- ***Save as much as you can.*** Proverbs 10:22 says, "The blessing of the Lord brings wealth, and he adds no trouble to it." When God blesses you with some extra money, put it away and save it. Don't go out

and spend it on foolish things. Some money experts say that you should save at least 10 percent of everything you earn. Put it into a savings account with a decent interest plan and leave it there. This is possible for some, impossible for others. Save what you can. If you can do more than 10 percent, do it. If not, save what you can. God will give you the increase.

- ***Give what you can.*** "A generous man will prosper; he who refreshes others will himself be refreshed" (Proverbs 11:25). Paul counseled the Corinthians to save up each week to prepare for worship when they would give it to the church (see 1 Corinthians 16:2). Giving is an important part of worship and service to God. While some say today that you should tithe (give one-tenth of everything you earn), the New Testament really does not teach tithing. It teaches proportionate giving. That is, some people, because God has so prospered them, may be able to give much more money to the church and God's kingdom. Others may only be able to give a small percentage. What matters is your heart. When you're sold out for God, you'll want to give all you can to advance his work in your world.

- ***Spend what you need.*** Refuse to spend your hard-earned money for frivolous things. CDs, DVDs, video games, and other things can suck up your wealth very quickly. Think wisely about everything you spend. The less you spend on unimportant things, the more you will be able to save for the really great things, and also the more you will have to give to the work of the Lord.

Roundup of Other Issues

Here is a roundup of a number of other issues and concerns you may have and some biblical insights on each:

Sex Education

You will be exposed to a lot of education about sex. However, much of the teaching may be skewed toward modern thinking, which embraces many unbiblical practices. Where can you go to get the real info if your parents won't discuss the subject with you?

- Try your youth pastor or other Christian leaders. They will give you straight answers and may have a number of texts you can refer to.

- Refuse to plug into worldly and secular teachings that do not accept the Bible as an authority and may be misleading about sexual issues.

- 1 Thessalonians 4:3–5: "It is God's will that you should be sanctified: that you should avoid sexual immorality; that each of you should learn to control his own body in a way that is holy and honorable, not in passionate lust like the heathen, who do not know God."

Gambling

The Bible does not say anything specific about gambling except its mention that the Roman soldiers who crucified Jesus gambled for his possessions. Keep these teachings in mind:

- Ephesians 5:15–17: "Be very careful, then, how you live—not as unwise but as wise, making the most of every opportunity, because the days are evil. Therefore do not be foolish, but understand what the Lord's will is." This passage instructs us to be wise in our use of time and life. Gambling is probably not a wise use of resources, money, or time.

- 1 Thessalonians 5:22: "Avoid every kind of evil." While some may argue about whether gambling is evil, the truth is that for a Christian, it is not good to be seen by others doing something that many consider wrong and foolish.

Healthy Lifestyles

What you eat and how you exercise are important issues. Here are some Scriptures to apply:

- 1 Corinthians 6:19–20: "Do you not know that your body is a temple of the Holy Spirit, who is in you, whom you have received from God? You are not your own; you were bought at a price. Therefore honor God with your body." This includes keeping in the best shape possible, not overeating, and learning moderation in all things.

- 1 Corinthians 10:31: "So whether you eat or drink or whatever you do, do it all for the glory of God." You can be sure that an unhealthy body will not be a good witness to others. Obesity in some people is genetic. For most, though, it's just a matter of controlling what you eat.

Here are some tips for nurturing a healthy lifestyle:

1. ***Eat healthy.*** Watch the junk food. Drink good things, not sodas and other high-calorie, low-nutrient concoctions. When you eat

out, avoid high-calorie processed foods you find at most fast-food outlets. Use common sense.

2. *Exercise regularly.* It can be difficult to maintain a strong regimen. But there are many exercises that are easy to do and pay high dividends in terms of building solid health. Walking, for instance, is an easy exercise for most people and can be done while listening to music or while praying. Since your mind can be occupied with things other than your exercise, walking is a good way to do both at the same time. Many other forms of exercise are good as well. Find something you like and stick with it.

3. *Avoid fad diets.* Think about this: Why is there always a new diet on the bestseller lists? The reason is that most of them don't work long-term for most people.

4. *Get serious.* It's your body. God will one day want to know what you did with it. Be prepared to give an answer that you and he will like!

You know, that's about it for this subject. It really comes down to two things—healthy eating and exercise—plus adequate hydration (water!) and sleep.

Reality TV

Remember one thing about this whole subject: Reality TV is *not* real! It's mostly staged, or at least edited down to its most dramatic moments. While much of TV is just a waste of time, there are some good things that come from TV. What are they? Shows that have some benefit to you or others. Educational shows. Relaxation and entertainment shows that are clean and do not defame Christian faith. Some sports.

The important thing is to not let TV dominate your life. Remember what Paul said: "'Everything is permissible for me'—but not everything is beneficial. 'Everything is permissible for me'—but I will not be mastered by anything" (1 Corinthians 6:12). When you decide what shows to watch on TV, just ask: (1) Is it beneficial? Does it help me grow as a Christian in some way? Does it benefit my life? (2) Is it mastering me? Have I become obsessed? Do I "have" to watch "my" show or my day will be "ruined"? If so, it's become a problem.

Fads and the Latest "Thing"

A new fad arrives just about every week. Whether it's a kind of shoe, a new outlet store's "stuff," something to wear, a place to hang out, or whatever, you can be sure someone is waiting to take your money and your time. You can apply the same question as you did to TV watching: Is it beneficial or just a waste of time and money? Will it master me, or can I control it and keep it in perspective? Only you can answer such questions.

Enjoying the Beat of Life

> **Psalm 150** ***Praise the Lord. Praise God in his sanctuary; praise him in his mighty heavens. Praise him for his acts of power; praise him for his surpassing greatness. Praise him with the sounding of the trumpet, praise him with the harp and lyre, praise him with tambourine and dancing, praise him with the strings and flute, praise him with the clash of cymbals, praise him with resounding cymbals. Let everything that has breath praise the Lord. Praise the Lord.***

Music can send a person into raptures of bliss or the depths of despair. It touches the heart and soul, not just the mind. This psalm speaks of the ultimate proper use of music—to praise and worship God. David worshiped God with his lyre. King Solomon wrote songs to be used in the temple. Music became an important and highly enjoyed element of religious life in the Bible. Jesus himself, though not a musician, may have led the disciples in song as they talked around their campfires or in the synagogue.

At the same time, music can be a means of destruction. Some heavy-metal and rap groups have become known for their songs about suicide, molestation, rape, and murder. These groups sometimes glorify violence and hatred, and they stoke in some people a desire to do wrong. Some bands have been known to promote, through their music, the most deadly and ghastly deeds.

> **How Others See It**
>
> **Martin Luther**
>
> Music is the art of the prophets, the only art that can calm the agitations of the soul; it is one of the most magnificent and delightful presents God has given us.[9]

How to View Music

check this out

make melody
Ephesians 5:18–22; Psalm 33

psalms
Psalms 22; 88

COLOSSIANS 3:16–17 ***Let the word of Christ dwell in you richly as you teach and admonish one another with all wisdom, and as you sing psalms, hymns and spiritual songs with gratitude in your hearts to God. And whatever you do, whether in word or deed, do it all in the name of the Lord Jesus, giving thanks to God the Father through him.***

Paul writes that we are to make music with "gratitude" in our hearts to the Lord." He says specifically that when our hearts are filled with God's word, we will do several things: teach one another with wisdom, sing, and make melody with our hearts, and overflow with thankfulness.

words to live by

The Bible extols music, as in Psalm 150, and calls it a means of worshiping God. In fact, some scholars believe that God originally created the angels to be a giant orchestra, belting out the tunes of heaven in crescendo after crescendo. God himself loves to be worshiped through music. He tells us to "make melody with our hearts to him" and to sing to him a new song.

How do you determine if the music you listen to is the kind that pleases God? Let's just say at the outset that music does not have to be overtly Christian to please God. Some psalms in Scripture are decidedly down and do not in any way reflect worship, and yet they're psalms in the Bible, music meant to exalt God before his people.

How Others See It

Amy Grant

The purpose of Christian music is to move us toward God, to articulate the experience of believing in God and how that affects our lives, and how we struggle, celebrate, worship . . . all of the above. It connects us with the community of believers.[10]

Phil Keaggy, a Christian rock guitarist and singer who is often listed with Eric Clapton, Stevie Ray Vaughn, and others as one of the five best guitarists in the world, said, "In the context of a concert situation, the whole point is to lift up Jesus."[11] Keaggy's concerts become acts of worship and create an emotional uplift of the soul that many say is far more beautiful and exciting than any rush one might get listening to Metallica, Korn, or N.W.A.

What's Left to Listen To?

> EPHESIANS 4:29 *Do not let any unwholesome talk come out of your mouths, but only what is helpful for building others up according to their needs, that it may benefit those who listen.*

check this out

lyrics
Ephesians 5:3–4
lifestyles
Hebrews 12:14–16
goals
2 Timothy 3:5–8

Paul tells us that we're to speak words that give grace according to what is happening at the moment. We are not to let any unwholesome word (cursing, dirty talk, put-down) come out of our mouths. Rather, we are to speak so that we build up others, help them, and give them grace. Here are five principles to measure bands against:

1. What are the lyrics about? What does the song say? If the song extols immoral thoughts and activities, it isn't good spiritually; it's evil. Turn off the song, and don't listen to any more of it. If you have the album, get rid of it.
2. What are the lifestyles of the performers? Sometimes not much is known about what the performers of the song believe, but often it's evident that the performers are into sex, drugs, drinking, and orgies. You have no need to be a part of their support.
3. What are the goals of the band or singer? This is often plain as well. Some bands, like Marilyn Manson, make it clear that their goal is corruption.
4. What are the graphics of the band about? What is portrayed in their albums and on the inside covers? Is there nudity? Is there lust and sensuality? Prince, Beyoncé, Blink-182, Pink, and numerous other male and female acts whose sensuality is on display are examples of this kind of appeal.
5. What are their concerts like? Do their concerts glorify God? Or do they work the crowd into a frenzy to the point where the crowd will do anything crazy, foolish, stupid, or violent?

When you submit much of today's music to these five principles, many modern musicians come up wanting. They can't bear the scrutiny of someone who will ask the hard questions. And if you will ask them, you'll find that many bands aren't worth the money you pay to listen to them.

check this out

parties
Exodus 32:1–10

parables
Luke 15

wine
John 2

> **How Others See It**
>
> **Dallas Holm**
>
> We are the most entertained society in the world, and our lives are so cluttered with meaningless, worthless things. People just indulge in so much of no value. . . . If we Christians would just listen to what these people [rock artists] are saying and listen to what their desires are . . . there is no question that we . . . should have nothing to do with it. . . . I don't think . . . you can listen to it and please the Lord or do yourself any good.[12]

Partying: If It's Fun, Is It Still All Right With God?

1 PETER 4:1–5 ***Therefore, since Christ suffered in his body, arm yourselves also with the same attitude, because he who has suffered in his body is done with sin. As a result, he does not live the rest of his earthly life for evil human desires, but rather for the will of God. For you have spent enough time in the past doing what pagans choose to do—living in debauchery, lust, drunkenness, orgies, carousing and detestable idolatry. They think it strange that you do not plunge with them into the same flood of dissipation, and they heap abuse on you. But they will have to give account to him who is ready to judge the living and the dead.***

The classic party girl and party boy have been around for centuries. In the book of Exodus, one of the biggest parties ever thrown is depicted. Moses had gone up on the mountain to receive from God instructions for the people of Israel as they lived in the desert. While gone, the people complained that he would never return, and they wanted Aaron, Moses' brother and his right-hand man, to create an idol that they could worship as their god. Aaron made a golden calf. The people worshiped by dancing, drinking, and having an orgy. Three million of them. That was the way parties were done in those days.

Scripture is clear about partying. God likes parties, but not parties that get out of control and foster sinful activity. One of Jesus' most famous series of parables talks about people partying when they've found a sheep that was lost, a coin that was lost, and a son who had gone astray. When people are happy, they throw parties. Jesus' first miracle at Cana was for a wedding party. When the wine ran out, Jesus created new and better wine out of water on the spot. Jesus frequently attended parties and was accused of being a "glutton and a drunkard"—a person who ate and drank too much. So clearly, God is not against parties.

It's only when people gather where sin is tolerated and even applauded that God says stop. Parties that turn into places where teens can have illicit sex and alcohol are wrong, and they can turn an otherwise normal person into a liar, a cheat, and a fornicator.

stay away
Galatians 5:19–21;
Mark 7:20–23

Biblical Parties

> EPHESIANS 5:18 ***Do not get drunk on wine, which leads to debauchery. Instead, be filled with the Spirit.***

Paul tells us not to get drunk with wine (or any other alcohol) because it's a waste of energy and time. Rather, we are to be "filled with the Spirit." That means to be controlled and led by the Spirit.

The problem with parties in God's eyes is that they often lead to excess. A sip of booze leads to a whole glass, and then to a whole bottle. Many teens simply can't control it. If that's your problem, then stay away from parties where you know the beer will be free, the girls loose, and the boys wild.

But that doesn't mean God doesn't want us to have some fun. Scripture is full of people throwing parties. Just remember one thing when attending a party: If it turns ugly, violent, sexual, or into a drinking bash, get out. Paul told Timothy to "flee from all this [the pursuit of money], and pursue righteousness, godliness, faith, love, endurance and gentleness. Fight the good fight of the faith" (1 Timothy 6:11–12). Why did Paul say "Fight the good fight of the faith"? Because it is a fight. Every day will in some ways be a battle for you. Temptations. Ways to waste time and money. Encounters with negative and sometimes evil people. Beware. Walk close to God, and he will lead you.

Final Thoughts

- To abort a fetus is a false and foolish way to solve a pregnancy problem. There are other solutions. Yes, you'll have to face the consequences of sex outside of wedlock, but you will also find the blessing of God on your life ever after.
- Homosexuality is not an easily solved problem. The first step, though, is commitment to God and his Word. Everything else will find its place when built on this foundation.
- To become entangled with drugs or alcohol is a foolish and useless

way to live a life. Beware of these realities. Shun them. Refuse even to experiment, and you will discover that God rewards you with a happiness far beyond anything in this world.

- Smoking is a dirty habit that has been made appealing by today's advertising world. Beware of its dangers. Don't become chained to a habit that will be hard to break and a pain to maintain in your later years.
- Parties are fun, and even Jesus went to them. But they're not everything. Keep your social life in perspective, and God will give you the time of your life in every area.

Questions to Deepen Your Understanding

1. What does the Bible say about things like abortion? Can you find specific truths that will help you make decisions about these things?
2. Does the Bible ever support music?
3. Why is the partying lifestyle mostly a waste of time?

read on

Some of Mark and Jeanette's favorite books about tackling the really hard stuff:

- *Demons, Witches and the Occult,* Josh McDowell and Don Stewart, Tyndale
- *The Edge of Evil,* Jerry Johnston, Word
- *God Allows U-Turns for Teens,* Allison Bottke and Cheryl Hutchings, Bethany
- *Keep 'Em Talking! Real-Life Dilemmas That Teach,* Mike Yaconelli, Youth Specialties
- *Life Is Like Driver's Ed . . . Ya Gotta Buckle Up, Stay to the Right, and Watch Those Turns! Devotions for Teens & Their Parents,* Greg Johnson, Vine
- *Life on the Edge: A Young Adult's Guide to a Meaningful Future,* James C. Dobson, Word
- *Life, Love, Music, and Money (Pretty Important Ideas on Living God's Way),* Susie Shellenberger and Greg Johnson, Bethany

Afterword

Open Your Bible and Go!

The Bible is a volume full of interesting information and help to Christians who sincerely desire that help. The Word of God was written to edify us, to build us up in faith, to make us more like Christ, and to inform us about God's great plan for humanity. It contains insight into nearly every aspect of human life. As one unknown person wrote long ago, "This book will keep you from sin; or sin will keep you from this book." It's your choice. How you handle and live out the Bible in your life is between you and God. Applying it diligently leads to life and hundreds of blessings you could not get otherwise.

For us, writing this book has been a thrilling experience. But the greatest thrill of all would be for you to take it and use it for God's glory. May God greatly bless you.

—Mark and Jeanette Littleton

Appendix A–Time Lines

Old Testament

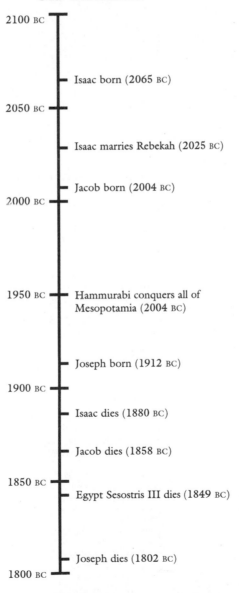

2100 BC

- Isaac born (2065 BC)

2050 BC

- Isaac marries Rebekah (2025 BC)
- Jacob born (2004 BC)

2000 BC

1950 BC

- Hammurabi conquers all of Mesopotamia (2004 BC)
- Joseph born (1912 BC)

1900 BC

- Isaac dies (1880 BC)
- Jacob dies (1858 BC)

1850 BC

- Egypt Sesostris III dies (1849 BC)
- Joseph dies (1802 BC)

1800 BC

Old Testament

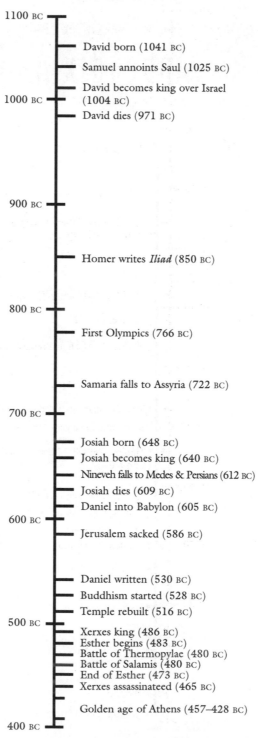

- 1100 BC
- David born (1041 BC)
- Samuel annoints Saul (1025 BC)
- David becomes king over Israel (1004 BC)
- 1000 BC
- David dies (971 BC)
- 900 BC
- Homer writes *Iliad* (850 BC)
- 800 BC
- First Olympics (766 BC)
- Samaria falls to Assyria (722 BC)
- 700 BC
- Josiah born (648 BC)
- Josiah becomes king (640 BC)
- Nineveh falls to Medes & Persians (612 BC)
- Josiah dies (609 BC)
- Daniel into Babylon (605 BC)
- 600 BC
- Jerusalem sacked (586 BC)
- Daniel written (530 BC)
- Buddhism started (528 BC)
- Temple rebuilt (516 BC)
- 500 BC
- Xerxes king (486 BC)
- Esther begins (483 BC)
- Battle of Thermopylae (480 BC)
- Battle of Salamis (480 BC)
- End of Esther (473 BC)
- Xerxes assassinateed (465 BC)
- Golden age of Athens (457–428 BC)
- 400 BC

New Testament

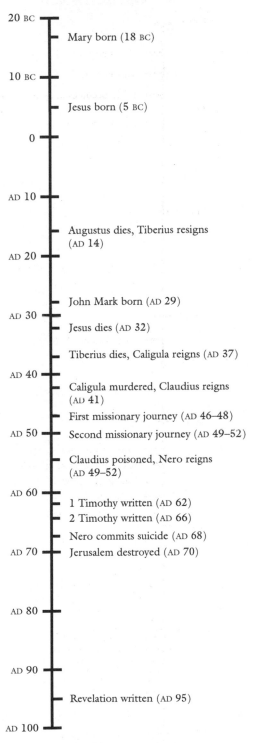

- 20 BC
- Mary born (18 BC)
- 10 BC
- Jesus born (5 BC)
- 0
- AD 10
- Augustus dies, Tiberius resigns (AD 14)
- AD 20
- John Mark born (AD 29)
- AD 30
- Jesus dies (AD 32)
- Tiberius dies, Caligula reigns (AD 37)
- AD 40
- Caligula murdered, Claudius reigns (AD 41)
- First missionary journey (AD 46–48)
- AD 50
- Second missionary journey (AD 49–52)
- Claudius poisoned, Nero reigns (AD 49–52)
- AD 60
- 1 Timothy written (AD 62)
- 2 Timothy written (AD 66)
- Nero commits suicide (AD 68)
- AD 70
- Jerusalem destroyed (AD 70)
- AD 80
- AD 90
- Revelation written (AD 95)
- AD 100

Appendix B—The Answers

Chapter 1: Is the Bible Worth Reading?

1. The Bible is God's unique word to us in the world. It has spoken to people throughout all generations, and it speaks to me personally as I read and study it.
2. The Bible can help the people I know gain peace and joy through faith in Christ, overcome bad habits and irritating problems in their lives, and transform them more into the kind of person God wants them to be.
3. Answers will vary. Many teachings from the Bible have helped me. For example, it has taught me to trust God when things go wrong, shown me how to have peace when I'm upset, and helped me see a way to overcome bad personal beliefs and habits.
4. Answers will vary. Several good ones: Proverbs 3:5–6 on trusting God no matter what the circumstances; Jeremiah 29:11, that God has a plan for my life; Ephesians 2:8–9, that faith is a gift from God; and John 3:16, that God loves me.

Chapter 2: Teens Who Helped Found Judaism

1. God led Rebekah through people like Eliezer, through his words known from the ages, and through her own heart.
2. When his father was sent to sacrifice him, Isaac didn't resist, but submitted himself, trusting both God and his father.
3. Answers will vary. Examples are lying, cheating, stealing, hating, and breaking relationships.
4. Because Joseph trusted God and knew God's plan would ultimately show the truth (see Genesis 50:20).
5. The principles that Naaman's wife's maidservant demonstrated are that God can speak through each of us; that when we love someone, we should pray for them; and that God loves all people, not just Christians.

Chapter 3: Teens Who Were Leaders in the Old Testament

1. By trusting that God would show me how to handle him and, through obedience, overcome.
2. Answers will vary. Examples: concerning a sin I may have committed or am committing, concerning my lack of commitment to him, and concerning my forgetfulness of keeping up with a close relationship with God.
3. Answers will vary. Examples: that God promises to be with us no matter what we have to face, and that God will speak through us if we listen and let him.
4. A personal answer is required here. Example: Risking your life for God is not a real risk because God is the author of life, and even if I were to die, I would still live forever!

Chapter 4: Teens Who Followed God in the New Testament

1. Examples of what you can learn from Mary's story include listening for God's voice and direction when he calls, and not being afraid of gossip or hatred when you're doing as God asks.
2. Possible answers include that God condemns no one for past mistakes or that God is always willing to start where we are and take us where we should be.
3. Answers will vary.
4. Possible answers might be to respond positively when God calls or to not let others' criticism or carping stop me.

Chapter 5: Jesus Christ: The Perfect Example

1. We can learn that God wants our fellowship and friendship. Examples of questions: What is God like personally? How can I grow in my relationship with him? What Scriptures should I turn to for help on specific problems?
2. Answers will vary. Examples: wisdom in obedience, wisdom in solving problems, wisdom in relationships and loving others.
3. Answers will be personal. Remember: (1) God is wise; he made you with wisdom; (2) God is all-knowing; he made you the best in this world for what he designed you to do and be; (3) God is love; he has and always will love you, and your design is from his heart of love.
4. Ways to grow spiritually include studying his Word about a problem and applying it, praying for friends and relatives on specific issues, and seeking ways to build relationships with unbelievers with the idea of leading them to Christ.
5. Ways to grow socially include learning good manners, conducting yourself as a gentleman or woman, and learning to converse and make small talk.

Chapter 6: A Jet Tour Through Theology

1. The most important teachings about God the Father are that he is holy, righteous, loving, and gracious.
2. The one thing everyone should know about Jesus is that he died for the sins of the world and lives today.
3. The Holy Spirit fills and leads and guides us in the circumstances of life.
4. Church is important because through fellowship we become friends, helpers, and encouragers, and we become accountable to someone.
5. You need to be baptized because it's an act of obedience to God in faith.
6. Examples of answers: What will happen at the end of time? When will Jesus come? What will heaven be like?

Chapter 7: Everyday Christianity

1. We can strengthen our relationship with God through the following: reading his Word and obeying it, spending time in prayer and meditation, listening to his Word preached and explained, encouraging other Christians, and loving people.
2. Here are ways we can truly understand the Bible: ask the Spirit to open our eyes and teach us, study it to discover meanings and applications, and let God speak to our hearts through it.
3. Different kinds of prayers include adoration, confession, thanksgiving, and supplication.
4. God forgives forever and immediately.

Chapter 8: Living in Your Family

1. The primary things we need to practice in relation to our parents are honor and obedience.
2. We should treat members of our extended family with love, acceptance, understanding, and kindness.

Chapter 9: Friendship, Dating, and the Big One—Marriage

1. Preparation for marriage begins with understanding how God has set up the process of leaving, cleaving, and becoming one, and remaining true to God's moral plans (keeping our virginity until marriage).
2. We know we're ready when we can answer these questions with a strong yes: Can I commit? Do I love? Can I support and honor my spouse?

Chapter 10: Life's Ingredients

1. The important things to remember are to study, learn, obey, and honor—our teachers, our parents, and our leaders.
2. Friendships are very important. The wrong friends can fell us; the right ones can launch us. Choose wisely among people who are good, kind, loving, and faithful.
3. Entertainment can cause us to waste our time in foolish amusements, and it rarely contributes to our growth as people.
4. Sports and physical fitness are good for physical development, but growth in holiness should be the highest priority, both in sports and outside of them.

Chapter 11: Tougher Issues

1. Lying destroys trust and friendship.
2. Many valuable opportunities are lost when we fail to use time wisely.
3. There are some apparent contradictions between science and the Bible, but with study and a right understanding, often God provides the right answers.
4. Answers will vary.

Chapter 12: Let's Get Serious

1. The Bible does not say much directly about abortion, but it does clearly state that a fetus is a real human being, woven in the womb by God himself.
2. Yes, the Bible is full of music.
3. The partying lifestyle often leads one into sin, and it does not build you up in faith and in relationship with God.

Appendix C—The Experts

Akers, Michelle, is a soccer pro who was a member of the U.S. Women's National Team that won the Gold Medal in the 1996 Olympic Games.

Arbuckle, Tiffany, is a member of the music group Plumb.

Bolton-Holifield, Ruthie, is a superstar for the Women's National Basketball Association.

Bonaparte, Napoleon, was a famous French emperor and conqueror who lived from 1769 to 1821.

Bryant, Anita, was a very popular Miss America in the 1960s who carried her fame into a singing career. She was also a very familiar face on TV commercials—especially those selling Florida orange juice.

Campbell, Serene, is one of the musicians known in the Christian music world as Considering Lily. Serene is the youngest of six kids in her family.

Carter, Joe, is a professional baseball player who played for such teams as the Cleveland Indians and Toronto Blue Jays. He retired in 1999 after finishing his last season with the San Francisco Giants.

Chambers, Oswald (1874–1917), was a Christian author and teacher. His wife compiled his lecture notes to form the famous devotional *My Utmost for His Highest.*

Crawford, Steve, finds his ministry being part of the music group Anointed.

Cyril, Saint, is often called the father of the church. He became bishop of Jerusalem in AD 350 and served there until the end of his life, although sixteen of his years as bishop were spent in exile. He picked up where the disciples left off.

Diemer, Bryan, is a runner who has been in the Olympics four times and won an Olympic bronze medal. He's also a pro at the Steeplechase.

Dobson, James, is a family psychologist and founder of Focus on the Family. He has written many bestsellers, including *When God Doesn't Make Sense.* He has worked with presidents and served on the President's Commission on Pornography. His organization produces magazines, including the teen-focused *Brio* and *Breakaway.*

Edwards, Jonathan (1703–1758), was an American theologian, minister, and writer who spearheaded a time of revival in America known as the "Great Awakening."

Einstein, Albert (1879–1955), was a popular American physicist who lived from 1879 to 1955 and developed the general theory of relativity. Einstein was considered a failure as a student but later was recognized to be a mathematical genius. He participated in the Manhattan Project, which was the American initiative during World War II to develop an atomic bomb.

Eli, is a Christian musician who enjoys challenging and encouraging Christians.

Evans, Tony, is a popular pastor of Oak Cliff Fellowship in Dallas, Texas. He has a radio program and several bestselling books.

Feder, Don, is a newspaper columnist, well known for his incisive columns about American culture and the political scene. A Jew, he has aligned himself strongly with the evangelical community.

Floyd, Heather, is one of the singers in the Christian group Point of Grace.

Fosdick, Harry Emerson (1878–1969), was an American Baptist liberal theologian, writer, and pastor. He played a prominent role in the debate between Christian conservatives and liberals. He became minister of the influential Park Avenue Baptist Church in New York from 1925 to 1946.

Franklin, Benjamin, was one of the founding fathers of our nation. He was known for his wit, wisdom, and pithy sayings. He invented the bifocals and started the United States Post Office system.

Furler, Peter, is a member of the music group the Newsboys.

George, Bob, is a Christian author and minister.

Graham, Billy, is a well-known evangelist. Graham first came to prominence in 1949 when his crusade in Los Angeles attracted thousands of listeners. Over the years, he has conducted many crusades. Recently, his autobiography, *Just As I Am,* was a bestseller and won the Gold Medallion Book Award. He has been spiritual adviser for most presidents since Harry Truman.

Graham, Ruth, was an author and speaker who had a very successful ministry. She was Billy Graham's wife.

Grant, Amy, is a well-known Christian singer. Grant is famous for crossing over into the mainstream secular pop audience and taking that audience by storm without compromising her faith. Her albums have won Grammy Awards.

Green, A. C., plays forward for the Los Angeles Lakers.

Harrington, Bob, was once known as the Chaplain of Bourbon Street for his ministry among people of the streets in New Orleans. He was well known for his ability to come up with creative, funny phrases that also packed a spiritual punch.

Hendricks, Howard, is an educator and author. He is also professor emeritus at Dallas Theological Seminary, where he has taught since the 1950s. He has made his reputation in powerful preaching and has participated as a speaker in Promise Keepers rallies. His books include *Heaven Help the Home, Say It With Love,* and *Elijah.*

Holm, Dallas, is a pioneer Christian rock artist. His most famous song, "Rise Again," won a Dove Award and is still a popular choice in churches.

Hostetler, Bob, has coauthored many books with Josh McDowell. Hostetler is also a former magazine editor and writes nonfiction and fiction books, scads of magazine articles, and even tackles poetry.

Jackson, Mike, is a pitcher for the Cleveland Indians who is well known for his saves. In 1998, he converted 40 of 45 save opportunities and compiled a 1.55 earned run average.

James I (1566–1625), was the first king of Scotland and then became king of England. He ordered the writing of the King James Version of the Bible. King James was noted for his faith and his commitment to the Christian faith.

Jansen, Jed, was a utility player for the Kansas City Royals.

Johnston, Michael, is a member of the Christian rock group the Smalltown Poets. They have several albums, including *Listen Closely.*

Jones, Denise, is a member of Point of Grace.

Jones, Terry, is Denise's sister and also sings for Point of Grace.

Knapp, Jennifer, is a great Christian soloist.

Landers, Ann, wrote an advice column that was probably the most well-read of all time. Known for her acerbic and thoughtful counsel, she won the hearts of many, and her column was carried by over a thousand newspapers.

Lewis, C. S. (1898–1963), was a Christian apologist, author, and educator at Oxford and Cambridge Universities in England. His many popular books include *Mere Christianity*, *The Great Divorce*, and *The Chronicles of Narnia*.

Little, Paul, was a Christian educator and author. He was a professor of evangelism at Trinity Evangelical Divinity School and wrote the book *How to Give Away Your Faith*, considered a classic on how to witness to your friends and family.

Longfellow, Henry Wadsworth (1807–1882), was the most popular poet of his day. He taught at Harvard for many years and is famous for his poems "The Song of Hiawatha," "Evangeline," and "The Midnight Ride of Paul Revere."

Lucado, Max, is a Christian author and minister who gained notoriety in 1986 when his book, *No Wonder They Call Him the Savior*, was published. He has written many bestsellers, including *In the Grip of Grace*, *When God Whispers Your Name*, and *God Came Near*.

Luther, Martin (1483–1546), was a theologian and a leader in the Protestan Reformation.

MacDonald, George, was a Scottish novelist and poet. He entertained the idea that unsaved people might have hope for salvation after death, and as a result he was eventually kicked out of his church. He made a meager living by writing, tutoring, and preaching.

Manuel, Jerry, was manager for the Chicago White Sox.

Max, Kevin, is one of the members of the Christian music group dc Talk. One of their most well-known songs is "Jesus Freak," which has received airplay on Christian and secular stations.

McDowell, Josh, has written many bestselling books that help people understand, defend, and define their faith. As a speaker for Campus Crusade for Christ, he has spoken to millions of college students.

McGinniss, Will, is part of the music group Audio Adrenaline.

Menninger, Dr. Karl, author of *Whatever Became of Sin?* was an American psychiatrist.

Meyer, Paul J., is an American businessman and author. He is a contributor to *Chicken Soup for the Golden Soul*.

Molitor, Paul, is a professional baseball player who played with the Milwaukee Brewers, Toronto Blue Jays, and Minnesota Twins. He retired in 1999.

Moore, Geoff, was lead singer for Geoff Moore and the Distance before launching a solo career.

Moore, Hannah, is author of *Religion of the Heart*.

Newton, John (1725–1807), was a Christian minister and author who wrote the hymn "Amazing Grace." Originally involved in the slave trade, a violent storm in 1747 in which his ship sank forced him to seek God. He later became a minister in Buckinghamshire, England. He befriended the poet William Cowper, and together they wrote many hymns.

O'Brien, Austin, is a Christian actor who gained fame on the cast of TV's *Promised Land*.

Packer, James I., is an English theologian and author. He is well-known as an Episcopal scholar and has preached often in American seminaries. He is best known for his book *Knowing God*.

Pettitte, Andy, is a pitcher for the New York Yankees. He has been one of the mainstays of the team and a reason for its success.

Phillips, Shelley, is a member of Point of Grace. The other members of the group say she's the bossy one.

Price, Eugenia, is a Christian author and speaker. She has produced many secular novels over the years and has been a beloved author of southern Christian romances.

Roberts, Richard Owen, is an American minister and author.

St. James, Rebecca, is a Christian pop musician and singer. She has won several Dove Awards.

Schaeffer, Francis, was a noted theologian and author. Known for his intellectual powers, he founded L'Abri, a Christian community in Switzerland. Schaeffer is best known for his books *He Is There and He Is Not Silent* and *The Mark of the Christian.*

Schlitt, John, is a member of Christian rock group Petra.

Scott, Sharon, is an American researcher.

Silesius, Angelus (1624–1677), was an American poet. He's known for his quotable phrases.

Smith, Branley, was a drummer for the rock group Hootie and the Blowfish. He left the group to become a youth minister.

Smith, Michael W., is perhaps the most prolific male in Christian music. His track record covers two decades and dozens of awards both in singing and songwriting. One of his classic hits is "Friends."

Spiers, Bill, was a fielder for the Houston Astros.

Steorts, Ken, is a musician with the Christian music group Skillet.

Stephens, Danny, is a member of the Christian rock group the Smalltown Poets. They have several albums, including *Listen Closely.*

Sutton, Larry, is a first baseman who played for the Kansas City Royals, St. Louis Cardinals, and others.

Swindoll, Charles, is a pastor, author, and president of Dallas Theological Seminary. He has written many books and was for many years pastor of First Evangelical Free Church of Fullerton, California, with a membership of over five thousand. He has written such books as *Laugh Again* and *The Grace Awakening.* Also featured on the radio program *Insight for Living,* Dr. Swindoll is popular with all ages because of his humor, honesty, and style of helping people apply Scripture to their lives.

Syrius, Publius, was a Roman writer.

Talbot, John Michael, is a Christian musician and performer who is well known for his contemplative music.

Tavern, A. B. Zu, is an American business man and writer.

Thomas à Kempis (1380–1470), was a German mystic and writer. He entered the Augustinian Convent of Mount Saint Agnes, where he became a priest and spiritual adviser to many. His book of meditations, *The Imitation of Christ,* is considered a classic.

Tozer, A. W., was a Christian author and speaker. He wrote many books, including *The Knowledge of the Holy.*

Twain, Mark, one of America's most famous authors and humorists, wrote such classics as Tom Sawyer and *The Adventures of Huckleberry Finn.* He was an avowed atheist, but toward the end of his life, after many bitter tragedies, he is said to have tried to make peace with God.

Vanauken, Sheldon, is an American author who has written several books.

Velasquez, Jaci, is a popular Christian musician among English- and Spanish-speaking listeners.

Washington, Booker T., was an African-American educator who founded the famous Tuskegee Institute, a school for African Americans, in 1881.

Wiggins, Steve, is a member of the Christian rock group Big Tent Revival. A recent album is Amplifier. They have been nominated for several Dove Awards.

Endnotes

Chapter 1

1. Edythe Draper, comp., *Draper's Book of Quotations for the Christian World* (Wheaton, IL: Tyndale, 1992), 677.
2. Chris Lutes, "Point of Grace," *Campus Life*, September/October 1996, 20.
3. Draper, 678.
4. Linda Wakefield Kelley, "Football Analogies," Brio, November 1998, 34. *www.family.org/girls/briomag/features/a0003323.html* (accessed May 13, 2000).
5. Mark Moring, "Out of This World," *Campus Life*, November/December 1998, 22.
6. Chris Lutes, "Poetry in Motion," *Campus Life*, September/October 1998, 26.
7. Dana Key, *WWJD Interactive Devotional* (Grand Rapids: Zondervan, 1997), 22.
8. A. C. Green, *Victory* (Lake Mary, FL: Creation House, 1994), 63.
9. Josh McDowell, *More Than a Carpenter* (Wheaton, IL: Tyndale, 1977), 123.
10. Rebecca St. James, The Parable Group, *www.parable.com/feature/rsj/Interview.html* (accessed June 3, 2000).
11. John Dodderidge, "A Witness for the Kingdom: Biblical Principles Guide White Sox Manager Jerry Manuel," *Sharing the Victory*, April 1999, *www.gospelcom.net/fca/stv-april99Manuel.shtml* (accessed June 2, 2000).

Chapter 2

1. Marty McCormack, "Catching Up With Some Way-Cool Chicas," *Brio*, March 26, 1999, *www.family.org/girls/briomag/features/a0004923.html* (accessed May 13, 2000).
2. Derek Wesley Selby, "Triple Time," *CCM Magazine*, May 1999.
3. Christin Ditchfield, "Bouncing Back: Sacramento's Ruthie Bolton-Holifield Counts on Faith, Family," *Sharing the Victory*, May 1999, *www.gospelcom.net/fca/stv-may99/Holifield.shtml* (accessed May 13, 2000).
4. Mark Littleton, *Sports Heroes: Baseball* (Grand Rapids: Zondervan, 1995), 38.
5. Rebecca St. James with Amber Weigland-Buckley, "Just Rebecca," *On Course* magazine, Fall 2000.
6. Michelle Akers with Judith A. Nelson, "Higher Learning," *Sports Spectrum*, June 1999, 10.
7. Ibid.
8. George Barna, *The Barna Report: America Renews Its Search for God* (Ventura, CA: Regal Books, 1992), 117.
9. James Bilton, "A Changed Heart," *Sharing the Victory*, August/September 1998, *www.gospelcom.net/fca/stv-augsep98/Napoleon.shtml* (accessed June 3, 2000).
10. Editors, "Odyssey of the Albatross," *Time*, June 25, 1979.
11. Michael W. Smith, *It's Time to Be Bold* (Nashville: Word, 1997), 119.
12. David Smale, "True Champions: The Royals Are Building for the Future With Solid Rocks," *Sharing the Victory*, October 1999, *www.gospelcom.net/fca/stv-oct99/Royals.shtml* (accessed May 13, 2000).

Chapter 3

1. Edythe Draper, comp., *Draper's Book of Quotations for the Christian World* (Wheaton, IL: Tyndale, 1992), 43.
2. Jody Davis, quoted in Chris Lutes, "Step Back From the Microphone," *Campus Life*, July/August 1999, 22.

3. Mark Littleton, *Sports Heroes: Baseball* (Grand Rapids: Zondervan, 1995), 15.
4. Dana Key, *WWJD Interactive Devotional*, (Grand Rapids: Zondervan, 1997), 111.
5. Ibid., 87.
6. Christin Ditchfield, "Bouncing Back: Sacramento's Ruthie Bolton-Holifield Counts on Faith, Family," *Sharing the Victory*, May 1999 *www.gospelcom.net/fca/stv-may99/Holifield.shtml* (accessed May 13, 2000).
7. Marty McCormack, "Heartache to Heart of Joy," Brio, December 1999, *www.family.org/girls/briomag/features/a0008733. html* (accessed May 13, 2000).

Chapter 4

1. Josh McDowell and Don Stewart, *Answers to Tough Questions Skeptics Ask About the Christian Faith* (San Bernardino, CA: Here's Life Publishers, 1980), 57.
2. Michael W. Smith, *www.parable.com/feature/mws/MWSTime_int.asp* (accessed July 20, 2000).
3. David Smale, "In the Saving Business," *Sharing the Victory*, October 1999, *www.gospelcom.net/fca/stv-oct99/Jackson.shtml* (accessed June 3, 2000).
4. Rebecca St. James, The Parable Group, *www. parable.com/feature/rsj/Interview.htm* (accessed June 3, 2000).
5. Dana Key, *WWJD Interactive Devotional* (Grand Rapids: Zondervan, 1997), 123.
6. Michael W. Smith, *www.parable.com/feature/mws/feature.htm* (accessed July 20, 2000).

Chapter 5

1. "20 Questions with Rebecca St. James," *www.rsjames.com.*
2. Dana Key, *WWJD Interactive Devotional* (Grand Rapids: Zondervan, 1997), 6–7.
3. Michael W. Smith, *It's Time to Be Bold* (Nashville: Word, 1997), 65.

Chapter 6

1. Jennifer Knapp, *www.imusic.com/show-case/ contemporary/jenniferknapp.html* (accessed July 27, 2000).
2. Curtis McDougall, quoted on *thinkexist.com* (accessed March 26, 2007).
3. Bob George, Boardwalk Chapel retreat, Wildwood, NJ, August 3, 1973.
4. Eugenia Price, *What Is God Like?* (Grand Rapids: Zondervan, 1960), 125.
5. Michelle Akers with Judith A. Nelson, "Higher Learning," *Sports Spectrum*, June 1999, 10.
6. *Reader's Digest* (Pleasantville, NY: Reader's Digest Corporation), March 1978.
7. Steve Peters and Mark Littleton, *The Truth About Rock* (Minneapolis: Bethany, 1998), 90.
8. C. S. Lewis, *The Best of C. S. Lewis* (New York: Iverson and Associates, 1969), 440.
9. Greg Weeks, "You Can Go Home Again," *Sharing the Victory*, April 1999, *www.gospelcom.net/fca/stv-april99/Spiers.shtml* (accessed June 3, 2000).
10. Peters and Littleton, 90.
11. Dale Reeves, *Some Kind of Journey: On the Road With Audio Adrenaline* (Cincinnati: Standard Publishing, 1997), 48.
12. Jed Jansen and David Smale, "True Champions: The Royals Are Building for the Future With Solid Rocks," *Sharing the Victory*, October 1999, *www.gospelcom.net/fca/stv-oct99/Royals.shtml* (accessed May 13, 2000).
13. Clive Price, "A Delirious New Sound," *Charisma*, December 1999, *www.charismamag.com/articledisplay.pl/?d=cm129926&MonthID=cm1299* (accessed June 3, 2000).
14. Derek Wesley Selby, "Triple Time," *CCM Magazine*, May 1999, 29.
15. George Sweeting, *Who Said That?* (Chicago: Moody Press, 1995), 237.
16. George W. Bush, quoted on *thinkexist.com* (accessed March 26, 2007).
17. Sweeting, 313.
18. Tony Evans, *The Kingdom Agenda* (Nashville: Word, 1999), 77.
19. Billy Graham, *Angels* (Nashville: Word, 1997), Introduction.
20. Jeffrey Bryant, quoted on *thinkexist.com* (accessed March 26, 2007).
21. Michael W. Smith, *www.parable.com/feature/mws/feature.htm* (accessed July 20, 2000).
22. A. C. Green, *Victory* (Lake Mary, FL: Creation House, 1994), 156.

23. Edythe Draper, comp., *Draper's Book of Quotations for the Christian World* (Wheaton, IL: Tyndale, 1992), 149.
24. Liz Kelly, "Second Hand Hack," *CCM Magazine*, December 1999, 44.
25. Draper, 307.
26. Ibid., 309.
27. Sherwood Wirt, *Topical Encyclopedia of Living Quotations* (Minneapolis: Bethany, 1982), 107.

Chapter 7

1. Derek Wesley Selby, "Under the Big Top," *CCM Magazine*, February 2000, 26.
2. Rebecca St. James, The Parable Group interview, *www.parable.com/feature/rsj/Interview.htm* (accessed June 3, 2000).
3. Ruth Graham, *Homemade Bulletin* (Colorado Springs: Focus on the Family), December 1982.
4. Howard Hendricks, "Your Bible Can Help You Grow," *The Christian Life for the Kindred in Sprit* (Portland, OR: Vision House, 1994), 63–64.
5. St. James, The Parable Group interview.
6. James I. Packer, *I Want to Be a Christian* (Wheaton, IL: Tyndale, 1977), 171, 172.
7. Edythe Draper, comp., *Draper's Book of Quotations for the Christian World* (Wheaton, IL: Tyndale, 1992), 67.
8. Ibid., 509.
9. David Smale, "More Than Winning," *Sharing the Victory*, October 1999, *www.gospelcom.net/fca/stv-oct99/Pettitte.shtml* (accessed June 3, 2000).
10. George Sweeting, *Who Said That?* (Chicago: Moody Press, 1995), 178.
11. Rebecca St. James with Amber Weigland-Buckley, "Just Rebecca," *On Course* magazine, Fall 2000, 13.
12. Vernon McLellan, *Timeless Treasures* (San Bernadino, CA: Here's Life Publishers, 1992), 142.
13. John Powell, *Unconditional Love* (New York: Thomas Moore, 1995), 90
14. Dana Key, *WWJD Interactive Devotional* (Grand Rapids: Zondervan, 1997), 10.
15. Ibid., 71.

Chapter 8

1. Chris Lutes, "Hanging Out With Jaci Velasquez," *Campus Life*, March/April 1998, 18.
2. Rebecca St. James, The Parable Group interview, *www.parable.com/feature/rsj/Interview.html* (accessed June 3, 2000).
3. Chris Lutes, "Point of Grace," *Campus Life*, September/October 1996, 20.

Chapter 9

1. Josh McDowell and Bob Hostetler, *Handbook on Counseling Youth* (Dallas: Word, 1996), 115.
2. Chris Lutes, "Point of Grace" (Chicago: *Campus Life*, September 1996), 20.
3. McDowell and Hostetler, 134–35.
4. James Dobson, *Solid Answers* (Wheaton, IL: Tyndale, 1997), 160.
5. Chris Lutes, "Point of Grace" (Chicago: *Campus Life*, September 1996), 20.

Chapter 10

1. Chris Lutes, "Point of Grace," *Campus Life*, September/October 1996, 20.
2. James Dobson, *Solid Answers* (Wheaton, IL: Tyndale, 1997), 160.
3. Nicole C. Mullen, interview, *www.parable.com/feature/mullen/mullen_bio.asp* (accessed July 20, 2000).
4. A. B. Zu Tavern, quoted in Alfred Armand Montapert, *Distilled Wisdom* (Englewood Cliffs, NJ: Prentice-Hall, 1964), 340.
5. Edythe Draper, comp., *Draper's Book of Quotations for the Christian World* (Wheaton, IL: Tyndale, 1992), 391.
6. Mike Jackson, quoted in Smale, "In the Saving Business," *Sharing the Victory* (Kansas City, MO: Fellowship of Christian Athletes), October 1999, 5.
7. Mark Littleton, *Sports Heroes: Summer Olympics* (Grand Rapids: Zondervan, 1996), 61.

Chapter 11

1. Bartlett, *Familiar Quotations*, 16th ed. (Boston: Little, Brown, 1992), 523.
2. Alfred Armand Montapert, *Distilled Wisdom* (Englewood Cliffs, NJ: Prentice-Hall, 1964), 193.

3. Sherwood Wirt, *Topical Encyclopedia of Living Quotations* (Minneapolis: Bethany, 1982), 103.
4. Ann Landers, "Hatred," *Bits & Pieces*, August 1983, 1.
5. Emmett Dedmon, "Pilgrimage," *Reader's Digest*, May 1979, 126.
6. George Barna, *Generation Next* (Ventura, CA: Regal Books, 1997), 32–33.
7. Montapert, 234.
8. Charles R. Swindoll, *Come Before Winter* (Portland, OR: Multnomah, 1985), 8.
9. Michelle Healy, "Cheating, Lying on the Rise," *USA Today*, 23–25 February 1996, 1.
10. Vernon McLellan, *Timeless Treasures* (San Bernadino, CA: Here's Life Publishers, 1992), 279.
11. Wirt, 14.
12. McLellan, 274.
13. Edythe Draper, comp., *Draper's Book of Quotations for the Christian World* (Wheaton, IL: Tyndale, 1992), 104.
14. Josh McDowell and Bob Hostetler, *Handbook on Counseling Youth* (Dallas: Word, 1996), 147.
15. Sharon Scott, *PPR: Peer Pressure Reversal* (Amherst, MA: Human Resource Development Press, 1985), 6.
16. Chris Lutes, "Hanging Out With Jaci Velasquez," *Campus Life*, March/April 1998, 18.
17. A. C. Green, *Victory* (Lake Mary, FL: Creation House, 1994), 127, 129.
18. Chris Lutes, "Living in the Promised Land," *Campus Life*, March/April 1998, 40.
19. Draper, 543.
20. Wirt, 200.
21. Eugenia Price, *What Is God Like?* (Grand Rapids: Zondervan, 1960), 121.
22. George Sweeting, *Who Said That?* (Chicago: Moody Press, 1995), 345.
23. Draper, 593.
24. Draper, 592.
25. Michelle Akers with Judith A. Nelson, "Higher Learning," *Sports Spectrum*, June 1999, 10.

Chapter 12

1. Edythe Draper, comp., *Draper's Book of Quotations for the Christian World* (Wheaton, IL: Tyndale, 1992), 54.
2. Ibid., 54.
3. Jean Staker Garton, *Who Broke the Baby?* (Minneapolis: Bethany, 1998).
4. Josh McDowell and Bob Hostetler, *Handbook on Counseling Youth* (Nashville: Word, 1996), 305.
5. Quotable Quotes, *Reader's Digest*, May 1987, 167–68.
6. Draper, 321.
7. McDowell and Hostetler, 381.
8. Draper, 14.
9. Ibid., 432.
10. Gregory Rumburg, "Somewhere Down the Road," *CCM Magazine*, July 1998, 46.
11. Steve Peters and Dan Peters, *Why Knock Rock?* (Minneapolis: Bethany, 1983), 219.
12. Ibid., 215–16.

Index

K

L